The Tradition of Household Spirits

The Tradition of Household Spirits

Ancestral Lore and Practices

Claude Lecouteux

Translated by Jon E. Graham

Inner Traditions
Rochester, Vermont • Toronto, Canada

Inner Traditions
One Park Street
Rochester, Vermont 05767
www.InnerTraditions.com

Originally published in French under the title *La maison et ses génies: Croyances d'hier et d'aujourd'hui* by Éditions Imago, 7 rue Suger, 75006, Paris
First U.S. edition published in 2013 by Inner Traditions

Library of Congress Cataloging-in-Publication Data

Lecouteux, Claude.
[La maison et ses génies. English]
The tradition of houshold spirits : ancestral lore and practices / Claude Lecouteux ; translated by Jon E. Graham.
p. cm.
Includes bibliographical references and index.
ISBN 978-1-62055-105-9 (pbk.) — ISBN 978-1-62055-144-8 (e-book)
1. Jinn. 2. Haunted houses. I. Title.
GR549.L4313 2013
133.1'22—dc23

2012046362

Printed and bound in the United States

10 9 8 7 6 5 4 3 2

Text design and layout by Brian Boynton
This book was typeset in Garamond Premier Pro with Barbara and Legacy Sans as display typefaces

All photos in color insert are courtesy of Nigel Pennick unless otherwise noted.

Inner Traditions wishes to express its appreciation for assistance given by the government of France through the National Book Office of the Ministère de la Culture in the preparation of this translation.

Nous tenons à exprimer nos plus vifs remerciements au gouvernement de la France et au ministère de la Culture, Centre National du Livre, pour leur concours dans la préparation de la traduction de cet ouvrage.

Contents

Foreword

In Jean Giraudoux's charming comedy *Intermezzo,* the druggist exclaims: "All symbols have their meanings. We only have to interpret them." (Act I, Scene 1) But it was man who created symbols when fashioning his sociocultural world. Human fantasy remains an excellent subject of study for those with a real desire to become immersed in the medieval imaginal realm. As Évelyne Patlagean points out: "The imaginal realm is formed by all the representations that pass beyond the limits established by the lessons of experience and the deductive sequences they authorize."[1]

Those seeking to solve the problems associated with studies of the Middle Ages are confronted by many almost insurmountable difficulties. For example, descriptions of folk customs and beliefs were provided primarily by the representatives of the scholarly culture, which is to say monks, priests, clergymen, and bureaucrats—essentially the spokespersons of law and order. But as a result of their tendency to write in Latin, the sources were made literary. At the same time, folk expressions were altered to agree with the grammatical and syntactical requirements of the Latin tongue. The Christianization of popular terms, often in dialect, represents a huge obstacle to understanding medieval civilization. We should also note the incorrect interpretations on the part of clerics who did not grasp the key terms of the vocabulary of preindustrial culture. There is a kind of dialectic at work between the clerical culture and the folk culture throughout the entire Middle Ages.

It is certainly inadvisable to exaggerate this social and intellectual distance between scholarly culture and folk culture, because there were ideas, sentiments, and attitudes shared by all. Every detail of daily life in the Middle Ages was fraught with meaning. The medieval man was surely greatly influenced by religion, but at the same time he maintained ideas with roots that are to be found in folk mythology. People believed that dwarves, werewolves, fairies, the undead, and other marvelous and grotesque beings were all around them. Legends, tales, and ballads are narrative forms that teach us about the mental attitude of the people of this time toward these supernatural phenomena. We should also observe the impact of secular literature—medical and pharmaceutical treatises, treatises on astrology, grimoires, herbals, lapidaries, bestiaries, and bird books—on popular culture. In any event, behind the inconsistency of the sources we have at our disposal, and behind the array of beliefs, we can see resilient structures and enduring ideas. These beliefs are clearly mental structures that embrace values, norms, and attitudes considered valuable by the different strata of society.

Claude Lecouteux is engaged for the long haul[2] because he is quite familiar with Jacques Le Goff's dictum that "the Middle Ages never ended." There is nothing paradoxical about this. There are customs, trends of thought, and sentiments dating as far back as classical antiquity that still exist today in isolated regions of Europe.

As a Germanic scholar, historian, and folklorist, Claude Lecouteux is first and foremost an expert on the Middle Ages, and this study proposes to provide an in-depth analysis of the relationship between the house and its spirits, between man and the supernatural world. The corpus collected here is rich and diverse. On this point, the author says it is necessary to shed light on the literature by means of the civilization and vice versa, by excluding no kind of writing, and he adds that we should not reduce the perspective to clerical literature and historical texts. Nor does he confine his research to the Latin elements (chronicles, literature, historiography, catechesis, and *exempla*). We should take into account folklore traditions and myths, and refrain from dismissing the human substratum that produced these elements.

Here in a few words is the scientific credo of Claude Lecouteux. He never ceases to emphasize the predominant importance of philology as an analytical instrument for understanding the content and value of the texts studied. The linguistic contribution is decisive in his work. It is the lexicon that interests him, and this book on household spirits provides an eloquent testimony to that fact. The etymologies of the terms used to label supernatural beings and often obsolete notions are extremely important for clearly grasping the corpus, according to Claude Lecouteux. The names of the domestic spirits indicate their origin, appearance, and functions. In his analysis of this corpus, he discerns the mental structures of a patrimony common to all of Europe, despite the heterogeneous nature of these spirits. The notion about the sacred nature of the house is certainly universal. The house is a microcosm of the world. These domestic spirits have a very long and extremely complicated history. Belief in them is a religious, social, ecological, and economic fact.

Thanks to the erudition and meticulous nature of Claude Lecouteux, we have a better understanding of the fundamental facts of the historical evolution of these spirits over the centuries. They definitely belong to folk religion. On countless occasions I have been able to see striking and significant resemblances between the continental ideas and those of Norway on domestic spirits.[3] In passing, I should note that the author uses Scandinavian sources in his study. This book serves as a sequel to his earlier book on dwarves and elves, which inspired him to examine the demons and spirits of the land more closely. Now we have a trilogy on place spirits, which provides us with an overall view of them. Regional studies already exist on this subject, but to the best of my knowledge this is the first time we have at our disposal a magnificent and folkloric work on *genii loci,* and it covers the whole of Europe.

Alas, domestic spirits no longer exist. In Norway, we say that the house spirit called the *nisse* has gone into hiding because no one believes that it exists anymore and no longer cares about it. However, in eastern Norway, we have a roadside sign depicting a specter in its shroud that says, "Watch out for the Ghost!" In Iceland, a major road was recently constructed but fear lingered about the supernatural beings in its vicinity. For this reason, additional expenditures became necessary to divert the road around the mound in which they had chosen to live.

RONALD GRAMBO
OSLO UNIVERSITY
FOLKLORE INSTITUTE

Ronald Grambo, Ph.D., is a Norse folklorist and a retired professor who taught at Kongsvinger College and the University of Oslo. He has received many academic awards including the Hedmark Author Award in 2006, and is the author of many books and academic articles including the *Folkloristisk håndbok.*

Acknowledgments

Like my other works, this one would not have been possible without the help of my friends, colleagues, and students. I would like to thank Ronald Grambo (Kongsvinger), who has long discussed domestic spirits with me and provided me with many Scandinavian studies that were unavailable in France. A huge thank-you to Bengt af Klintberg (Lidingo, Sweden) for his repertoire of knowledge on the types of Swedish legends. Herfried Vögel (Munich) was kind enough to supply me with several German documents. Francis Conte (Paris-Sorbonne) opened my eyes to the Slavic traditions. My students Florence Bayard, Astrid Guillaume, and Anne-Hélène Delavigne discovered many survivals of beliefs out in the field and provided me with an excellent dossier of photographs that, alas, could not be reproduced. I also owe many thanks to Philippe Gontier (Graulhet, Tarn), a great admirer of folklore, who pulled everything from his library that reflected my concerns and sent me copies. Thanks to them, this study was able to come into being, and I wish to express all my gratitude.

I should not forget my French publisher, Thierry Auzas, who continues to believe that what I write is worth publishing and who, book after book, helps me unmask the secrets of the figures of popular mythology for a wide audience.

INTRODUCTION

More Than a Simple Building

In this world, the sole land worth dwelling in is that of chimera.

Jean-Jacques Rousseau, *The New Heloise*

At a time when our individual dwellings bear such poetic names as F2, F3, F4, or "studio apartment," formerly sacred spaces are now located in a depersonalized collective space, where the shifting fortunes of our economic position impel us to move house rather frequently, a time when "Home Sweet Home" smacks of an almost inaccessible ideal as the bonds between the inhabitant and his house have vanished. But where the desire to have a hearth of one's own still remains very strong, it could be helpful to rediscover those links that once united man to his *domus.*

Ethnologists from a wide variety of European countries have closely examined what they call the rustic house, essentially drawing their examples from peasant culture because in the city all this has been erased and the habitat has become standardized and anonymous. Unfortunately, they have most often dealt with this subject from a synchronic perspective, drawing up a depiction of the state of the premises at one given moment. Rare are those who attempted a diachronic approach and sought to see to what extent nineteenth-century folk traditions reflected far older considerations. The main research has been conducted in the Baltic, Scandinavian, and Slavic countries, for these studies could only bear fruit in lands that had been slow to evolve and where urbanization did not come about until much later. In Western Europe, industrialization at the end of the nineteenth century brought about large movements of the populace from the countryside into the cities, which ensured the disappearance of many ancestral traditions connected to habitat. In the city, the dwelling place became functional and impersonal, more a temporary place to lay one's head than a true home that was passed down from generation to generation. It was no longer a dwelling in which everything recalled the former inhabitants. Today, the fundamental symbol of the hearth has practically vanished from the house—the hearth, the fireplace that simultaneously served to provide light, cooking, and heat.

However, I should point out that a substantial discrepancy exists between cities and the countryside. In fact, fragments of the rites of olden times survive in the rural regions better than anywhere else, rites that are based on a set of homogenous beliefs whose origins are lost in the dawn of time. This is why in France, when someone settles into a house, their housewarming party is called the hanging of the chimney hook (*on pend la crémaillère*), and when someone moves away, they are said to be not only changing home, but changing "household gods" (*on change de pénates*). Other fragments include the custom of the young bride being carried into the newlywed's new home over the threshold by her husband, and that of hanging mistletoe above the main entrance at Christmas, or decorating that door with branches of spruce. Sometimes houses are still baptized with a name, which bestows an identity and personality upon them, or an old horseshoe is fixed to one of the walls.

A glance at old rural houses reveals many other elements whose meaning has disappeared: gothic inscriptions on the beams of half-timbered dwellings, a niche with the statue of a saint or the Virgin Mary, a sculpted keystone, gables in the form of horse heads, or the sun and moon painted on the facade. The interiors of these old houses are often noteworthy: a mantelpiece adorned with mysterious or symbolic figures, a cast-iron frying pan or earthenware tiles bearing a device on a banner, or a blessing carved on the main beam of the house. If we think about it and ask ourselves the reason for all this, we shall soon see that the home was more than a simple building.

The aim of this study is to present the house and its spirits. It follows my earlier investigation of elves and dwarves, and that on demons and land spirits in which we looked at rites for taking possession of land, for expropriating the spirits of place, and the choice of a territory for building a house—and I then pointed out the difficulty we have in making a clear distinction between the *genius loci* from the domestic deity, inasmuch as this latter can be a former place spirit that has been tamed or satisfied by the offerings or worship it has been given. This book should give the contemporary reader a more rounded view of all those creatures, often inappropriately described as elves or dwarves, about which folk tradition has informed us.

To explain the mental background of the connections between people and their houses, it is necessary to place our reliance on sure elements and assemble a corpus of material, which is where the difficulties begin. My predecessors' investigations essentially deal with the nineteenth and twentieth centuries and focus on different civilizations. Comparison of these studies reveals that we encounter fundamental constants from one end of Europe to the other; the similarities are astonishing, for it is impossible to postulate any genetic bonds between them. These constants emerge from the vast mass of rites and beliefs connected to the house, and they allow us to sketch out—through comparison, superimposition, and cross-checking—a typology of representation that makes it possible to understand the rare medieval accounts whose fragmentary forms are filled with gaps that discourage any immediate interpretation.

After a quarter century spent studying folk beliefs, I have been able to verify many times that they survived into the onset of the twentieth century (something other researchers have also demonstrated) and form a logical and coherent ensemble—once one has discovered the common thread that ties them together. At the archetypal level, this ensemble scarcely evolves over time and it reflects a distinctive conception of the world. The "essentials" are hardly affected by the law of ecotypes and it is therefore permissible and even advisable to erect a bridge between eras and cultures once they have been given serious attention. This is in no way an indulgent attempt to reconstruct the past, but rather to decipher it with the help of the traces it left behind.

We do not have a great many sources on these beliefs at our disposal. We can find elements of the remote past in the collections of laws and customs, in chronicles, and in the lives of the saints, but the only first-hand information concerns the rites for taking possession of a piece of land or for the founding of towns and cities. Once we tackle the subject of the house in the ancient past, the information becomes diluted and fleeting, and historians have never taken this fundamental aspect of daily life into account. It is therefore necessary to comb through every possible text and the resulting meager harvest—together with what has already been gleaned by the ethnologists—makes it possible to decipher the constituent elements of beliefs concerning the household. Then a great many things can emerge from the shadow that has gradually hidden them from view over time.

A house is much more than a building. It is a microcosm, a living being with both a body and a soul. It speaks, even if its language is only creaking and cracking noises for the profane. Its wailings are evidence of an attack by hostile forces. If uncared for, it can also grow old and die and, once abandoned, it crumbles away, leaving its skeleton visible to all. Commonly used comparisons testify to its anthropomorphization. In French, we refer to a leprous or seedy house, a blind or one-eyed wall, and, conversely, a decrepit old dame. The house establishes a bond between itself and its inhabitants. It becomes the family seat; a very clear trace of this sense remains when we refer to nobility by using the phrase "the house of so-and-so." Moreover, the medieval Latin term *domus* means both "house" and "family." The ancestors continued to live there because this (or somewhere very close by) is where they were once buried. The home is a multivalent space that encompasses notions of symbol, religion, patrimony, and law; it is also very telling that the phrase "without hearth or home" was an expression referring to banished persons and other outcasts. The house resembles a tracing of human life; all the major moments of existence from birth to death are connected to specific places. Various expressions reveal which parts of the house were important enough to be

Sweden, late Neolithic period

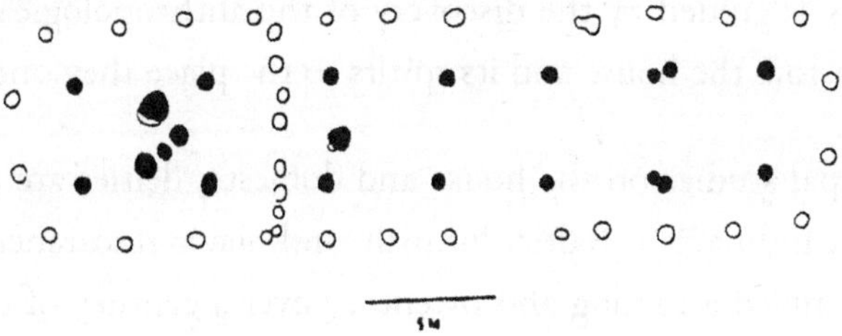

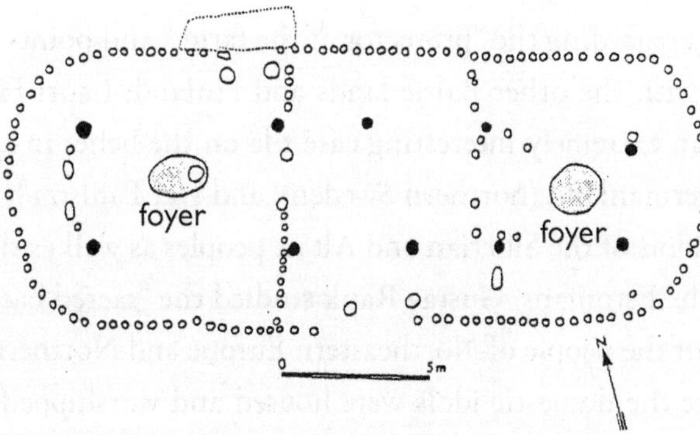

Denmark, Bronze Age ground plan

made part of the popular lexicon: "to have a roof over one's head," the "hearthwife" (*la femme au foyer*),* "to take someone out to the woodshed," "to throw something out the window," "to be on the threshold of life," "to hang the chimney iron,"† "if you can't stand the heat, get out of the kitchen," and so forth.

When we study the house over the centuries, we come across several building types, from the single-room edifice to the farmhouse and its outlying buildings grouped around a central courtyard. It is therefore necessary to take the entire habitation and its dependent structures—barn, stable, and so on—into account, because the house spirits would be as likely to find shelter near the fireplace as in the stable, sty, or hayloft. By means of what are mistakenly labeled superstitions, we will extract the principal components of the house, those connected to rites and beliefs, after which we will consider everything we find reflected back explicitly or implicitly in an attempt to find an explanation. It is therefore an inner journey on which we are inviting the reader in search of his roots, a veritable pilgrimage on long-forgotten paths. This campaign of mental archaeology is guided by the discovery of the anthropological structures that will restore the house and its spirits to the place they once held.

The principal studies on the house and domestic deities are the work of German, Scandinavian, Baltic, Finnish, and Slavic researchers who have largely assembled a catalog and inventory over a century of ethnological investigations. Andrejs Johansons has devoted himself to the rich traditions of Latvia regarding the "protector of the farm," and points out all its relationships with the other Baltic lands and Finland; Lauri Honko has put together an extremely interesting case file on the belief in spirits and genies in Ångermanland (northern Sweden); and Iver Paulson has studied the domestic idols of the Siberian and Altaic peoples as well as the domestic deities of the Estonians. Gustav Ränk studied the "sacred back-corner" of the homes of the people of Northeastern Europe and Northern Eurasia, the spot where the domestic idols were housed and worshipped. Aukusti

*[An old-fashioned expression for "housewife" —*Trans.*]

†[Idiomatic expression for being given a housewarming party —*Trans.*]

Vilho Rantasalo concentrated his research on stables and the beliefs relating to them among the Finns and Estonians, but he also drew connections to the Germanic peoples. Martti Haavio devoted a very fine study to the domestic deities of Finland, whose traditions are inseparable from the traditions cited above. By grasping the traditions of people whose historical evolution was slower than that of the Western world, these six major studies reveal that every construction possesses its own spirit, and that its adherents regard this belief as an obvious fact. They also describe the rites connected to this belief. And they show us that the mental attitudes of the people of these regions demonstrate a confounding kinship, to such an extent that we can envision a common anthropological substratum based on archetypes or, if you prefer, "psychic unity."

For Scandinavia, we have the monographs on the spirits of house and farm written by Inger M. Boberg, Reidar T. Christiansen, David Allen Rabuzzi, and Hans F. Feilberg. John Pape retraces the history of the house spirit that inhabits a church (the *kirkegrim*), while Cornelia Weinmann examines that of the home, from the Neolithic period into the Middle Ages, drawing up a precise picture of the evolution of the house.

For the Slavic region, we find valuable information on our theme in the far-ranging studies by Jean Cuisenier and Francis Conte. The important bibliography in Russian that these two researchers compiled has remained inaccessible to me, unfortunately, for simple linguistic reasons.

We are fortunate to have two recent books on Germany at our disposal. One is a highly specialized work by Dagmar Linhart focusing on household spirits in Franconia, and the other is a more general work on the same subject by Erika Lindig. Basing their efforts on a large body of legends, these two scholars drew up a typology of spirits, outlining their appearance, role, and duties, with both authors arriving at the same conclusions.

Paul Sebillot's work touched upon building rites and their legends and beliefs in France, and Paul Sartori has studied the sacrifices that once accompanied the construction of every building. His general study should be rounded off by that of Ion Talos focusing on the Romanian domain, a marvelous work of synthesis that goes well beyond this geographical region. Charles Higounet has given us a fine monograph on the historical geography of the village and the rural house, and Paul-Henri Stahl another on the magical organization of Romanian village territory, which clearly demonstrates the enduring nature of rites and beliefs. Stahl's findings match those from other countries that also are revealing about the vitality of certain mental attitudes. Oskar Loorits concentrated his studies on all the beliefs connected with the domestic fire, whose spirit will seek vengeance for any offense. Mircea Eliade and Jacques Merceron focused their attention on the roof, and Richard Wolfram has studied the gables sculpted with horseheads. Quite recently, Pierre Dubois wrote a marvelous French compendium on the Little People, in which the domestic spirits are strongly represented.

I am only citing the fundamental studies on this subject because there are a plethora of books dealing with the house from an architectural or historical perspective. These studies pay hardly any attention to the domestic spirits. They are helpful, though, because they provide us descriptions and ground plans that allow for comparison and, therefore, a better grasp of the actual surroundings for the beliefs. For example, when the farm consisted of just a single building that was at once a dwelling, stable, cowshed, pigsty, hayloft, and granary, there was only one household spirit. When the farm consisted of a dwelling house and dependent buildings, we find specialized spirits for each structure. Thus, in France for example we find the *faudeur,* or *fouloux,* the spirit that minds the haylofts.

I should also mention the *Handwörterbuch des deuschen Aberglaubens* (Dictionary of German Superstitions). Although its conclusions and interpretations are often outdated, it nevertheless remains a collection of references and traditions with such entries as "threshold," "door," "roof," "gutter," "hearth" (and "frying pan," "oven," "utensils," etc.). The commentaries in the *Atlas der deutschen Volkskunde* (Atlas of German Ethnology) also provide some noteworthy information.

Putting together a corpus on the Middle Ages is quite difficult because the information is concealed amid an array of all manner of texts. The inventory of data unearthed remains extremely sparse, but the traces detected show that domestic spirits were a reality in this time period. The vocabulary is there to inform us of this, and behind the diabolized accounts in which the clergymen castigated certain rites that they viewed as pagan we can discern the presence of the household gods. My previous studies have taught me this: folk beliefs have extraordinary longevity and barely evolve as long as social and material conditions do not change. They vanish when extinguished by major historical upheavals—industrialization, for example, or a war. Closely connected to the rural world and, in our case, to the peasant world, they endure. The studies by Ion Talos clearly show that Romania is an extraordinary repository of ancestral beliefs. The investigations undertaken by Charles Joisten have shown evidence of the same thing for the Alpine regions. Then we have Thekla Dömötör demonstrating the same thing for Hungary, and Boris Rybakov for the Russian region. Therefore, although we are missing some of the links in the chain connecting the Middle Ages to the traditions

Peasant house from Transylvania, Romania (nineteenth century)

collected in the nineteenth and twentieth centuries, it is permissible to compare the two temporal extremes of our investigation in order to shed light on the content of the accounts, especially as we have at our disposal rare but expressive bits of information that surface, terracelike, from the sixteenth to nineteenth centuries. With the help of the tradition of the "sacred corner of the house," I shall demonstrate how this belief endures through the ages.

PART ONE

The House and Its Grounds

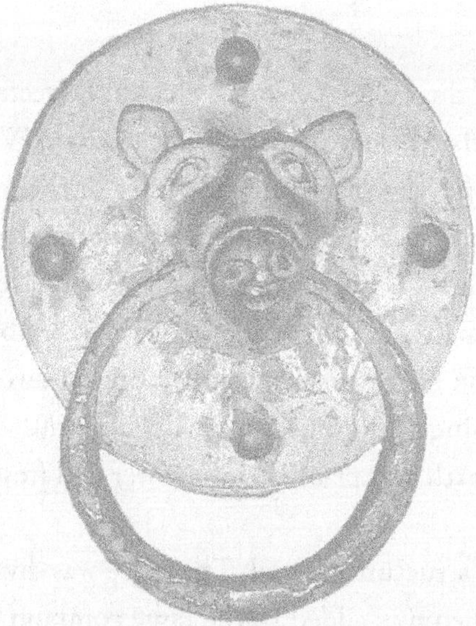

1

The House and Its Construction

The rural house of the more ancient past could be rectangular or round, and essentially consisted of a single room with a door. Windows were only added later. A fire pit was placed in the center of the room and the roof was pierced by a hole for the smoke, which could be shut by a detachable flap. Benches used as beds ran along the walls and household objects were stored beneath them. This house of a bygone age resembled the *bourrines** of the Vendée region or nineteenth-century Breton dwellings—rectangular buildings of a single room that were divided into an upper end (the gable where the hearth was placed) and a lower end (reserved for milking and tool storage).

Gradually, this structure evolved. The space was divided up according to function; a kitchen was added to the large common room, along with one or two additional chambers and a cellar. They often included detachable partitions, namely those that separated sleeping areas from general living areas. A different form of this separation can be seen again in the box beds of ancient Breton dwellings, which were placed at one end of the

*[An earthen construction with a thatched roof built in the marshy areas of this part of France (Vendée region) —*Trans.*]

single room. The fire pit became a fireplace, stove, or oven, depending on the region. Sometimes the kitchen was a separate building outside of the main house. The master of the house and his wife soon had their own room that was separate from the servants' sleeping quarters. In short, the house was subdivided into small, specialized living units.

As the activity of its inhabitants evolved, the house grew to include dependent areas designed for specific elements. The farm animals were separated from one another and given their own quarters: stable, cowshed, pigsty, and henhouse. The harvests were stored in barns and haylofts and silos; drying rooms and attics housed the grains, and the plow and other tools were housed in equipment buildings. At the seaside, we find smokehouses for fish or a hall for drying them along with the nets. In the countries of Northern and Eastern Europe, the bathing cabin, widely known by its Finnish name *sauna,* was located a short distance from the house.

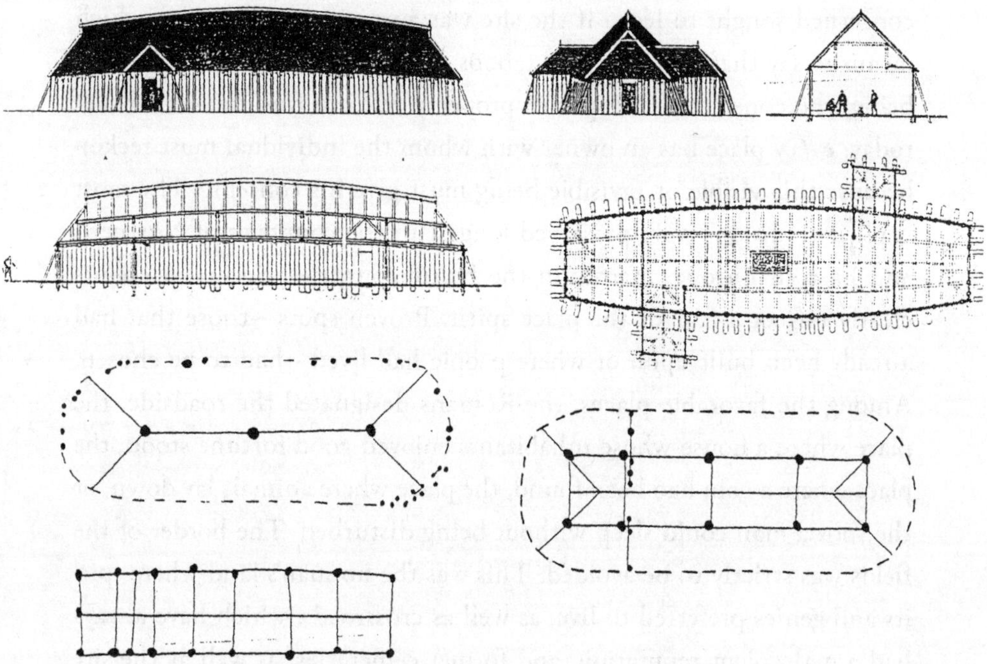

Ground plan for Scandinavian dwellings based on the pillars holding up the roof.

I should also make mention of the temporary dwellings, the chalets for the seasonal displacement of the herds to mountain pastures or the huts located near remote fields. They were arranged like the main house although in a much more rudimentary fashion, and were undoubtedly more similar to the dwellings of a much older era. The single room was dominant and housed the hearth. Activities took place outside or in the common room where the tools were stored and where, once, the livestock were only separated from the people by a half partition, because the heat released by the animals contributed to the heating of the room.

THE CHOICE OF THE HOUSE'S LOCATION

In my study on place spirits, I provided information on the rites for taking possession of a piece of land collected from a large number of sources. When any kind of building was being planned, the individuals concerned sought to learn if the site was auspicious or unlucky, which means to say that there were no taboos there imposed by a supernatural being who considered the spot its property. We can find the same belief today: every place has an owner with whom the individual must reckon because this visible or invisible being must give his consent.[1] The most explicit traditions were preserved longest in the countries of Northern and Eastern Europe, mainly in the Baltic countries. Several accounts clearly reflect a fear of the place spirit. Proven spots—those that had already been built upon or where people had lived—had to be chosen. Among the favorable places, the Romans designated the roadside, the place where a house whose inhabitants enjoyed good fortune stood, the place where a coin had been found, the place where animals lay down, or the spot a man could sleep without being disturbed. The border of the fields was strictly to be avoided. This was the no-man's land where spirits and genies preferred to live, as well as crossroads, which have always had a malevolent reputation, and former cemeteries, as well as the site of a suicide or a place where animals were slaughtered, because death is contagious. The Estonians regarded the site where a house burned down as cursed,[2] and the site where human bones were discovered was believed unlucky by the Sámi, who also avoided settling on spots where a bear or wolf had devoured its prey. For the Finns, Swedes, and Estonians, it was necessary to avoid the passage of a path or an underground waterway as well as the border between two domains, because a spirit (*rajamies*) made this spot its home. A similar belief exists in Sweden regarding places where an unmovable stone is found, or where a house has burned down.[3] In Denmark, the site where a building once stood was avoided because the former spirit lingered there, something that was quite visible because whenever old houses were demolished, a snake would be found beneath the floorboards. The Slavic Ruthenian people of the Carpathians, the Votyaks, and the Russians all refrained from building alongside a path or road.[4]

In Sweden, it was necessary to request permission from the earth spirits (*jordvättarne*) to build, and it was equally important to avoid offending them.[5] The Russian Votyaks asked the spirit of the place for authorization to build and consulted a magician before starting any work.[6] An anthill indicated a good site.[7] Before building a house, it was necessary to spend a Thursday or Friday night at the desired construction site. If the spirits did not drive you away from the spot, you could put a dwelling there.[8] The site on which a farm was to be built had to be courteously greeted first and foremost. This was an absolute necessity; otherwise the construction would be unsuccessful. The individual would say, "Hail earth, hail spirit of the land (elf, sprite, dwarf), hail family mother" (*perehen emäntä*).[9] In this way, the place spirit was recruited to serve as the house spirit.

In Estonia and among the Votes of Laukaa Bay in Finland, "when a house was raised, one started by tracing furrows in a cross in the ground that would be included in the house; in this was the spirit blessed."[10] Among the Votes of Jœnperä, "when someone began construction of a hut, it was necessary to bless the ground with salt, exactly as if the farm was bothering the spirit." Before building, the ground would be worked while holding a black rooster by the wings, because it was said evil spirits feared the color black.[11]

In 1777, A. W. Huppel stated that the Latvians and the Estonians

> never build a house on an evil site where a building has burned, and if a spark leaps up from the ax when placing the first beam, they deduce that a new conflagration will occur and seek, if possible, another spot for the building. Before building a stable, they carefully verify whether the land is auspicious or unlucky; they lay down rags and plants and make their decision based on the ants they find on them. Black ants are in fact a good sign; red ones are the sign that the spot is worthless.[12]

This account is, in its own way, a veritable summa, and the role played by the insects is decisive. According to other traditions, a piece of tree bark would be laid down and if, on the next day, any kind of insect was found on it, that was a good omen. For a stable, a shaving of wood would be set out and checked several days later to see what might be beneath it. If it was an earthworm, one should not build there; if it was a slug, the site was good because the horses "would be equally as supple." It was also said it was propitious to build where three mice were found nesting. Another tactic was to build a tiny wood house and if a beetle was found sticking on it the next day, it was a sign that livestock would prosper there.[13]

There were other tests such as placing four piles of grain in the four corners of the future house. If something touched them during the night, the site was propitious, and it was then acceptable to mark out the placement of the dwelling, in other words, draw a frontier between the surrounding space and the one to be created. Among the Romanians, on the other hand, verification regarding the favorable nature of the terrain was determined by placing slices of bread or cheese, or glasses of schnapps or water on it. If they remained intact, one could build there. Here is another test that was once used in Finland: one had to place the four cornerstones of the future house and sleep inside the space they marked out, especially in the corner that would be home to the crucifix. No fire or fire starter should be brought there, or else a fire should be kindled with the oakum of a living tree and a charm recited, after which the property would be circumambulated two times from east to west while reciting charms and prayers, The fire should burn for three days and three nights while a Christian remained permanently in the center of the circle that had been marked out.[14]

It was also necessary to clearly determine the orientation of the house.

> An old woman observed the direction of the houses from the sky and predicted whether happiness would come to them or not. The place of the doors in the walls was then decided. The location of the cowshed should not be to the north for the animals to prosper; the door of the sauna should open on the south.[15]

This orientation was so fundamental that when a man bought a house, he would change the site of the doors so they would be the same as the ones in his former home, in order that the spirits could come and go as they were accustomed to. It would take far too long to list the traditions of different peoples on the nature of the cardinal points, so I shall content myself with noting that in Japan the directions of northeast (*kimon*) and southwest (*urakimon*) are reputedly unlucky. The phases of the moon and the wind and the cardinal points were also taken into account. Construction essentially was started at a full moon when the wind was out of the north.[16]

Sometimes it was the actual construction material that determined the site of the future building. This belief is encountered most often in connection with churches.

> The church of Siuxt (Kurland, Russia) is now at a lower level. Originally, people wanted to build it on a hill near the current territory of Gute Siuxt, but the first stone forced them to change their plans. Brought to the top of the hill during the day, that night the stone rolled down, finally coming to a halt where the church now sits. They ultimately decided to build it there. The first stone was originally walled up in the altar, then beneath the pulpit. Today it can be found in the pavement beneath the entrance portal.[17]

In certain cases, an animal's behavior clearly indicated the site for construction. Here is a Courland (Latvia) legend that associates this motif with that of a human sacrifice.

> When the people decided to build the church of Skrunda, in Courland, two pastors left on horseback to select the site. They first passed by the Krievukalns, where one horse dislocated a hoof; then by the Pilskalns, where a horse started bucking. They finally came to the spot where the church now stands. Here one of the horses went down on its knees, and they saw that the site was intended for the building. But during this period it was not possible to build a church without walling up a chaste young girl or child in a pillar, otherwise whatever one built during the day would collapse at night, which is what happened with the church of Skrunda. Messengers were sent to ask young boys and girls if they wanted to look after the keys of the church. The children had been warned to say no if anyone asked them this question. But one little girl responded: "I would really like to keep them." She was taken away and walled up in a pillar of the church. And look, what was built during the day no longer collapsed at night.[18]

The construction sacrifice, which is well substantiated throughout the whole of Europe, became proverbial in Latvia: "Every church demands a sacrifice." Furthermore, it was assumed that the victim transformed into a supernatural guardian spirit.

From his study of a vast body of legends concerning the construction of churches, Dag Strömbäck summed up the various rites as follows:

> The placement of the church is: 1. Indicated by animals (ox, sow, colt, and so on) allowed to wander as they pleased: the building would be placed where they stopped, knelt, and so forth; 2. A tree trunk was cast into a lake or river and wherever the current took it was the most appropriate site for the church; 3. The construction material was transported by supernatural means from the site where building had begun to another spot that had to be the best one according to the prediction.[19]

On each of these occasions, supernatural forces come into play. In the case of a religious edifice, it is obvious that the entities that would find lodging there would refuse to be neighbors to creatures of another religion, who were considered to be demons and pagans. Every building should therefore be erected in a magically pure place, which is to say one without a supernatural owner, whether it is a spirit, a demon, or a dead soul. This notion can be found in the Far East in a similar form. In China, for example,[20] appeal was made to a geomancer to determine if the spot lent itself to construction because it was especially important not to build on the tail of a telluric dragon.

A person could not remain ignorant for long about whether the place selected was auspicious or harmful, in other words, whether or not it irritated the spirits. In fact, most often a very clear sign was displayed: the livestock died. There are a thousand stories repeating this same thing. Here is one example.

> When the Undergrounders [*Untererscher,** the name for domestic spirits in the Lubeck region of Germany] still lived here, it was impossible to raise calves on a Stocksee farm because they always died within a few days of birth. Just as the folk there lost another one, an extremely tiny woman appeared who told them: "You should know that you cannot raise calves here because my bed is located just beneath the cowshed. When the manure flows over it, the calf has to die." The folk moved the stable and their misfortune came to an end. [21]

The Sacrifice for the Building

As the sacrifice for a building has already been extensively studied by various scholars, I will not dwell on it and simply noting certain aspects will suffice here. Depending on the time and the place, it could appear in a wide variety of forms: actual sacrifice of a human being or an animal, or a simulation of such a sacrifice. In the latter case, the shadow or its life-size approximation was buried in the foundations, and even today a photograph

*The term can also be translated as "subterraneans."

may be used to perform the same function. Whatever the case, the person will die forty days or even a year later, which is why a stranger to the village is often chosen for this purpose. In the southern Slavic countries, the victim can be the first person to walk past the construction—his or her shadow will be walled up—a form of sacrifice condemned by the *Nomocanon* (legal canon) of the Byzantine Church.

> It was customary when building a house to put a human body in the foundation. May he who places a human being be punished with

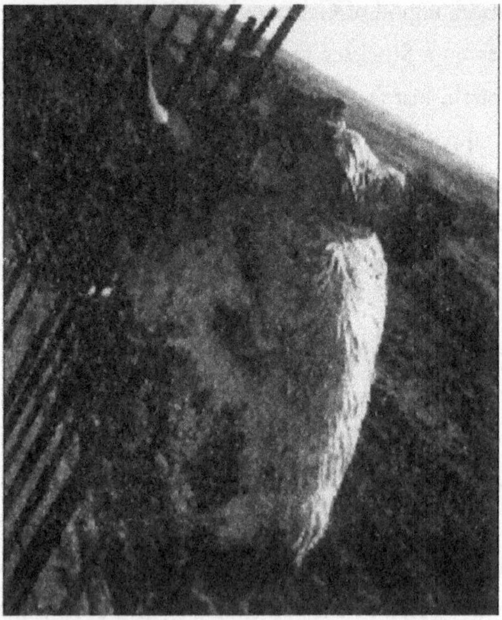

Building sacrifice at Agia Marina, Greece, spring 1998 (above). A close-up of the head impaled at the upper right (below).

twelve years of penitence and three hundred genuflections. Let a wild boar, bull, or goat be placed in the foundation instead.[22]

This ambiguous prescription therefore accepts the ritual sacrifice of an animal as a substitute for a human being, while not condemning the overall practice!

In Romania, the legend of Meşteru (Master Builder) Manole celebrates the memory of an atrocious act: Manole had to sacrifice his own wife to permit the construction of the Cathedral of Curtea de Argeş to move forward.[23] The original sacrifice was gradually euphemized. The immuring of a cat, or even a frog (*anjou*), replaced that of a human being. The foundations were sprinkled with the blood of an ox or a rooster, or even with wine (Upper Brittany). In Catalonia, broken eggs were placed within the foundations.

Among these animal sacrifices, the oldest verified beast is the horse. Ethnologists cite the sacrifice of roosters and hens as more recent. This is why archaeologists almost everywhere in Europe have unearthed bones when excavating the sites of old houses. In Novgorod, in the excavations of tenth-century buildings, horse skeletons have been found. In the hill fort of Talsi, Latvia, the bones and skulls of horses that had been placed between the foundation stones of various buildings dating from the tenth and twelfth century were discovered in 1936. The skull of a horse flanked by ox bones from the thirteenth century was also discovered, as well as a pig's head beneath the corner of a tower next to a gate. In Dundaga, in the Latvian region of Courland, it was recommended to enclose a duck beneath the house one wished to build.[24] In Russia, a black rooster would have its neck wrung, then be placed beneath the threshold of the bathing cabin, and expressly consecrated to the spirit of the sauna. White Russians would bury a rooster's head in the ground on which they wanted to build.

In Baltic countries, the sacrifice took the form of a coin placed in a specific spot during the construction: beneath the threshold, the floor, between the stone foundation and the wooden wall, between certain beams, or between two logs. Once this coin has been placed in its proper spot, the house belonged to the peasant. In the cowshed, the stable, and the sauna, mercury, black wool, and a spoonful of butter were introduced into the construction.[25] In France, substances with a reputation for turning bad influences aside and for driving evil spirits away were incorporated into the construction materials, and a coin bearing the date of the year the building was built was placed in its foundation.[26] Even today, in Greece, one can see a cow's head stuck on a piece of rebar protruding above the edge of the roof once the basic structure has been erected.[27]

Various interpretations have been provided for these building sacrifices. It is first and foremost a purchase price, a compensation to the invisible owner of the site that has been taken and whose potential anger the new owner thereby seeks to appease. Next it is a means of obtaining the neutral or benevolent feelings of the place spirit; if the spirit's disposition can be swayed, it will thus restore the balance that has been broken. Finally, it is the transmission of a soul into the new building, giving life to a new creation. Sacrifice is therefore a primordial act and should be compared to the major cosmogonic myths that evoke the dismemberment of a supernatural being, as was the case with the giant Ymir of the ancient Germans, whose body parts became those of the earth.

For Andrej Johansons, the sacrifice is purely apotropaic as its purpose is to obtain a tutelary deity for the new building,[28] an assessment that Harald Sjövall clarifies more specifically as follows: "It does not so much involve taming the place spirit as it does changing his mood; if he is pleased with the sacrifice, he will accept his new role; the genius loci will transform into the protector of the house and even the entire farm."[29] Thanks to other accounts collected by Georg Sverdrup, the accuracy of these interpretations is confirmed. In Norway, the *tomtegubbe,* meaning the "Old Man of the construction site," regularly transforms into the *tunvord,* the "Guardian of the farm."[30] We will revisit this extremely important point.

THE MATERIALS

The accounts we possess mainly concern wooden buildings that we can imagine as the old chalets or the log cabins from the time of the winning of the American west. These dwellings could be taken apart, like the Russian izbas (traditional log houses), and we can find a trace of this in the *Sachsenspiegel* or *Mirror of the Saxons,* a collection of laws and customs assembled by Eike von Repgow in the twelfth century. When a widow was not the owner of the site on which her house stood, she had to leave it "to vacate the land without harming it"; if she was unable to purchase the land, she could "remove the construction from the ground and plow it, leaving it in tillable condition."[31] These stipulations clearly demonstrate that it was possible to take the house apart. The trees that provided the basic construction material were chosen with care because it was believed that they were inhabited by spirits, which brings to mind the verses of the French poet, Pierre de Ronsard:

Stay woodman, stay thy hand awhile and hark—
it is not trees that thou art lying low!
Dost thou not see the dripping life-blood flow
from Nymphs that lived beneath the rigid bark?[32]

Ronsard is referring here to the traditions of Classical Antiquity, to the dryads, hamadryds, and other nymphs that Ovid depicted so wonderfully in his story about Erythichthon. When this individual struck an oak sacred to Deo (Demeter) with his ax, "red blood poured from the rent he made in its bark."[33] Ronsard was unaware, however, that this belief was widespread throughout all of Europe. A tree is a living being that is respected, to whom fate has alloted a certain lifespan; therefore, people refrained from chopping it down without rhyme or reason, as that could be dangerous. It is close to man and sometimes his personification; it sings, speaks, bleeds. A tree was planted at a birth, a veritable plant double of the child, and if it died, that individual would also perish. In Westphalia, the beech tree was known as the baby tree because it was believed they were taken out of its hollow. The same thing was believed about the ash in the Tyrol, and in both cases it signifies that trees are the "reservoirs of souls." Furthermore, in Germano-Scandinavian mythology, the names of the first two human beings are Ask and Embla, meaning Ash and almost certainly Elm. Wilhelm

Wundt has shown how widespread the belief is that the soul can move into a tree.[34] In Germany, the woodsman starts by asking the tree's pardon before he cuts it down.[35] In the Slavic regions it is said that every new house demands a victim in compensation for the trees that were cut down to build it.[36] In Siberia, the Russians bring a young juniper into the izba that has just been built, install it there roots and all, and then address the *domovoj*, the domestic deity, saying, "This is for you, father and neighbor, a truly warm house and a shaggy juniper."

The tree was kept in the front corner of the izba, and it was believed that the *domovoj* established his patron spirits there. Near Vjaznikov, a tree taken from the forest (a birch or rowan) would be planted after the site of the future house had been determined, and the same was true for the stables. It was considered as the sacrificial tree in compensation for the trees that had been cut down for the construction. At the same time, this planting rite aimed to profit from the tree and its vitality in order to protect the people and animals living there. In the region of Vologda, a spruce tree was planted in the middle of a newly built stable, in the belief that it would protect the livestock from epidemics targeting animals. It is likely that the last remnants of these beliefs can be seen in the *cérémonie du bouquet* still practiced in modern France. As an indication that the construction of the house is finished, a small spruce or some branches from a tree are fixed to the roof ridge or chimney.

In Russia, pains are taken to avoid using a tree that has been struck by lightning, one that is dry or been brought down by a storm, as well as trees growing near a crossroads or on the borders of a property. Some trees, like the aspen, have an evil reputation. In the Baltic countries, the trunk used should not have its shoots turned toward the sky, otherwise the house will burn down, and if it has an outgrowth, it should be turned to face the outside of the house, otherwise its inhabitants will always be sick.[37] This latter belief is easily explained once we know that some Russian sorcerers, when treating certain diseases such as hernias, did so by transferring them from the patient into the trees of the forest. This outgrowth is thus an indication that such a transfer did indeed take place. But people operated this same way in many other countries as well.

In Germany, it was even claimed that three different kinds of wood should be used: stolen wood, purchased wood, and wood offered as a gift, otherwise luck would flee.[38] In the Harz region, the wood served as an oracle. The master builder had to be the first to strike the wood for the construction with the carpenter's ax; if sparks flew, it was sign that the house would burn down and was therefore unsuitable.[39]

The precautions taken in the choice of the building material have their roots deep in the same source as the legends that describe how a woodland spirit transforms into a household spirit and enters the house with the first beam. Among the Swedes of Finland, it is said a homonuculus can be seen sitting on the final beam after a house has been destroyed.[40] This belief can be found again in Switzerland, in the Upper Valais, and in the Canton of Uri in a different form. The elements of this belief have been heavily Christianized, and the spirit seen in the ruins is a lost, lamenting soul.

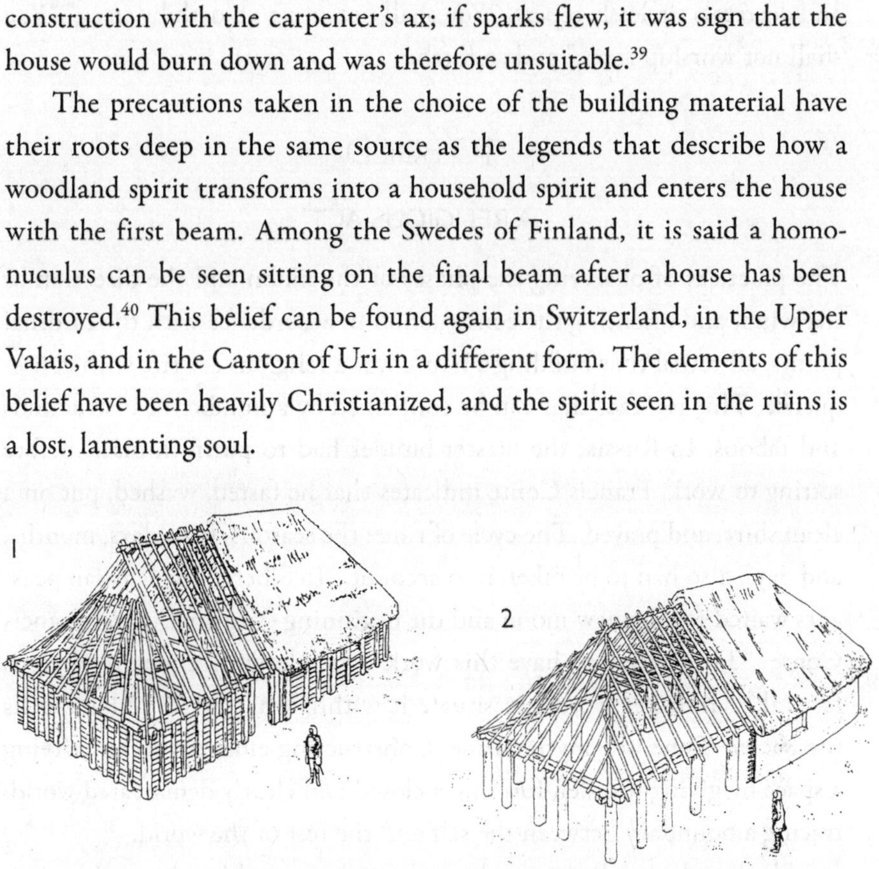

(1) England, Anglo-Saxon period; (2) Denmark, Middle Ages; (3) Denmark, Viking Age

All of these elements match what the medieval texts tell us about the worship of trees. When Sulpicius Severus informs us in his *Life of Saint Martin* (chapter 13) about a tree sacred to demons, it obviously involves a tree inhabited by a supernatural spirit and, like a leitmotif, the penitentials and decretals tirelessly repeat, "You shall not swear an oath by trees," "You shall not worship trees," and so forth.

TO BUILD

A RELIGIOUS ACT

The practices of observing the phases of the moon and the direction of the wind, and orienting the construction in accordance with the cardinal points, all reveal that building a house was a religious act rife with consequence. This is a fact that can be confirmed by a number of instructions and taboos. In Russia, the master builder had to purify himself before setting to work. Francis Conte indicates that he fasted, washed, put on a clean shirt, and prayed. The cycle of time: the seasons, feast days, months, and days, also had to be taken into account. "In Siberia, the Russian peasants waited for the new moon and the beginning of spring," notes Francis Conte. "They strive to have this work coincide with a major religious festival,"[41] in other words, to situate it within what Mircea Eliade calls the Sacred Time, the mythic time. Constructing amounts to sanctifying a space by giving it order, forming a closed and clearly demarcated world, tracing a boundary between the self and the rest of the world.

Eliade, who studied everything that relates to this sphere with great perspicacity, realized that every construction is a creation, a beginning, the reiteration of a mythical act, a cosmogony, and therefore requires precise rites so that it conforms to the archetype. The house is a new center of the world and possesses a religious value. Is it any coincidence that the ancient name for a dwelling in the Germanic languages (*hof*) can mean "farm," "house," and "sanctuary," and that the keystone is still called Heaven's Gate" (*Janua Coeli*)? Eleazar Mélétinskij points out that the Yakut epics attribute the building of the first house to Er Sogotoh, the son of the supreme god Yurong Ayi Toyon.[42] Russian traditions also tell us that the house is a microscosm: in the izba, the corner where the icons are kept is the dawn, the ceiling represents the celestial vault, and the large center beam represents the Milky Way.

The house is also a center in the sense that it is a principle of unification of men and goods, and simultaneously of building and family, as Emmanuel Le Roy Ladurie notes.[43] It is therefore hardly surprising to come across gestures of consecration, namely with the help of a hammer or ax that is thrown over the roof of the house. In Christianized countries, a priest would bless the house. In Namur, Belgium, the first stone was sprinkled with holy water using a bough of boxwood that had been blessed.

Invested with sacredness by the rites and by the presence of a spirit, the building should not be destroyed, no matter what, under pain of punishment. Latvian accounts provide proof of this belief.

> A peasant owned a barn that was falling into ruin where he left his food for the Dievins [deities]. When he died, his son ordered one of his servants to knock the building down, but once this individual began tearing down the thatch roof, he was struck with madness, and there matters rested. The son's children inherited the farm in turn, and the new owner wanted to get rid of the barn. The worker responsible for this task went mad. And the same thing happened repeatedly until the building was left alone.[44]

Moving In

When the building was finished, the act of taking possession was performed with a specific ritual, which the French called the *remise du corré,* the "handing over of the bolt," or even of the pull, the threshold, the hinges, and the lintels of the door. A notarized writ states:

> Today, the twenty-third day of December 1656, in the presence of the royal notary . . . his lordship Gilles Lucas, Marquis de Saint-Marc, Saint-Charier, etc., has taken and apprehended the true, real, and current possession of the property of Ponthion . . . and this by

> play of the *corré* [bolt] of the principal door and by the entry and exit he made in one of the dilapidated apartments of the noble house of the said site of Ponthion, by the breaking of the branches of the trees of the enclosed garden that sits before said house, as well as those of the fruit trees in the orchard of said site; the entire mill of said site by the entrance and exit he made there, the opening and closing of the windows, and by all the other customary solemnities called for in such cases, said lordship declaring aloud that he has come to take true . . . possession of said site and noble fief of Ponthion . . .[45]

Other seventeenth-century charters inform us that the new owner of a property would also be accompanied by a priest and that in the case of taking possession of a priory, he would have to kiss the main altar of the church, open and close the missal, and enter and leave while the bells were ringing. Sometimes this included the sprinkling of holy water and the singing of the *Veni Creator mundi.*

It was imperative for the new inhabitant to faithfully follow the ancestral rites because the building presented a danger. Among the beliefs recorded by Jacob Grimm, one says this: "Whoever moves into a new house should start by throwing a living creature—a dog or cat—inside. Whoever enters first shall be the first to die."[46] Lauri Honko has made the same observation about the region of Ångermanland.[47] The orthodox Russians, for example, toss a rooster into every new building before a priest arrives to bless it. It was a common belief throughout all Europe that every new building required a victim—I provided a glimpse of this earlier—which brought about a proliferation of legends on this theme, mainly those concerning the building of bridges. The construction would repeatedly collapse and appeal was made to the devil for assistance. As wages, he demanded the soul of the first living being to cross over the bridge. Once the work had been completed, the devil would have to be satisfied with a cat or some other animal that had been let loose on the bridge.

In 1901, in Deville, two miles from Rouen, a man witnessed the following rite.

An old woman holding a black chicken in her hand entered the first room; once she passed over the doorsill, she secured the bird between her legs and slit its throat with the blade of a knife. She poured its blood in front of the house and when the animal was on the verge of expiring, she spilled the last drops on the threshold. The dead bird would then be roasted and served at the meal following the sacrifice.

The witness questioned the old woman, who answered him as follows.

> It is to avoid one of the inhabitants of this house dying during the next year. I do the same thing for all new construction, and there is no one hereabouts who would consent to living inside a new-built house unless a few drops of blood from a pigeon, duck, or rabbit had been spread over the doorsill beforehand.[48]

The moment chosen for moving in is important and suggestive of commencement rites since it is augural, foreshadowing the future of the dwelling and that of its inhabitants. In seventeenth-century France it was said people should move into their new lodging "when the moon was a crescent in order to increase their property,"[49] and in Germany, "one must move in during the new moon: their food supplies will increase."[50] In Bohemia, on the other hand, the new moon was strictly to be avoided. The weather and events are also highly meaningful: if it is raining, no one in the new home will know happiness, but if the rain falls on the procession, one will be rich; if an object is broken when moving out or if someone brings an egg, this brings misfortune; if someone brings a cat, a family member will die; if one brings the stove first, quarrels will ensue.[51]

Often moving in assumes moving out of one's former dwelling to set up house in the new one. In Germany, Monday, Wednesday, Friday, and Saturday were advised against, which became the source of a number of proverbs: "Who moves out on a Wednesday will have little food" (*Mittwoch gezogen kurz gegessen*); "who moves out on a Saturday will not stay there a long time" (*Samstag gezogen, bleibt nicht lange*).[52] Holy week is also to be avoided. In the Transylvanian mountain region of the Muntii

Metaliferi, Sunday is the recommended day, which is odd since the church forbids any work on this day. In Norway, it is said people should change domicile on Thursday; in Holland, it is May 1; and in Scotland, Pentecost. In Ångermanland, people did not move on Sunday, Wednesday, or Friday (days of rest) because "Sunday is the Sabbath; the week begins to grow smaller on Wednesday, and Jesus suffered on Friday."[53] Saturday was therefore the preferred day, with Tuesday and Thursday as possible stand-bys. The prescriptions are quite restrictive, but judge for yourself.

> On this day, one should not bring all their belongings into the new dwelling so that it may continue to swell with them later. One should therefore leave some of their things behind and go retrieve them several days later. The dishes should enter the house with their openings facing the sky in order that one does not become impoverished. When moving out, the farm wife carries some fresh dough, some soot from the stove and the sauna oven, and manure from the stable. She tosses all this underneath her clothes from the hem of her dress to the top of her shirt. Once she reaches the boundary of the grounds of her old house, she allows some of it to fall out. She then waits for all the livestock and people of the farm-stead to cross this boundary line before following them. At the border of the new farmstead, she takes the head of the group and lets the rest of what she has been carrying fall to the ground, walks on the path in four directions making a cross, then makes a slight incision in the ear of the lead animal of the flock and touches the blood that flows from it with her tongue while saying: Here as over there!" This means: I was the mistress over there, I am the mistress here as well. On entering the common room, the farm wife says, "Greetings! Peace be with you! So that we live in good health and die with honor." Next she throws salt and breadcrumbs into the hearth that a magician has given her for this purpose. For his part, the farmer brings his horses to a halt in the courtyard of the new house, unharnesses them, and strikes the ground with his whip, saying: "Tamp down the soil, reheat the land!" He, too,

has salt, which he places in the manger. Everyone who has helped them to move from their former home carries an armful of wood into the common room and the oldest among them says: "That's enough, may those living here always have bread to eat, heat for when you sleep, and sturdy clothes to wear!" Then everyone will sit down to eat so that the place spirit can see the entire group right from the very first day. After the meal, each of them will place some money in the plate of the farmer or his wife, stating: "May you have no need of money, may your gold collect here; outside of God you need no other assistance." A verse of a canticle is then sung as a signal that the ceremony is over.[54]

In Germany, a person should start by installing the table and placing a slice of bread on it. A lit candle should be placed to the right and left side, with a crucifix behind it. Another order is: a crucifix, a table, bread, salt, and silver. It is necessary to put a new broom in the house as well as salt, or else sugar, salt, and pepper, if one wishes to be happy.[55] Other accounts indicate that it is necessary to invite the domestic spirit of the former house to follow you into the new one, otherwise it will be left weeping in the abandoned home.[56] But it is also possible to go back to retrieve it. If you wish to be rid of this spirit because it is a pest, and to prevent it from following you, place two tiles in the form of a roof over the site where the house you have dismantled once stood. It will remain in this simulacrum of a dwelling.

Among the Siberian Votyak people, a small number of cinders or live embers are carried away; otherwise the hut is entirely taken apart to be rebuilt elsewhere.[57] Virgil tells us that Aeneas carried his household gods into Italy, which is something we should compare to the discovery made in Pompeii of a woman's skeleton holding her jewels and a clay statuette. In Volhynia and Podilskyy, the old home is swept in order to ensure no happiness is left behind. The sweepings are carried to the new home where they are shoved into the icon corner or under the stove.

All of these rites are the expression of an extremely ancient and simple mental attitude. It involves the transfer of the happiness and luck of the house one is leaving into the new home. Many different peoples share the custom of carrying cinders or live embers, symbols of the hearth in every sense of the word, inasmuch as domestic life was totally organized around it. It was commonly said that a person should go back into his former house before seven years have passed, unless something was left behind, even if it was just a nail in the wall. Leaving something behind acts as a good luck charm as it shows the house has not been totally abandoned.

It has also been observed that all living creatures are included in the rites and animals are treated just like human beings. Manure is brought from their former stable, and their new home is introduced to them for their approval, for it was common knowledge that if they did not like it they would not prosper, which could also be a sign that the farm was ill placed and was irritating a spirit who would take it out on the animals.[58] This detail shall be more fully examined later.

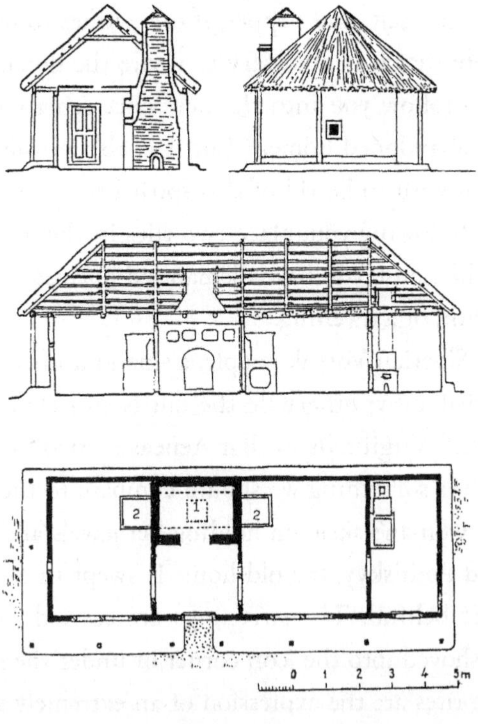

Wallachian farm. Interier view at bottom: (1) hearth; (2) blind stoves.

I noted earlier that to build is a cosmogony, and a Russian moving ritual confirms this observation.

> On the first night, a chicken and a rooster is moved in; on the second, a goose, a dog, or a cat (preferably black); on the third, a pig; on the fourth, a lamb; on the fifth, a cow; and on the sixth, a horse. If no animal has perished or even suffered, the masters of the house will spend the next night there, the seventh, which would correspond in some respects to the culmination of the creation of the world.[59]

We can thus also see the polysemy of the precautions that are taken. By this means, assurances are sought that the site is not malevolent; an archetypal action is repeated and a new center of the world is created—which is confirmed by the German names that divide the world into the Middle Enclosure (*Miðgarðr*), the earth of men; the Outer Enclosure (*útgarðr*), the world of giants and monsters; and the Aesir Enclosure (*Ásgarðr*), the domain of the gods.

Humans clearly occupy the center of this mythical geography. This mental attitude is particularly obvious in how the Russian peasant views his izba. As I mentioned earlier, the icon corner represents the dawn and the ceiling the celestial vault. The large central beam of the ceiling stands for the Milky Way. Thus, the dwelling is also a microcosm.

Concerning the rite described above, Francis Conte rightly notes: "We see that the animals were placed in the izba in a specific order, which did not correspond to their size but to their proximity to human being. The rooster and hen were considered by the peasant to be the most distant from him while the horse and cow were the closest."[60] The peasant therefore tests the new house before moving in, which clearly shows he dreads something—the presence of an invisible and dangerous being.

THE HOUSE MAN

The house is not only a center and a microcosm; it is also a living being and it is treated like a person. In ancient times did it not receive a soul—that of the sacrificed individual placed in its foundations? The anthropomorphism of buildings is solidly attested among the Slavs. Relying on the works of Dmitrij Sergeevic Lixacev and Paul Castaing, Francis Conte summarized the Russian's metaphorical interpretation of the church as follows.

> In Russian, the outer dome of the church is called *glava,* "the head"; the lower part of the cupola is *lob,* "the forehead"; the molding above the windows, *brovki,* "the eyebrows"; the louvers are called *sluxi,* "ears"; the windows, *okna* or *oko,* "eyes or eye"; the blind drum is *sejalsejka,* "the neck or throat"; the roofing that slopes gently down from the base of the "neck" is called *pleci,* "the shoulders"; the pilasters dividing the façade are *lapatki,* "the shoulder blades"; the "kidneys" of the vault, *pazuxa;* and finally the foundations, or rather, the lower part that touches the ground, is *podosva,* "the sole."[61]

Presumably, what is valid for the church should be likewise for the house, but there is no information available in this regard and I cannot do more than speak hypothetically. We should note that the Chinese call the roof opening Heaven's Gate and also use this term to describe the foramen in the skullcap, which in Sanskrit is called the *brahmarandhra.*[62] It is nonetheless worth recalling something that I already mentioned in the introduction: that numerous metaphors treat the home like a human being. It can be one-eyed, blind, leprous, or like an animal, as shown by that round opening called an *œil de boeuf* (bull's eye).* For poets, a thatched roof is like a head of hair, and a house without a roof is described as "decapitated." A room is amputated from a house, and so forth. All this reveals that the house is considered to be a living organism, and we shall see that its heart is the hearth.

*[A circular window, also called an oculus —*Trans.*]

Farm: Holstein

Haller House in Rauhensass (left); note the stag antlers. Roof ridge of a farm in Lower Saxony (top right). Details from farms of Lower Saxony and Westphalia (bottom right).

2

The Building

Every element of a building possesses magic and religious meaning. We gained a glimpse of this in the preceding chapter. The walls and roof hold great importance because they are the elements that make a building a closed and therefore sacred space, a space in which one feels safe. In her study of the tale in Eastern Slavic peasant life and culture, Tatiana A. Bernstam noted a revealing clue.

> It is indisputable that a magic motivation is concealed in the way fairy tales are habitually told from inside when dark and threatening weather is occurring outside, a place and time when "impure forces" are activated. The wonders described in the fairy tales seem to be incorporated into the behavior of "impure forces" and the house is isolated from [evil influences].[1]

THE WALLS

We do not have very much information concerning the treatment of walls because it is often difficult to distinguish the rites concerning the whole building—circumambulation and sweeping, for example—from those that concern only the walls. Pliny the Elder tells us that a dwelling could be protected from all evil spells by sprinkling dog blood on its walls and burying the penis of that animal beneath the threshold.[2] In the Sologne region of France during the nineteenth century, once the construction of a farm had been finished, the owners hastened to slit the throat of a rooster and sprinkle its blood on the walls of the common room; then its body was tossed into the courtyard as food for the devil.[3] Throughout Western Europe, people offered protection to their dwellings by nailing *billets de Sainte Agathe* to their walls, powerful Christian charms on parchment that were intended to protect the home from fire. We should keep in mind another practice for curing toothache: in the Tarn region of France only a century ago it was said that all one had to do was to drive a nail in the wall.

In the Middle Ages, a house would be breached by making a hole in one of its walls, in order to prevent the defilement of the threshold,[4] and this fundamental notion was the basis for many accounts. Ancient German judicial decrees recommended that suicides be removed from the house "by a hole in the wall" (*men maiken sale en gat in den want des huis*) for this reason. In Denmark, one door was reserved for the dead (*likport*); the stones that customarily sealed it off were removed for taking out the coffin and then put back in place after the burial. In medieval Scandinavia, a hole was made in the wall to bring out the bodies of those whose deaths were somewhat suspicious and gave the impression that the deceased would transform into a revenant,[5] a rite that was followed in Scotland well into the nineteenth century.

Walls were used to place curses on humans and livestock. Around 1890, a man known as Little Gregory kept an iron tip on hand that he would hide in the wall of people he was upset with; as long as the piece of iron remained there, a misfortune befell the house every day.[6]

THE CORNERS

Jean-François Simon has rightly shown that "the four fundamental stones in the life of every individual" are the "corner stone, the hearthstone, the baptismal font stone, and the tombstone."[7] But one of the most important parts of the house is the corner formed by two walls and not simply the corner stone. It is a sacred space—of which there are several in the home, but not all share the same importance—as shown by archaeological discoveries and building rites.

In 1955, archaeologists in Novgorod unearthed horse skulls inserted between the foundation stones of houses built in the period spanning the tenth and the fourteenth centuries. They were always found in proximity to a corner and had been intentionally placed at that spot.[8] In Lejasdopeli in Semigalle, the ancient Duchy of Courland, the skull of a pig was found under the corner of a house. When laying the first stones of new house, the Russians buried the head of a hen at the same spot, while in Poland a black rooster was placed there.[9]

Corners are ambivalent locations as they are the abode of benevolent or malevolent forces. Various liquids can be sprinkled in them, or this or that item will be placed in them. During the process of construction, one or more coins or a horseshoe would be buried beneath a corner of the house, or else mercury would be poured into the mortises of the corner beans in order to protect the dwelling from lightning and other misfortunes.[10] During the nineteenth century in the Russian region of Kostroma, the head of a rooster would be cut off on the threshold of the drying house or the bath house and its blood would be spread in the corners in order to disperse any malevolent forces they might be sheltering. In order to evict an evil spirit, bear fur would be placed in the corners of the house, and in order to rid the house of fleas, the German farmer had to go to his field in spring, dig the first furrow using a plow without a cotter pin, and place the dirt from it in the four corners of the common room.[11]

We should note that these rites can be divided into two types of measures: some are apotropaic (defensive), while the others have a sacrificial value. Thus, they illustrate the belief that corners were home to supernatural powers.[12]

THE ROOF

Without a roof, the house does not exist because it is open to all winds, which is a general sign it is uninhabited because evil spirits could take possession of it. This is why the Eskimos destroy the roofs of their igloos when the move away. Because a home has been anthropomorphized, the destruction of its roof is the equivalent of its death. The ancient rules governing the exile of criminals from the community attest to this with their instructions to remove the roofs from their houses, to seal off the door, cover the well, and to break the oven.[13]

The covering of the house was regarded as an impassable border, as shown by numerous beliefs, and its strength was reinforced by sculptures, carvings, horse heads, or deer antlers. In Russia, the roof ridges were carved in the forms of birds and horses,[14] and in Japan, the roof ridge of the castle tower was always adorned with two gold fish with tiger heads and dolphin bodies—called *shachihoko*—which were attributed with the power of protecting the house from fire. But it seems that such strength required constant renewal. In Bohemia, the roof of the house was watered at the first ringing of the bells, and in Germany the same was done at Easter, for protection against fires. Branches that had been blessed and other charms were also attached to the roof for the same purpose. In the United States, in California and some other states, a wood or plastic owl can be seen on roof ridges today. The inhabitants may view this as offering their homes protection against earthquakes, lightning, and storms.[15]

In many places, including southern China, three tiles are removed from the roof in order to ease the passing of a dying person. This allows his or her soul to take flight; this custom was condemned by Bernardino of Siena in the fourteenth century. In England, the ridge tile was called the "soul window." In central Russia, roofs were sometimes decorated with two small horses that would be removed when it was learned that a sorcerer was on his deathbed, as this would facilitate his death. The Scandinavian sagas tell us that revenants scale the roofs and seek to bang or knock on them as if they wanted someone to let them in.[16] We should compare this detail with a belief recorded by Plutarch—that a person believed the dead could only return to his former home though a hole that had been made in the wall—and a German custom of removing the body of a suicide from the house through the roof. All of the evidence indicates that the roof is connected to ideas about the beyond. Perhaps this is because, like a tree, it lifts toward the sky while its foundations remain in contact with the domain of telluric spirits.

This link with the other world is evident from a ban promulgated by the Spanish church: it was forbidden to climb on your roof and to sit on it with your sword in order to foresee what the forthcoming year had in store. Earlier, in the tenth century, Burchard, the Bishop of Worms, scolded those who performed healing and divinatory rites on their rooftops,[17] where they would spend the night of Saint Sylvester after drawing a circle with a sword around themselves. In his critique of superstitions, Jean-Baptiste Thiers mentions this practice as still being widespread in the eighteenth century.[18] A variant of the rite involves throwing the patient's shirt over the roof at a certain hour during the night, a detail that, alas, is not provided.

Throwing something over the roof is a precaution common to many peoples. In the Montagne Noire region of France, it was thought all misfortune during funeral ceremonies could be averted if all the hand towels used by the guests were thrown onto the roof. In Haute-Saône, the husband tosses an egg over his roof when returning from the marriage ceremony: if he throws it far, he will be the dominant partner; if it does not reach the other side, his wife will be the dominant one![19] In Silesia, a hen's first egg is thrown like this while making the sign of the cross three times in the air,[20] and elsewhere the same is done with the "witch's egg," which can be recognized by its soft shell.[21] Harvesting the mushroom of the wild rose (*fungus cynostati*) in autumn brings misfortune, but it can be transformed into good fortune if tossed over the roof while standing with your back to it.[22] The Bukovine Gypsies (Romania) think that if a handful of beans is tossed over the roof on the morning of Pentecost, witches and devils will not be able to enter the house.[23] To obtain protection from a curse, the milk that has been charmed must be boiled in a pot, then the entire affair thrown over the stable roof.

This throwing rite was also used for divination. In Scotland on the evening of All Saint's Day, a shoe would be cast in this manner. If it landed upside down, it was a bad omen.[24] We should note that this ritual was practiced during the Middle Ages without using the roof, and I should also point out that it is a fertility rite. Bread, apples, or some other food item would be thrown in the hopes that the item thrown this way would not be lacking in the coming year. This act is, in fact, an offering based on the principle of *Do ut des* ("I give so that you will give").[25] To prevent hawks from attacking the chickens, the stove broom would be tossed over the roof.

The roof is associated with birds and therefore has augural value. In Bielefeld, it was common opinion that if an owl landed on a roof, hooted, then flew away, someone would die.[26] A similar notion is still widespread today, particularly in Brittany, where the bird in question is a magpie. In Picardy, it is said if bats are flying around the house, it will be necessary to move out soon as it will soon be destroyed by fire.[27] It is also thought that if a crow caws over the house of an ill master, he or she will soon die, but if the crow is followed shortly thereafter by the chatter of a magpie, he will be healed.[28] If they soar over the house, it is a foreshadowing of death (Brittany). The call of magpies heralds very bad news[29] or a visit.[30] Birds are therefore sometimes considered to be psychopomps, which is connected with the belief of the soul in the shape of a bird and even that of the individual's animal double. Among the Swedish Sámi, the double of the visitor will announce the arrival of a person long before he or she arrives.[31]

We should also recall that seeing a burning roof crash toward you indicates the owner of the premises will die in the coming year, and that leaving the house while looking at the roof and walking backward will allow for the realization of whatever next catches your eye.

Furthermore, this spot was a kind of altar where noodles, waffles, and hard-boiled eggs would be deposited as sacrifices on the eve of Epiphany. The notion of sanctuary becomes apparent from a magical practice that Jean-Baptiste Thiers recorded: "To speak certain words on the roof of the house so that a laboring woman will give birth easily."[32]

To whom were such words being addressed, if not the supernatural beings who ruled over life and death?

Lastly, the roof is one of the entrances used by the spirits. This is why an opening must be put there so they may come and go as they please.

The spirits here are obviously domestic deities and not malevolent powers.

The symbolic value of the roof is expressed in a custom based on the anthropomorphic principle of the house and that of the magical principle of *similia similibus* (like affects like):

> Pierce the roof of a pregnant woman who is in labor, with a stone, or with an arrow that has slain three animals, to wit a man, a boar, and a she-bear, struck several times, to make her give birth at once; which will occur even more assuredly when the house is pierced with an ax or the saber of a soldier, wrested from the body of a man before he hits the ground.[33]

The roof is made up of beams and rafters, which are the object of revealing beliefs. Among the Siberian Goldi people of the Amur River region, the central beam that supports the roof is identified with the domestic spirit.[34] Jacob Grimm speaks of those who, in Germany, on "Saint John's Night, place as many mugwort plants inside a beam as there are inhabitants of the house, naming the plants with their names," to ascertain the order in which they shall die. The plant of the first to die will wither first.[35] In France, to countermand a curse, the procedure below is followed.

> Without saying a word, obtain the entire heart of a cow from a butcher. Pay for it without heed of cost. . . . From there go to a nail-maker's shop and take a handful of nails. . . . Next, return home while maintaining absolute silence. Between eleven o'clock and midnight, hammer the nails into the heart and firmly attach it to the main beam of the house. As the heart dries out, the sorcerer, with no way to defend himself, will also wither away.[36]

To strengthen the apotropaic properties of the stable roof, an old scythe blade or other sharp tool is placed between the ceiling and the beams. There was one found in a house in Thônes, in Upper Savoy as recently as 1965, and it is common knowledge today that spirits cannot stand iron. In Finland, a bloody cowhide cast on the roof of the cowshed will prevent witches from entering.[37]

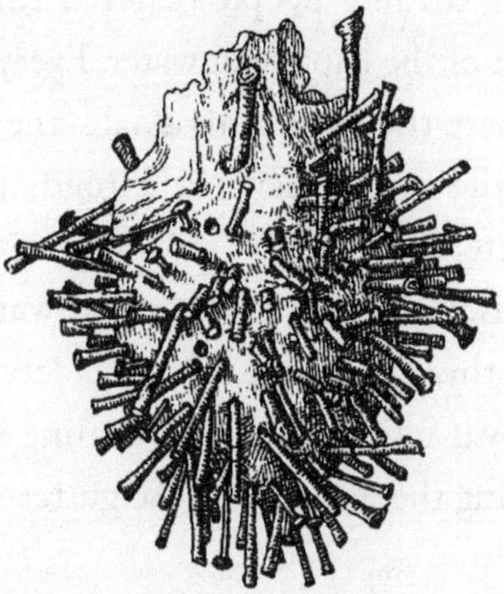

Heart stuck with pins, Devon, nineteenth century

A word must be said about the materials used to cover the roof, although we have very little information at our disposal. What we do have essentially concerns the tiles. We have seen that one or three tiles were removed from the roof in order to allow the soul of the dying individual to flee. The opening of the ridge tile has another meaning. In Catalonia, during the festival of Saint Felix of Africa, this same procedure is used to allow sunlight to enter the house, and the opening is called "hole of the sun" (*forat del sol*).[38] Jean-Louis Olive interprets this rite as a call to the solar virtues and the souls of the dead who dwell above the heavens.

An opposite effect is obtained in northern and eastern Catalonia where a curved tile is placed in the roof ridge, and whose unusual shape and name evokes its function: it is a "Witch scarer" (*espanta bruixes*) or "Witch horn" (*banya de bruixa*). It is used to snag and tear the skirt of the witches as they leave on Sabbath night.

THE GUTTER

The gutter that catches the water from the roof is a legal boundary line that is clearly set down in the ancient texts. Among the Romans, the children who had died before their fourth day—the *lustricus dies*—were buried there, for they would not be accepted in the family tomb and it was believed that the Lares *grundules* or *grundulii* lived in this spot.[39] Among other peoples of Europe, the women who had died in labor and their unbaptized infants were buried there because people believed that the rainwater would perform the function of the baptismal water. Everything that had been used to wash and prepare the dead individual—the straw on which the body had lain, the needle used to sew the shroud, and so on—was buried beneath the rain gutter.[40] The same was done with the placenta, the objects that had been used to treat illnesses and warts, or an ax that had injured someone. In this latter case, if it was left there for eight days while the Our Father was recited each day, healing would ensue. It was also believed that drinking the water from the gutter would cure headaches.

In addition to these rites for healing wounds and illnesses and for protection against death, there are others that clearly indicate the rain gutter is a boundary line. If a mole tunnels beneath the gutter, in other words, if it makes a breach in the defenses of the house, someone will die soon. Burying a cross beneath it will prevent revenants from entering the home; if one of these undead individuals leaps upon your back when you are returning home one night, the victim, if you carry him beneath the gutter, will be freed from his endless wandering. We know that water is one of the surest means of getting rid of the returning dead because water purifies all that it comes into contact with. In 1960, several miles to the southeast of Caunes-Minervois, the sepulcher of a pilgrim of Saint James of Compostela was discovered next to the walls of the church in Trausse. The man had been buried beneath the gutter with a rich funeral array, and Jacques Berlioz noted: "Now, in the ninth to eleventh century . . . important individuals of a religious type (rectors, pilgrims) were buried against the walls of churches beneath the rain gutter, so that the rain water that fell from heaven upon the divine building, thus two times purified, would water the grave of the blessed one."[41] We can safely assume that Christianity retained a much older custom here that it invested with a new meaning.

Among the ways for driving away storm and thunder, we may note the burial of objects beneath the rain gutter. In Bohemia, an ax would be buried with its cutting edge aimed toward the sky, as if a threat, and in Switzerland, a cover or a triangular cloth was buried. This linen, in fact, hints at another, much more magical sphere, and we have examples of witches causing substantial damage by waving a cloth. To ward against hail, the Germans laid a tablecloth in the gutter and placed a knife and fork on it in the shape of a cross, and for protection from lightning, Transylvanian peasants placed bread or dough on the roof.

None of these precautions is simple; each is in fact a combination of different elements, with the metal being the most important, and all of them reveal that the rain gutter is only the extension of the roof and therefore shares its virtues.

THE OUTSIDE OF THE HOUSE

The rural house quite often consists of several buildings situated around a courtyard, and this also forms part of the domestic space. The courtyard therefore warrants a brief discussion, as we will encounter various beliefs that relate to it in the contexts we have already discussed. In Estonia, if a rooster or a hen drags a piece of straw behind it in the yard, this signifies an imminent death, and the sex of the dead person will correspond to that of the animal pulling the straw.[42] In Russia, a spirit that can assume the shape of a snake with a rooster's head, called a *dvorovik,* lives in the courtyard. This spirit has a connection to the household spirit (*domovoj*), whose provocations can be dispelled by placing the foot of a goose there.[43] We should recall that the *domovoj* is almost always a dwarf, whose face is covered by hair except for his nose and around the eyes. The soles of his feet and the palms of his hands are also covered with hair. According to one legend, these dwarves were among the overly numerous descendants of Adam and Eve, who concealed their children from God; the ones that were hidden in the house, the bathhouse, and the barn transformed into the spirits of these places.[44]

The entire dwelling is protected on the outside by various practices that can be classified under two major rites: circumambulation and sweeping. The first is performed while holding an object—for example, the chimney hook—or while sowing the seeds of certain plants. The second is done with a broom whose sweeping material is made from the twigs of certain trees. The two actions take place at sunrise or sunset, and in the sunwise direction, which corresponds with acceptable white magic, or in the opposite direction, which makes it unacceptable black magic.

In Basque country, the cinders from the Yule log are spread around the family house and the barnyard to avert livestock diseases.[45] In Romania, the house was decorated with linden, maple, birch, or rowan branches when in flower at Easter as protection against burglars and mice.[46] In the German-speaking regions, however, thieves were well aware how they could get away with their misdeeds: if they were able to silently pilfer the "dead man's measure"—the stick that was used to take the dead person's measurements—and prop it up at night against the door of the house, the inhabitants would not wake up.[47] In France, the turret of the house was sprinkled with chitterling sausage broth on Thursday or on Mardi Gras, to prohibit foxes from eating their chickens.[48] In Anhalt, a crow slain in March would be hung on the exterior of the house to drive flies away, or an owl, bat, or wolf skin following the same rule of *similia similibus.*[49] Serviceberry branches hung over the door to the house and the stable prevented the flying *drac* spirit from entering.[50] The Russians placed a bear skull on top of the stable to protect the animals from the evil eye.[51] In the sixteenth century, Olaus Magnus reported that nailing a bird of prey to the house drove nightmares away.[52] To ensure good fortune, a wheel should be hung above the main door[53]—a custom that can still be seen in rural areas today, although it has been stripped of any meaning beyond its aesthetic qualities. In the upper Aude Valley, mothers spread barley and wheat in front of the house when a strong wind rises because it is believed that the *follet,* a kind of spirit, can make itself as invisible as the air in order to attack a girl.[54]

Objects, plants, and animals are used based on the symbolic or religious value they have been accorded and the principle of analogy. The folk botanicals divide plants into two major groups: those that are pure and those that are impure. Among the second group, there are many magical plants whose common names imply the idea of witchcraft. Folk zoology does the same. All the components of the universe have their own stories, which explain the mental backdrop of the practices I am citing, and it forms the natural order of things. Unfortunately, we only possess some of these stories—but enough of them, however, to realize that we are dealing with a logical world, even though it may seem rather irrational to us. Nothing is left to chance, and the absolute rule is that of tradition: our ancestors did things this way and it worked out well, so why change? The meanings fade but the practices continue.

3

The Openings of the House

The house therefore forms a protective cocoon, one that is sacred and magical, with its own organization. It only exists thanks to its walls and its roof, which mark off a space horizontally and vertically, isolating it from the rest of the world and, notably, from all malevolent forces. On the vertical plane, the border with the sky is formed by the roof, and its border with the earth and the chthonic world is formed by the elements that were buried in the ground while it was under construction. In the words of the old Germanic laws, the building is inviolable (*Hausfriede*) and no one, for example, can pursue a malefactor into the latter's own house or that of his neighbor. Whoever breaks this law will be sentenced to capital punishment.[1] The Icelandic sagas and Scandinavian legal texts explicitly state that the individual enjoys the benefits of his house's sacred nature when inside (*mannhelgi*) and to banish him amounts to stripping him of it, making him "deprived of sacredness" (*óheilagr*). But the dwelling necessarily has to remain open to the outside in order to receive the necessities of daily life, and its openings thus amount to so many open breaches in this sacred and protective envelope. It is hardly surprising, therefore, that we encounter such a plethora of beliefs surrounding them.

THE DOOR

At one time the door was the sole opening of the house; windows made their appearance later. The door consisted of a doorframe (the lintel and uprights), a hinged section (or sections), and a threshold: in other words, the permanent and solid parts of the construction along with the movable and detachable parts. In Germany, the door was fortified by performing a sacrifice, such as of a cat. In the folk beliefs discussed, the term "door" essentially designates the whole, but when necessary they specify exactly which part of the door the rite affects. Distinctions will be made between the door of the farmhouse and those of the outbuildings.

Accounts dating back as far as classical antiquity make it clear that the door was more than simply a material obstacle erected to block intrusion or as a means of ensuring privacy. Among the Romans, the door was placed under the protection of the gods, as I noted earlier. It was also thought that the Manes spirits liked to stay there. It so happens that in the Upper Palatinate, it is said that the recently deceased linger in the

Main doors of a German farm in Schleswig-Holstein (1629). The inscription reads: "Anno 1629. May the Lord grant me entry and exit in his mercy. May God be with us."

door hinges every Saturday, and in Bohemia, that souls in torment live in doors. This explains a curious piece of advice that we come across in eighteenth-century Germany: "You should not slam a door because souls are performing penitence there."

The Biblical account of the establishment of Passover gives us one of the oldest accounts of purification and sacrifice affecting a door: "Thou shalt smear the blood [of the lamb] on the two uprights and lintel of the door in the house where thou doth eat" (Exodus 12:7). Pliny the Elder noted that newlyweds rubbed the doorposts with pig fat when entering the conjugal home,[2] and, according to Arnobius,[3] it was the goddess Unxia who presided over the ritual anointing. This rite survived in Crete and among the southern Slavs, although honey was used instead of fat. It can be interpreted as an oblation by referring to a similar rite performed by the Siberian Yugakure people who do the same when leaving their summer hut, saying: "Spirit of the house, eat and always give us good fortune in this place belonging to you."[4] The ancient Romans attributed a religious power to wool and encouraged newlyweds to touch the doors of their house with it.[5] According to Plutarch[6] and Lucan (II, 355), the bride crowned her husband's doorway with wool, which was undoubtedly intended to avert illnesses, as wool possesses medicinal properties according to Dioscorides.[7] Diogenes Laertius and Ovid report that branches of hawthorn were attached to the doors of houses to expel grief, illnesses, and spells.[8] In France, blessed hawthorn blossoms or boxwood seem to have once served a similar function.

Specific dates are connected to the rites concerning the door. Antoninus of Florence attacks a "superstition" according to which the door of the house was blessed at the calends of March and something was hung on it. In Catalonia, this blessing took place on Holy Saturday with holy water, salt, and eggs. In antiquity, the door was decorated with garlands at the calends of January, one of laurel for Hermes and one of wheat for Ceres. The rite survives in France on Christmas, and in Scandinavia on Santa Lucia's Day, now stripped of any meaning beyond the decorative.

Because it offers malevolent forces the possibility of intrusion, the door requires protection, and the number of prescriptions that have come down to us is a testimony to the profound fear inspired by these irruptions. "The laurel," says Pliny the Elder, "is propitious for our dwelling places. It stands guard at the door and protects the surrounding area." And Ovid specifies: "It stands as a faithful guardian over the portal of the emperors."[9] Branches of holly or buckthorn were placed there for the same purpose.[10] In the Germanic countries, a pentagram was drawn on the door along with the naive inscription, "If fever comes, I won't be in" or "Fever, don't come in, so-and-so isn't here!" Around the year 1500, it was recommended to write following citation above the door for protection against theft.

> *Beda mbeda conpendias perpendias, furem redde in domum vnde exiuit.* The cross of God should report it before sunrise. Say an Our Father. The cross of God was hidden and discovered by Saint Helene. In the same way any property shall be recovered. When Our Lord went to his martyrdom, return the same way to us. I conjure you, earth and sea, and all that is in you, by God the Father, the Son, and the Holy Ghost, and the virtue of the Holy Cross, to not tolerate this thief upon the earth. Once you have said this, attend the mass of the Holy Cross on the following day.[11]

Wooden snake above a farm door in Sarrétudvari, Hungary.

To protect against livestock epidemics, the peasants of the Isle of Worms (Estonia) nailed a sheep's head on the stable door. In the German area of Vogtland, godfathers would stick a fork or two knives in the door to the birthing room, or place a prayer book there before going to church. To prevent the eruption of the Pesadilla,* the Basques set a plate of lentils in front of the entrance of the house. If it sought to enter, this nightmarish entity would feel compelled to count them one by one before the end of the night, and since this is an impossible task for him to fulfill, those sleeping inside can rest at ease!

The Story of Thorsteinn House-Power (*Bœjarmagn*), written in Iceland at the beginning of the fourteenth century, shows us how a cross will prevent the intrusion of a revenant.

> One night Thorsteinn got up from his bed and saw Agdi [the revenant] passing by. He dared not enter by any of the doors because each had a cross in front of it. Thorsteinn went to the mound; it was open. . . . The Jarl Agdi then entered the mound, but Thorsteinn came racing out and placed a cross on the doors; the mound closed back up and Agdi was never seen again. (*Þorsteins þáttr bæjarmagns,* chapter 13)

Most recommendations make reference to witchcraft and concern the doors of all buildings. In an early account from antiquity, Apuleus described witches entering a house and when they left, "the doors reverted undamaged to their previous position. The hinges settled back in their sockets, the bars were restored to the doorposts, the bolts jumped back into the locks."[12] In 1411, Hans Vintler remarked in this regard that "many evil folk enter at night through locked doors,"[13] and we know from other sources that witches and spirits (*Walridersken, Scgrättele, Alp, Mahr*) enter through the keyhole, which should therefore have their keys left in them at night. In Appenzell canton in Switzerland, it is said that "witches can slip inside through the keyhole" (*Häxa chönid dör-ena schlüselloch döra schlüffa*).

*[The word also means "nightmare." —*Trans.*]

In Thuringia, the lock should be bound with blue apron string until the newborn child has been baptized. During childbirths in Hungary, the keyhole is plugged and all the doors are sealed with an undergarment string for fear of a substitution of the child (*changeling, cambio, Wechselbalg*) by a spirit or witch. For protection against a nightmare (the German *Mahr*), a Bible or other pious tome is placed in front of the lock. In the Hautes-Alpes region, it was still believed in 1962 that witches often assumed animal form and entered houses through the chimneys, keyholes, or cat doors. When in the form of a cat, it would sit on the chests of those who were sleeping and press down on them, preventing their breathing. You would be freed of their oppressive presence if someone spoke your name aloud or uttered the name of Jesus.[14] A tradition from the Upper Palatinate tells us that a witch can conjure up the dead through the keyhole of the church door until they boil up from their graves in a fury and fall upon the house of her designated target, where they will become a heavy weight on the sleeper and slay him.[15] We should note that the intruder can be captured if the keyhole through which it entered is plugged up, but here we are verging into the territory of the Melusine legends. The imprisoned entity is often revealed to be a beautiful young woman who has been married and even given birth to children, but one day the hole is unplugged and the woman disappears forever.

To prevent witches from entering, a new broom should be placed upside down behind the door,[16] and if a pentacle is drawn upon the door, witches will keep their distance (Swabia).[17] According to Pliny the Elder,[18] a dried wolf's head nailed to the door of farmhouses will counter all evil spells, and touching the door posts (*tactis postibus*) with the blood of a hyena will fight off the spells of sorcerers.[19] In Germany, the same result can be obtained with the head of a horse or billy goat, or with the horns of the latter animal,[20] or even with elder.[21] Against witches, Russian women placed branches of aspen, nettles, burdock, or thistle against the stable entrance. In spring, when the animals were first let out after their winter confinement, the peasants of the German-speaking regions would set axes, hatchets, saws, and other pieces of ironwork in front of the stable door, which would then be assurance against any enchantment.[22] In Anhalt, as an obstruction to witches and lightning, a bag with nine herbs, or red mugwort, would be hung from the lintel of the stable door on the evening of Saint James' Day and Saint Philip's Day.[23] In the fifteenth century, the inquisitors Heirich Kramer and Jacob Sprenger noted that in Swabia, "on May 1, women leave the village before sunrise and return with branches taken from the forests and trees (willows, for example), which they weave into the shape of crowns and hang at the stable entrance to ensure that all the animals living there will remain healthy and protected from all evil spells."[24] In 1771, garlic (*Allium victoralis*) prevented wizards and sorcerers from remaining inside the building,[25] and marjoram and mugwort prohibited them from entering.[26]

All Christian symbols allegedly provided effective protection if carved on the door.[27] In Germany this opening also possesses apotropaic virtues: following a birth, three crosses were drawn upon it at the height of the newborn's head. When the child had outgrown these marks, it was believed he was protected from hexes and jinxes. In the Upper Palatinate, three other crosses drawn in chalk above the entrance door to the stable prevented witches from entering it.[28] In his book, Jean-Loïc Le Quellec

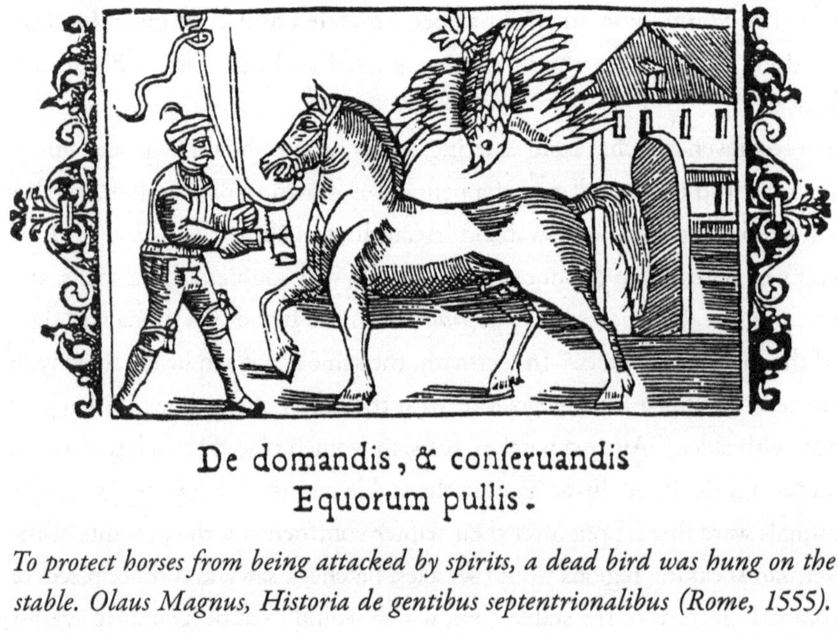

De domandis, & conſeruandis
Equorum pullis.

To protect horses from being attacked by spirits, a dead bird was hung on the stable. Olaus Magnus, Historia de gentibus septentrionalibus (Rome, 1555).

A stone in the shape of a missal discovered in the foundations of a Hungarian house.

reproduces a photograph of the smallholding of La Petite Motte in Frosse de Corpe (the Vendée region of France), on which a small white cross can be seen painted above a door in order to keep evil spirits at a distance.[29] The same thing can be found in Latvia, where crosses are carved on the foundations or the entablature of windows.

In the sixth century, Gregory of Tours indicated that the peasants of his era used the cross, which they called Tau (*hic scriptos Thau vocabatur*) to protect their homes. Damien Vorreux notes:

> The Tau, as an emblem of health, had already long been an article of faith in folk religious culture and belief. This is why when the plague was ravaging southern France in 546, Saint Gall organized a solemn procession. Immediately a sign that all the peasants recognized as the Tau appeared on all the houses and churches, and the epidemic ceased.[30]

The letter T is used as a protective sign on the door and we come across it above the door to a cell in Bebenhausen Abbey as part of a Latin inscription: "The Tau above these doors sends the enemies fleeing."[31] On an encircled cross crafted around 1175 in Lower Saxony, the Tau is interpreted this way: "The Tau that marks the door is the cross that sends the enemy fleeing."[32] The word "enemy," which is often encountered when the virtues of the Tau are enumerated, refers not only to the devil but to all demons, especially those that are disease carriers. In southern Italy, a broom is placed behind the door so that the witch will waste her time counting the straws and either become discouraged or be caught by surprise by the coming of day.[33]

Witches and their evil spells were not the only things people feared. In Norway, on the night of Imbrelaurdag, which is the Saturday before Christmas, an ax or an iron object was hung above the entrance to every stable, and a cross was drawn in chalk or tar above all the other doors in order to prevent the eruption of chthonic entites.[34] In Germany, serviceberry branches were placed in the same location on Saint Walburga's Feast day* to prevent the flying *drac* from entering.[35] Jean-Baptiste Thiers notes that in his time (the eighteenth century), people rubbed the doorposts of the house where newlyweds went to sleep together,[36] but he does not indicate the reason. In other locales, a cross made of two knives, or an open pair of scissors, was set there.[37]

To get rid of mice, people inscribed "Nicaise" in chalk on the door during the evening of this saint's feast day, [38] and in the Upper Palatinate, to prevent sheep from getting the staggers, the most beautiful lamb would be buried beneath the sheepfold. In other locales, it was recommended that a dead domestic animal be buried upright beneath the main door of the house, with its head facing the house so that no others would die.

Protection was also sought from the dead and from revenants. Two ancient sagas depict the return of a dead man who knocks on the door, which causes more deaths, or who waits in front of the door to strike down any who step outside.[39] According to more recent Swiss traditions, we know that in theory the dead person cannot enter unless some-

*[Better known now as Walpurgisnacht, April 30. —*Trans.*]

one opens the door to him. To prevent his or her return, the corpse was removed from the house by a special door; in Italy, this was the *porta di morti* that was always kept locked.[40] In the Mecklenburg region, the dead man should lie with his head facing the door and, once he has left the house, the sealed door is knocked on three times to ensure he never returns. The Russians sometimes remove the coffin through the window so that the deceased will not be able to find his way back to the house,[41] a precaution taken in Germany for suicides, sorcerers, small children, and hanged men.[42] The corpse of a suicide was regularly taken out through the roof, but ancient German legal codes also indicated the body should be removed from his home through the window (*ut dem venstere*) or by a hole in the wall (*men maiken sale en gat in den want des huis*).[43] This brings to mind what Jeremiah said about the dead man coming in through the windows: *mors ascendit per fenestras nostras* (Jeremiah 9:21). The fear of revenants is regularly coupled with a religious action: no one wants the dead person to contaminate the threshold of the house. Later we will discuss what lies behind this fear.

The entrance door is not the only one to play an important role in folk beliefs. To protect the woman giving birth, it is recommended that a wisp of straw that has been plucked from her mattress be placed at each door to her room. In this way the Jüdel* and other spirits will not be able to get in.[44] Jean-Baptiste Thiers mentions a similar Jewish superstition.

> Do as some Jews do, according to Maiolus, who bind to their heads and left hands, and hang at the right side of their doors, parchment they call *Tephilin,* in a way that the third part of these bands are facing the bed in the house, so that the Demon can cause them no harm. And who, in the same way, make a circle in charcoal or chalk around the room in which a woman is in labor, then writing on all the walls of the room: *Adam, havah, Chutz, Lilith,* and on the inside of the door, the name of three angels, or rather devils, *Senoi, Sansenoi, Samangeloph,* which they learned from the famous witch Lilith, when they tried to drown her in the sea.[45]

*[The spirit's name translates as "Little Jew." —*Trans.*]

Giving birth has always had a connection with a potential eruption of malevolent beings, hence the desire to protect the door to the birthing chamber by placing an upside-down broom in front of it or by sticking a knife into it.

Lastly, the door has been used in amorous divination. The *Distaff Gospels*[46] say that the first thread of the day should be stretched before one's door: by doing so, one will learn the name of the very first man to walk past.

THE THRESHOLD

The majority of the prescriptions that have been discovered—of which I am providing only a small sampling—establish a close bond between the door and the threshold. Entering a home or building is a kind of rite of passage, the crossing of an invisible frontier that has been made physical by the stone or the step of the threshold. The threshold has legal significance: in medieval Germany, when demanding payment of a debt from the debtor, it was necessary, in the event that the debt was contested, for the creditor to swear an oath with his right foot placed on the threshold while the *Schultheis* (head municipal official) stood to the right of the house.[47] The threshold is sacred, and in Estonia a husband making an offering to the tutelary spirits of the house will let spill a few drops of beer on it.[48] In Vedic India, it was the dwelling place of Pûsan, the god of pastures; offerings to the god were left on the threshold, and the husband would enter his new house without touching it.[49] It is an obstacle against which hostile and malevolent forces will collide, so in Latvia people place burdock, nettles, scythes, and other sharp instruments there.[50] The threshold gives material substance to the opposition between the household and what is foreign to it, whatever that may be. Then in Brittany we have Ankou, the personification of Death, who settles in this spot after the house construction has been completed, lying in wait for the first person of the family to cross it. This is why an animal is often introduced into the house first, or else a grandfather, full of familial devotion, will volunteer to enter the house first.

In earlier times in Lithuania and Russia, "people who were moving out of their homes would take with them two roosters, one old and the other young. They would slaughter the old cock on the threshold of the new barn so that the cows would prosper there,"[51] which is a propitiatory sacrifice. In Sweden, a snake would be buried near the threshold or inside a hole that had been bored in it, and this snake was sometimes called the "spirit of the house serpent" (*tomt orna*).[52] Pliny the Elder pointed out that placing the head of the dragon, a kind of reptile, underneath door sills (*limini ianuarum subditum*) after gaining the favor of the gods through a prayer, would attract good fortune to the house.[53] In eighteenth-century France, to prevent the untimely death of animals, a horse, an ox, a cow, a goat, or a sheep would be buried with their legs up beneath the threshold of the stable or sheepfold. Jean-Baptiste Thiers cites this other rite.

> Bury a [?] beneath the threshold of the barn or stable, or hang buildings bricks in the shape of a cross in either of these to prevent the horses and other animals from becoming sick or afflicted by evil spells, and the cows running dry of their milk.[54]

Alas, he does not tell us just what we should bury. In Germany, it is recommended that a piece of alder wrapped with the hair of a billy goat be stuck in the stable threshold to protect it from witches. [55] The hair obviously represents the malevolent women in her pact with Satan, the Great Goat, who is thus literally fixed, nailed down, and unable to do anything.

I have pulled two interesting magical recipes from a German grimoire that was quite popular in the eighteenth century. It is titled the *Romanus Büchlein* (Booklet of Romanus). The first, which is to be "placed in the stable as protection from the witches that enchant livestock, or written on beds for protection against men of evil intent and the spirits that assail both young and old at night, something that will free and save them," states,

> Witch, I forbid you my house and yard, I forbid you my horses and my stable, I forbid you my bed so that you shall cause me no affliction! Go afflict another house! Begin by crossing all the mountains, by counting all the hedge stakes, by crossing through all the waters

until dear light of day enters my home. In the name of God the Father, the Son, and the Holy Ghost. Amen![56]

The second should be placed in the same spot, "so that evil folk can do nothing to the livestock."

> Take absinthe, black cumin, cinquefoil, *asa foetida,* two pieces of each, take broad bean stems, the ordure from the rear ends of stable animals, and a little salt. Bind it together in a small packet and place it in a hole you shall drill in the threshold over which the animals cross when entering and leaving the building, and seal it up with a plug of alder. This works.[57]

For their part, medieval accounts inform us that if someone seeks to enchant the members of a household and cause them harm, it is necessary to place the evil spell beneath the threshold. Several examples are provided in the *Hammer of the Witches* (II, 1, 14). Here are two of them.

> Agnes of Regensburg said during her interrogation that she caused the death of animals by hiding the bones of different kinds of animals beneath the threshold of the stable entrance in the name of the devil and other demons.
>
> A person complaining of having been enchanted consulted a specialist, who said:
>
> Your illness comes from an evil spell, and an instrument of this curse is hidden beneath the threshold of the door to your house. Let us find and remove it, and you will feel better. So my husband and the specialist went to remove the evil spell. The potter lifted up the sill and commanded my husband to put his hand in the hole beneath it and pull out whatever he found. This he did: he first brought out a wax figure the length of a palm, pierced all over and stabbed through the side with two needles just at the spot where from left to right and vice

> versa, I felt my pains. He pulled them out. There were also little bags containing various grains, seeds, and bones. Everything was tossed into the fire and I began to feel better. (II, 1, 12)

The dead, meanwhile, received a special treatment with regard to the threshold. In more ancient times, the dead were buried beneath the lintel, and the *Laxdæla Saga* cites the case of Hrap (chapter 17), who asks his wife to have him buried upright in a hole dug beneath the lintel of the kitchen door. Suicides and heretics were removed from their homes through a hole dug beneath the threshold. In the thirteenth century, the preacher Bertold of Regensburg provided specific instructions on how to proceed: a rope was wrapped around the feet of the corpse with the help of a pitchfork. It was then dragged under the lintel and taken to a field, where it was abandoned. The clear efforts made to avoid touching the dead body and to deprive it of a Christian burial are suggestive of postmortem punishments. In Goslar, in the Harz region of Germany, suicides were still removed from their homes in the same fashion in the nineteenth century.

In Russia, the coffin was knocked against the lintel three times so the deceased would take leave of his home and not return again,[58] and in Germany, the corpse was placed in the threshold three times, which must have the same meaning. Once it had left the courtyard, the gate was closed, and three piles of salt were made in the common room. They were then swept up, and sweepings and broom alike would be cast away in a field,[59] which is the equivalent of an expulsion of the dead person who will therefore no longer be in any position to contaminate anyone. In Estonia, it was customary to stick as many nails in the lintel as there were dead people in the house,[60] which underscores the memorial function of the spot at the same time it allows an image of the family to appear.

Sometimes the belief is barely comprehensible and Jacob Grimm notes that "someone who wants to say something and then forgets what he intended to say, should go over the threshold then return, it will come back to him."[61] Might this not be a plunge back into the protective sphere where one enjoys the aid of the invisibles?

THE WINDOWS

Originally the window was an opening that allowed some light to enter the building as well as to aerate it. The English "window," which derives from the Norse *vindauga,* "wind eye," and which has a parallel in the Sanskrit *vātyāana,* "wind passage," allows us to grasp this concept. It is furthermore a breach in the protective cocoon of the house, so it also must be protected against the entry of hostile forces. It is hardly surprising to find almost exactly the same beliefs we have seen concerning the door. Pliny the Elder records that if one walks with a bat around the house three times and then nails it upside down above a window, it will be an amulet (*amuletum esse*). This animal is used in particular for sheepfolds, where it is hung by its feet above the threshold.[62] A bouquet of foliage hung from the window drives witches away, and in the Tyrol region, a dried toad is reputed to provide protection from contagion at times of plague. During the feast of the Assumption in Bavaria and in the Upper Palatinate, a bouquet that has been blessed is affixed to the window to avert hail and lightning. This bouquet is made of the flowers that were thrown during the passage of the holy procession and that have been woven into a crown. But in Estonia, three knives placed in the same spot grant this same protection. Lastly, the Germans stick a baking paddle out the dormer window to divert storm gusts.

The window is also a magical location. Writing on a fogged window causes discord, but in the seventeenth and eighteenth centuries the condensation that forms on a glass pane was said to be a remedy against warts. In charms against colic and fever, the illness was expelled out the window. This magical place is sometimes a kind of altar where offerings of food are laid out for souls during the Twelve Days of Christmas.

This aperture is closely linked to misfortune and death, either because it allows such forces to enter or to escape, or because it is an alternate opening used when there is a desire to avoid contaminating the threshold. In the Harz region, it is said that a woman in labor should not look out the window, otherwise the first team of harnessed animals that passes by will carry away her happiness.[63] In Romania, and Bukovina in particular, it is believed that it is dangerous to look into the common room through the window because someone will die. Among the Ruthenians, dead children would appear at the window, requesting baptism; it was then necessary to make the sign of the cross and give them a name; in other words, to perform a simulation of a baptism so that they might find peace. Throughout almost all of Europe, the windows were often covered before a birth to prevent the eruption of malevolent forces, mainly those of demons attracted by an effusion of blood.

In East Prussia, when a man has lost several wives, it was said that the new bride must enter by the window; undoubtedly because the earlier deaths were interpreted as the result of hostility from the threshold spirits. If several children of the same family had died, the most recent newborn would be taken from the house though the window to be baptized, otherwise, it was said, he would pass by the bodies of his brothers and sisters—meaning those who linger beneath the lintel—and he had to be carried back into the house by the same way following the ceremony.[64] Another explanation was advanced by the people of classical antiquity: if someone follows this procedure, the child will be all the healthier for it and will have a long life.[65] In the eighteenth century, Jean-Baptiste Thiers criticizes those who:

> when a woman has given birth to a stillborn child, do not wish to have it removed from the chamber through the door for burial, but instead through the window, out of fear that all the woman's subsequent births will be stillborn.[66]

Suicides, witches, hanged men, and dead infants were all removed through the window where the devil would come looking for them,[67] although the former customary law of Goslar only applied this measure to suicides. In Switzerland, however, removing the coffin through the window is avoided for fear that the deceased will not find rest, whereas the Russians sometimes do the opposite so that the dead individual cannot find his way back to the house.[68] What emerges from all of these contradictory elements is that the devil or death is lurking at the window.

Among a great many peoples—for example, Germans, English, Armenians, and Slavs—the window is the passageway taken by the soul at death. It therefore needs to be opened, otherwise the dead person will appear in the room in the form of smoke, and once the soul has left, the window is slammed shut. The window is kept shut because the soul will return to knock on it the night after the body was buried. It is crucial not to open the window at this moment, because this will bring about the deaths of more people. The window is therefore also a passageway to the beyond. A legend from the British Isles confirms this, although in the case, the other world is the kingdom of the fairies.

> In Caerlaverock, a family is seeking to get back their child who had been kidnapped by the fairies and replaced by one of their own. They plugged up the chimney, missing not a chink or cranny, meaning they hermetically sealed the dwelling and reinforced its sacred, intangible nature. The child was then tossed on the burning coals, and he began shrieking. Immediately, the fairies could be heard moaning around the house, knocking at the windows, doors, and chimney. The serving girl then cried, "In the name of God, bring back the bairn!" The window flew open and the real child was laid in his mother's lap, and the fairy child flew up the chimney laughing.[69]

Incidentally, we may note an inconsistency in the story: although the chimney had been sealed up, the changeling went out through it.

I would like to conclude this section with a charming Estonian belief: "Thunder occurs when God, who is chasing the devil, catches and pulverizes him. Doors and windows are therefore shut during storms to deny the devil refuge in the house and prevent the latter from being struck by lightning."[70]

THE CHIMNEY

The chimney is primarily an opening that has been made in the roof. In the remote past, before there were masonry chimneys, the smoke of the hearth exited through a hole in the house's exterior that could be opened and shut by a trapdoor. Later, chimneys were made from stones, but the notion of a breach in the sealed, domestic space persisted, so it, too, required protection to prevent any unwanted intrusions or outbreaks. Medieval legends centered on the theme of the union of a mortal and a supernatural being under the weight of a taboo inform us that the latter being will fly up the chimney once the taboo has been broken.[71] According to one legend, Ghengis Khan's ancestor was born from the sexual relations of his mother with a divine being who entered the tent through the smoke hole via a trail of light that entered her belly.[72] The unmasked changeling flees up the chimney, the Buryat swan-woman vanishes through the smoke hole, and fairies enter the house via the same route. The Russian *samodiva,* a fairy or swan-woman who finds her clothing—the disappearance of which had obliged her to couple with a human—will flee up the chimney:

> *He took her clothes, took and then returned them*
> *And Marika made a pirouette, then flew up the chimney,*
> *Perched on the house and whistled in the manner of the samodivy.*[73]

says one ballad. Among the Balkan Slavs, demons called *karakondzul* try to enter houses through their chimneys at certain times that bear evocative names: "the evil days," "the nights of the enemy," "the unblessed days," and "the days of the demons."[74] In Austria, the devil comes to claim the dead person through the chimney hood.

As a dwelling place for supernatural forces, witches use the chimney to leave for the sabbat or to get rid of the people they hate. Jacob Grimm tells us that "the old women often cut a foot's length of the grass their enemy has walked upon. They hang it down the chimney pipe and their foe wastes away."[75]

The chimney is thus a link between heaven and earth. At its base, it is anchored in the hearth, and its smoke rises up to heaven. This confers upon it the quality of an *axis mundi,* which explains its ties with the other world, either lower or higher, that it connects to our own. This is where elves play at night and where souls in torment gather, which demonstrates well the chimney's chthonic value. It is regarded as a gate to heaven that allows the soul to fly away. Its bond with the hearth makes it a center, which is why in Tuscany, the umbilical cords of newborns are buried there to ensure they never leave the family home and to also spare them from falls. It also holds an augural value, and it was believed in the fifteenth century that the collapse of the stovepipe was an indication of an imminent death,[76] an opinion that was still widespread in the Metalliferous Mountains during the nineteenth century. In France in the nineteenth century, it was believed that some people were able to tell from the smoke rising from the house where a dead person lay, if the deceased would go to heaven, purgatory, or hell.[77]

We should note that an analogous notion can be found in a civilization quite remote from our own, that of China, as François Delpech points out:

> In the theory of the ancient Chinese house, which was partially underground, the hole in the roof and the central drain well in the ground defined, through their correspondence, an axis that allowed Heaven and Earth to communicate, and to which was associated the god of the household grounds (who would be replaced by the god of the hearth).[78]

Who can deny that we are dealing with archaic mental structures here?

To protect the chimney, it was equipped with a hook on which were placed talismans, for example, ceraunia (thunder stones), which prevent all evil spells. Its base serves as a family altar and the evening prayer (whose participants kneel) takes place in front of it in Brittany, and elsewhere. It is fairly common knowledge that if a stork builds its nest on the chimney of your house, you shall live long and be rich.[79] We should finally note a recipe from the Morteau Valley of France that never fails to be a regular topic of interest for those suffering from the flu. They fight the illness by drinking a decoction made from the soot scraped from the chimney!

4

The House Interior

All the places inside the house do not share the same value: it is readily observable that the components of the space are assigned a hierarchical and a semiotic value. Combined with this are the religious and magical value of certain objects. We will begin by taking a look at everything that relates to the fire and the hearth, which was an object of worship for our ancestors, before more closely examining the associated utensils.

THE FIREPLACE AND THE FIRE

Among the Indo-European peoples, the fire and the hearth chain give physical expression to the bond between the living and the dead, which explains rites of aggregation like the following: "A servant should, on entering the house, see if there is a fire in the fireplace and stir it up; in this way her position will be secure there for a long time."[1] "If someone has stolen something from you," says Johann Georg Schmidt, "affix a horseshoe that you have found by chance to a spot where the fire is constantly burning, and you shall get it back."[2] We shall see more like this further on. The fire is the symbol of the *ignis communio* and the center of the house. It is an altar around which everything is organized and it is helpful to note that in Catalan, the hearth is called *Llar,* a term that recalls the Roman *Lar*. In earlier times in Scotland, the different configurations of fire were considered to be a variety of spirits called hearth spirits (*coracha cagalt*); the blue glow caused by stirring the ashes is a confirmation of their existence.[3] A sign of life and human activity, they hold a specific place in legal rites: the extinction of the fire accompanied by the scattering of its ashes in the street indicates the eviction of the owner. We also know that houses were once taxed based on the number of their fireplaces and the censuses of earlier days counted them.

The extinction of the fire was a bad omen. In Thuringia and Vogtland, it was especially important not to allow the fire to go out on January 1 if one wishes to be happy throughout the year.[4] Elsewhere it was said that the fire in the stove should be allowed to burn through the entire Christmas night.[5] Throughout Europe it was commonly believed that lightning would never strike a house as long as the fire was lit,[6] and its apotropaic virtues were enhanced by tossing blessed herbs, and the branches or coals from the fires of Holy Saturday. In Catalonia, when the younger son married or moved out of the paternal house, he took with him a burning brand of the "heir's fire" (*Foc de Hereu*) to light his own fire; otherwise he was at risk of being struck by lightning.[7] The purpose of this custom was to emphasize there was no rupture between the old and new hearths, a time-honored theme that can be found in the Bible (Amos 4:6–11). We should note that the Silesians were in the habit of blessing the fire with a sign of the cross before leaving their homes, and an old proverb asserts that "the house whose rooster, cat, and dog are black shall never be lacking for fire."[8]

Among the ancient Germans, all the village fires would be extinguished whenever there was an epidemic that struck animals or humans, and they would be relit after it had passed through. This sacred, prophylactic rite is called *nothfiur*. Antonius of Florence (fifteenth century) scolds those who refuse to give fire away on certain dates, claiming they would therefore be giving away their own good fortune. Lighting the fire was a magical act accompanied by the recitation of phrases, some of which have come down to us.[9] To light the winter solstice fire, the children of Barcelona used to say:

Catric, catroc	*Catric, catroc,*
Catch fire	*encén-te foc,*
Because there is a poor soul	*que hi ha un pobret*
Dying of the cold.	*Que es mor de fred.*

The hearth should never be defiled as that would amount to sacrilege. According to the *Distaff Gospels,* throwing bones into the fire after eating causes toothache,[10] and pissing on it causes apoplexy or urinary gravel.

THE HEARTH

Hearth is a generic term for designating the place where fire burns. The hearth can mean different things depending on the era and the region; it ranges from the simple fire pit of primitive dwellings to the more modern earthenware and cast-iron stove, and includes the open chimney, the fireplace, the oven, or the furnace. The hearth is the center of the house even if it sits elsewhere than the geometrical center of the premises. In Russia, the farther one is from the hearth, the more negative the supernatural elements become and the greater the danger, according to Francis Conte. It is the symbol of the life of the house, a meeting spot and a place for convivial gatherings. It is here that the Savoyard shades, the souls of the dead, and supernatural entities come at night to get warm. It is here where the dead were buried, especially infants in classical antiquity, in Russia, and in the Tyrol. In 1951, in Haute-Nendaz (Valais canton of Switzerland), the table was set for Christmas evening with bread, white wine, water, milk, cream, and a lit lamp—which is to say, the "white alms" that are offered to the good souls who come there to get warm on that night. As recently as 1969, a candle was left burning near a partially open window in a house in this same village, and its owner confided to someone who asked: "I am imploring the good souls who come here to get warm, and for whom I pray, to give me their aid."[11] When the Latvians build a fireplace, they enclose three eggs, the symbols of life, in the corner located on the right side—that is to say, the "beneficial" side.[12]

The hearth is also a means of communicating with hell—using the word here without any Christian connotation—as several necromantic rites indicate. In the third century, Heliodorus reported how an old woman made an incision in her arm, wiped up her blood with a laurel branch, and sprinkled the hearth with it, then performed a few bizarre rites, leaned over the corpse of her son, murmured something to him, and succeeded in getting him to stand up and answer her questions.[13] The hearth allows for communication with the chthonic realm and Russian ethnologists studying healing rituals have noted that the aperture of the oven is consecrated as an entranceway to the world of the dead.[14] In Russia, the souls of unbaptized children dwell in the oven,[15] and in Germany, the area behind the stove was called hell (*Helle, Hölle*). In Czechoslovakia, prayers for the hanged were said there, which overlaps with the same belief insofar as suicides are among the damned. For protection from the Bretoune, a kind of fairy, the Savoyards broke a dozen eggs, put water in their shells, and decorated the chimney hearth with them.[16] The same thing was done to successfully discover whether the child in the cradle was a changeling, an infant that had been substituted by fairies or demons. In Brittany, for example, this individual will then cry out:

> I am more than one hundred years old and I have seen the acorn before the oak, and the egg before the chicken, but I have never before seen so many little boiling pots.

Numerous aggregation rites take these meanings into account. Almost throughout Europe, the serving maid who has just been hired has to look in the stove, the chimney, or the furnace when she first enters the house.[17] In the Caucasus region, the young husband must walk around the hearth three times. In order to keep cats and dogs from escaping, they were made to walk around the hearth three times, before they were rubbed against its wall,[18] a rite that was also practiced with other household animals. If the animals fled despite this, the Transylvanian Saxons would call them through the stovepipe hole.[19] Sometimes the aggregation rite takes the form of a sacrifice: among the Slovenes of Lower Styria, the new bride would toss pennies into the furnace before the wedding supper.[20] In France, a cross is drawn on the chimney to prevent the chickens from leaving the home.[21]

Fire is a purifying agent, so it is hardly surprising to find healing rites associated with it. Around 1006, Burchard of Worms forbade the placement of ill individuals on the oven,[22] something that still is done in Russia. In Germany, a person will place his hand on the stove Sunday morning, while saying for protection against chills: "May clay and stone take my chill, first for a month, then for a year, then for as long as the sun travels the sky. In the name of the Father . . ." In Saxony and Lusatia, one greases the stove mouth after being burned and says, "I am greasing you, heal me!" In Norway, chapped lips are cured by embracing the stovepipe of the earthenware stove.[23] To contend with udder pox, the inhabitants of Mecklenburg in the sixteenth century drew a triple circle around the hearth cinders while reciting a spell that healed the cows. Among the Slavs, the healing was also achieved with the help of incantations spoken in front of the oven with the flue closed, so they would not fly off before they could take effect.[24] In Germany, the pregnant woman prayed on her knees in front of the furnace before going into labor; she had to avoid touching it before her lying-in period of rest was over; otherwise she would feel the icy hand of a dead person and die soon afterward.[25]

The hearth is linked to methods for rendering witchcraft inoperative and for quelling any hostilities. To protect the newborn from the evil eye, visitors were asked to look into the stove first.[26] If children or animals were under a spell, an animal heart would be hung to dry above the heart with the thought that by means of sympathetic magic, the heart of the witch would also dry up. In northern Russia, the wizard sent his helpers (*ikotas*) to seize a part of the targeted individual's body, hair, for example, which they would cast behind the oven, saying, "As this hair dries up, so shall so-and-so wither away!"[27] In Germany, this advice was given: "If several chickens, ducks, pigs, and so on die within a short period, light a fire in the oven and toss an animal of each species inside. The witch will die with them."[28] In the Upper Palatinate, the new furnace would be sprinkled with holy water and hawthorn burned in it in order to expel witches from the chimney. In 1951, an inhabitant of the village of Ribes in the valley of Freissinières (in the French Hautes-Alpes region), stated: "When a person dies as the result of an evil spell, his *fricassée* (all the major viscera) will be removed and hung in the chimney. This will provoke the sorcerer to come forth," undoubtedly in order to punish him for his malicious action.[29]

According to Pliny the Elder, the wolf will never attack any animal in a field where the first furrow of the year is plowed with a plowshare that has been burned in the hearth of the household *Lar* god.[30] The furnace is also used for protection against a storm: all that is required is to cast blessed objects inside it.[31]

As the hearth is a means of communication with the other world, it is a component in divination rites. Antonius of Florence provides us with one of the questions the confessor should ask the fifteenth-century sinner: "Have you placed within your family hearth blessed olive branches or a grain of wheat taken from a manger to learn if someone shall live or die?" According to Anatole Le Braz, the following rite is practiced in Cornwall.

> To learn whether someone should die within the year, one places in a vase filled with water as many ivy leaves as there are people whose fate one wishes to know. The vase is placed on the hearthstone and left there over night. In the morning, the leaves are examined. Those that have turned black foretell a death in the near future (no later than twelve days). If the leaves have red spots, they predict a violent death.[32]

In East Prussia, the stove is silently contemplated on Christmas and New Year's Day, and in this way one may learn what will occur in the year to come.[33] I should point out that this "furnascopy" is essentially used for love divination and it is in fact a form of pyromancy. The noises made by a stove also have augural value. If the fire in it crackles, there will be a quarrel in the household.[34]

THE ACCESSORIES OF THE HEARTH

The Chimney Hook

Like the hearth in which it hangs, the chimney hook possesses a sacred quality. The Ossetians believe that the theft of one is a worse crime than killing the son of the house.[35] It has legal significance and important symbolic value. In the Middle Ages it was ceremoniously handed over to the new owner of the house in an action called *per andelangum tradere.*[36] It even served as an emblem, a family name, and a coat of arms. When the Counts of Lippe changed, their chancellor visited all their holdings and reaffirmed them by touching the chimney hooks of the houses and castles. In 1609 in Cologne, the lifting and lowering of the chimney hook was the ritual for taking ownership of a building. In some countries, the lawbreaker who touched it obtained right of asylum. In the fourteenth century, a legal proceeding in Dortmund would be announced by striking it with a sword.[37] In 1360 in Turin, the young bride would take possession of the *catena,* symbol of managing the household, a rite also practiced in Westphalia.[38] In various regions, oaths were sworn while touching the chimney hook.

The sacred nature of the chimney hook is clearly visible in a Latvian account recorded by Andrejs Johansons.

> Every person entering the kitchen of a house touched the chimney hook saying: "Hello, chimney hook, hello!" Similarly, anyone who came to take fire from the hearth would thank it. If someone neglected to do so, the fire god (*unguns diev*) would avenge himself, and the guilty party would fall sick or die.
>
> A new house owner had the old kitchen hut (*nams*) demolished and threw away the venerated chimney hook. His stomach immediately began burning like fire, and a charlatan managed to reduce his suffering. One day, a manservant noticed something moving at the edge of the hedge: it was a very old minuscule man with a white beard, a black mouth, and red eyes. Making a face, he shook his fist at the manservant, who fled in terror and came back with some

other people. They searched in vain for the old man and only found the chimney hook that had been tossed in the hedge. It was picked up and hung back in the kitchen above the fire. The next morning, the master of the house woke up fresh as a daisy.[39]

Other admonitions confirm the ill advisability of mistreating a chimney hook. In Latvia, it is said one should not swing one back and forth under penalty of stomach aches,[40] and on Christmas and New Year's Day, it was smeared with a small sample from every dish so that it could take part in the feast.[41] It is sometimes specified that this is an offering intended for the *pūkis,* the domestic spirit. In the Morbihan area of Brittany, when fire refused to catch for some unknown reason, table salt was given to the chimney hook, which is also a form of sacrifice.[42] I should add that secrets that could not be entrusted to any human beings were confided to it, and people even confessed to it!

The chimney hook is a representation of the house according to metonymy and plays a major role in aggregation rites that correspond precisely with those we noted regarding the hearth. In Languedoc, the young bride is spun three times around it while at the same time she promises to remain loyal to the house and fulfill her wifely duties. In numerous German provinces and in Transylvania, the bride is asked to circle the chimney hook three times after the wedding, or else it is swung around her three times, which is reminiscent of the ritual gesture of the Christian priest with the censer. Among the southern Slavs, the bride then bows before the four sides of the stove and kisses the cauldron stand,[43] which should be interpreted as a sign of veneration and respect.

Elsewhere in France, in England, and in French-speaking Switzerland, the newborn was carried around it three times,[44] and the Ossetians passed it underneath the infant three days after birth at the same time as they left offerings for the hearth spirit. In the seventeenth century, in the German regions east of the Rhine, it was said: "Whoever wishes their dog or cat to stay at home and not run away, must lead them three times around the chimney hook," a belief that was also widespread in fifteenth-century Picardy, Russia, and the Nordic countries.[45] Jean-Baptiste Thiers devoted two sections to this in his *Traité des superstitions*.[46] Latvian cows could find their way back to the barn without any trouble if they had been led around the chimney hook three times, in a counter-sunwise direction, with the food one wished to give them.[47] The direction of this circumambulation indicates that we are dealing with a magical rite here. Finally, in order to keep hold of a beloved individual, a person would brandish the chimney hook three times around his or her head.[48]

The chimney hook comes into play in healing and protection rituals. To get rid of sore throats, people rub the hook against their throats in Latvia.[49] According to a witch trial held in Wittenberg in 1689, it is necessary, when healing this same affliction, to breathe on the chimney hook while saying: "Jode, Joduth, I cannot swallow the hook of the chimney hook. In the name of . . .[50] To treat swollen lips, Icelanders kiss it while asking if the master of the house is about.[51] In 1709, the inhabitants of Sarkau, an East Prussian village located on the Kurische Nehrung (Curonian Spit), a band of land separating the Curonian Lagoon from the Baltic Sea, protected themselves against the plague by carving a furrow with a chimney hook. The plague was unable to enter the village because "it was protected by a hedge."[52] Around 1650 in Lower Saxony, a Wendish peasant encountered the Plague and spoke with her. Finally she promised to spare him, commanding him: "Strip yourself bare, keep not a stitch of clothing, take your chimney hook, leave your house and run around your farm in the direction of the sun, then bury it beneath the lintel."[53] Implied in this account is a simple notion: with the chimney hook gone from the house, it is a sign that it has been abandoned, hence the plague has no business in an uninhabited house. Furthermore, the final destination of the object aims to increase the forces that prevent any intrusion.

It is not only illnesses that are averted thanks to this accessory of the hearth. The Livonians protect themselves from fires by splattering the chimney hook with a ladleful of soup three times,[54] which strongly resembles a propitiatory offering. Bernadino of Sienna (1380–1444) tells us that storms can be driven off by throwing the chimney hook outside the house, and Jean-Baptiste Thiers records the same rite in eighteenth-century France.[55] Over a long period in England, France, and Italy, bad weather was averted by hanging the chimney hook at the entrance door or outside, although we have no further details.[56]

In France it was widely believed that a comparage (the marriage of a godfather or godmother with his or her godson or goddaughter) would either produce no offspring or engender diabolical children who most often appeared in the form of little, hairy monsters. As soon as they emerged from their mother's womb, they would hide under the bed from which they would be dislodged with the help of a pitchfork.[57] They would then leap on the chimney hook, balancing on it for a time while making horrible grimaces, before disappearing up the chimney flue—thus confirming that this conduit is truly a means of communication between the worlds.

The chimney hook seems to have possessed augural qualities, but the accounts are extremely rare, and I can only cite one: if the chimney hook falls down of its own accord, it is announcing a visit.[58]

We are slightly better informed about the role this object played in combating witchcraft. In the northern regions of England, witches were repelled by drawing a cross on the chimney hook or by hanging it upside down on the last Sunday of carnival season. Its sharp ends pointed toward the top of the chimney obviously formed an obstacle to their intrusion through this opening. In France, houses were exorcised by revolving a chicken around the chimney hook three times.[59] In Montsardier in the Languedoc, it was said that doing the same thing to an animal that had fallen victim to an evil spell would dispel the curse.[60] The Latvians healed an bewitched child by making him or her drink holy water in which flakes from three chimney hooks and three lintels had been grated.[61] In Catalonia, when someone was suffering from an inflamed lymph node, a malignant angina, or a goiter attributed to the witch Mirmené, the following incantation was chanted:

Mirmené	*Mirmené*
You have done me harm	*mal me fas*
I shall do you harm	*mal te faré*

With three knocks I shall sign it	*Tres cops te senyalaé*
With the hook of the chimney hook	*Amb el ganxo del carmeller*
Amen	*Amen*

The Trivet

The trivet on which the cauldron sits upon in the fireplace plays a large role in folk beliefs because the dead crowd near the chimney at night to warm themselves. In fact, some of the dead retain their ties with their original home, visiting it every Saturday, even going so far as moving back into their former rooms.[62] They are predisposed to stand guard over their still-living relatives while they sleep, and grandmothers come back to see their grandchildren.[63] In Pomerania, this most commonly occurs on Saint Sylvester's feast day. In Masuria (Mazury in Polish), people know this to be true because they sprinkle the ground with ashes and find their footprints there the next day.

But spirits, often identical with the dead, also come seeking warmth at the hearth. Whatever name they bear—fairy, shade, sprite, or elf—these supernatural beings take a seat on the trivet and if they burn themselves they vanish forever, which is never a good omen.[64] This belief explains certain admonitions that we find from the fifteenth century forward. Echoing this, the *Distaff Gospels*[65] say that leaving the trivet or grill on the burning coals without putting a firebrand on the coals or something on the trivet will cause the lady of the house to age prematurely, undoubtedly because the supernatural being who gets burned will seek to avenge itself this way. In Germany, the trivet or grill should never be put over the fire without anything on it. If a women does this, she will get a wrinkle on her face.[66] The consequences of this unconscious act thus draws down a punishment on the part of the creatures who are burned because nothing has drawn their attention to the heat of the object.

At night, if a trivet is placed upside down with its legs in the air, a sign of disorder and disrespect, the devil will sit astride the house,[67] but a pot set on it will repel nightmares.

The Cauldron

The hearth is the headquarters for numerous divination rites, some of which involve the cauldron. In Vogtland (Germany), for example, it is filled with water on Christmas, New Year's Day, and Epiphany, and left on the fire. The next day, it is checked to see if the water overflowed or decreased. This would indicate whether the price of grain would increase or decrease over the next three trimesters, with each feast day representing one trimester. Furthermore, if the water evaporated away entirely, it is because a soul in torment used it to purify himself.[68] In the Montagne Noire in Brittany, a pot should not be left to boil without putting any salt in it; otherwise everything that is in the house will waste away as the water evaporates.

Another object sometimes takes the place of the cauldron. In ancient houses, a copper kettle was left permanently in the hearth, one surface of which was cut lower to receive liquid, and it was said that its song heralded the coming of the cold or the death of a family member.

Poker, Tongs, and Brush

The poker provides protection against hailstorms and other kinds of bad weather if placed above the farmhouse door. In the early Middle Ages, it reputedly was used by witches as a mount, and Hans Vintler alludes to this belief in his critique of superstitions.[69] The tongs were also used in a rite to break spells cast on cattle; the Silesians circled their farms three times astride their fire tongs, and this allegedly restored everything to order.

Like the other hearth utensils, it is most important to never place the poker upside down between the Day of the Dead and the Ember Days, to prevent the dead visitors to the house from hurting themselves—at least this is what the Franconians maintained.

The brush was employed as a mount by witches, too, but an ancient account informs us that it was also apparently used to ensure the health of young children by being placed in their baths. This claim was made by Brother Rudolf, who wrote between 1236 and 1250.

The Stove Bench

Throughout Europe, the stove bench is regarded as either the headquarters of dead ancestors or the place they best like to revisit. In Eastern Prussia and in the Allgäu region of Bavaria, it is left free for them from ten o'clock at night to three o'clock in the morning on January 1. On the shores of the Baltic Sea, the newborn is placed on it so that he or she will be pious and sensible,[70] undoubtedly so that he or she will share the qualities of the ancestors.

Sometimes the stove bench is replaced by a wooden stool that has the virtue of keeping hold of the nightmare that sits on it until daybreak, at which time the light will send it fleeing.[71]

THE BACK WALL AND THE CORNERS

The back wall and one of the corners of the dwelling are intended for the worship of the household gods; it is there a kind of altar is placed that sometimes appears in the form of a shelf or table. In the Catholic farms of southern Germany, there is a corner called the *Herrgottswinkel,* meaning the "Lord God's corner," that consists of a small domestic altar with a crucifix, several images of saints painted on the walls, or statuettes on the table.[72]

Incidentally, we should note that the "Lord God's corner" is located diagonally opposite the earthenware stove, as if we had heaven facing hell, which is also a way of depicting the opposition between Christianity and paganism. Furthermore, this diagonal line certainly gave structure to the space in these older times and represented a symbolic path. This supposition finds support by comparing it to a Breton tradition. In Armorica, the right-angle course leading from the lintel stone to the hearth—in other words, from the cold opening to the hot opening—was called the dog's path,[73] for this animal could travel between the worlds, and souls coming at night to warm themselves near the hearth followed this path, which was also earmarked for them. Details like this, together with what we have learned from Russian beliefs, clearly indicate that there is an internal structure of the house, at the heart of which are routes connecting this world to the beyond.

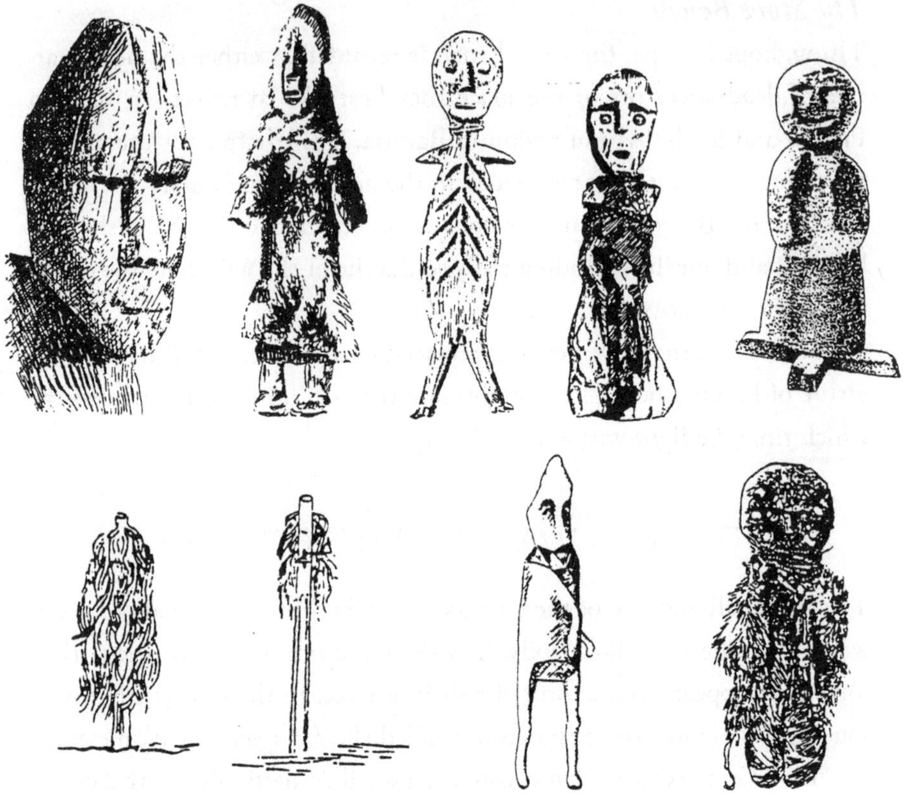

Domestic idols. (Top) from left to right are those of the Samoyeds, the Yuroks, the Ostyaks, and the Vogels; the final one is a domestic deity of the Setukese. (Bottom) from left to right: Inao and chisei koro of the Ainos, séva of the Samagirs (Tungus people of the Amur River), alalt of the Yeniseian people.

Among the Siberian Chukchee and the Koryak peoples, house spirits (*yara-vairgit*) stayed in the dark corner of the house and were inseparable from it. If the hut was destroyed, they no longer existed. But those in an abandoned house would transform into dreadful, evil spirits.[74] Among the Vogel and Ostyak peoples, Russian orthodox saints have replaced the house spirits, but the Vogel keep them in a sideboard placed near the back wall of the house on which icons of Jesus, the Virgin Mary, and Saint Nicholas are hung. The offerings made there are addressed to all three, but if sacrifices are made to the spirits, the icons are covered.[75]

We should not assume that the beliefs just cited are that far removed from those of Western Europe. Infinite traces can be found from the eighth century onward, indicating that this region also worshipped household gods. Texts often ignored by ethnologists are rich with criticisms of an apparently widespread practice: oaths should be sworn *ad cancellos* or *ad angulos.* If we examine the penitentials collected by F. W. H. Wasserschleben, Hermann Josef Schmitz, and Raymund Kottje,[76] we will readily see how frequently such references appear:

Pæn. Burg (ca. 700–725), c. 29: *ad cancellos* (K. 65)
Pæn. Simplex, c. 21: *ad cancellos* (K. 76)
Pæn. Bobb (ca. 700–725), c. 26: *ad cancellos* (K. 70; W. 409)
Pæn. Oxon I (tenth century), c. 24: *ad cancellos* (K. 90)
Pæn. Floria (ca. 775–780), c. 27: *ad cancellos* (K. 99; W. 425)
Pæn. Hubert (ca. 850), c. 24: *ad cancellos* (K. 110; W. 380)
Pæn. Merseburg (late eighth century), c. 27 (Mel) and c. 32 (V23, W10): *ad cancellos* (K. 133; W. 394)
Pæn. Paris (ca. 750), c. 21: *ad cancellos* (W. 414)
Pæn. Ps.-Romanum (between 817 and 830), c. 4, § 5: *ad cancellum* (W. 368)
Pæn. Ps.-Theod. (between 830 and 847), c. 12, § 18: *ad cancellos* (W. 3597)
Pæn. Ps.-Beda (ca. 850), c. 18: *ad cancellos* (K. 110; W. 254)
Ordo pænitentiae, c. 14, § 93: *ad cancellos*
Pæn. Vallicell, II (tenth–eleventh century), c. 61: *ad cancellos* (S. I, 370)
Vita Eigii (MGH Script, rer. Merow. IV, 706): *ad cancellos* variant: *ad cellos* (Grimm III: 402)
Excarpsus Cummeani (eighth century), c. 7, § 6: *ad angulos* (W. 481; S I, 633)
Pæn. XXXV capit. (eighth century), c. 17: *ad angulos* (W. 424 and 517)
Pirman v. Reichenau (died 753), Dicta c. 22: *ad angulos*
Ratio de cathechizandi c. 2: *ad angulos* (Heer edition, 81)

We can see that this information falls into two groups, with four texts, compiled in Germania, that read *ad angulos* and stand in contrast to the others. What do these two terms, *cancellus* and *angelus,* mean? In classical Latin, *cancellus,* primarily used in the plural, designated "bars, a trellis, a balustrade," and in Pliny the Elder's work (*Natural History* VIII, 30), it has the meaning of "boundaries, limits." According to the Du Cange dictionary, this term also referred to the church chancel in the Middle Ages.

If we take the German lexicons, vocabularies, and glosses, the term has the meaning of "iron gate, door" (*gadder, gater, valva, ostium*), "cupboard" (*schang/schrank, toreuma*), "trestle" (*gestell*), and "stake" (*stackh*). It is annotated by *fenestra reticulata.*[77] The polysemy of the term makes it possible to imagine the following hypothesis: wishes were addressed to an object—perhaps one that had been carved (*toreuma*)—placed behind a grill or trellis, or in a cupboard or on a pedestal, a notion confirmed by the Faksar, domestic idols of the Norwegian Setesdal region. There was a small cupboard or chest near them in the houses where the food offerings made to them were placed.[78] It could also involve worship directed at the entrance door, as suggested by *valva,* "door panels," and *ostium,* "the entrance, the door." The presence of *stackh* (stakes) is more likely to refer to the notion of the support of an object. We should note here that the ancient Norwegians worshiped stakes (*stafr*) as domestic deities, and did so despite the ban of the practice recorded in the *Eidsivathings Kristenrett* in 1152. In the twelfth century, the *Hernoss,* an idol mounted on a stake that had a human head but no arms, still existed in Sörum and Rike. In other places the Faksar, wooden statues depicting a bearded man the size of a twelve-year-old child, were worshipped. They were called "wights, spirits" (*vätte, tusse*) and food offerings were made to them at Yule (*jól*).[79] We have the following important account from the Cistercian brother Rudolf of Silesia, a valuable source we heard from earlier. He wrote:

> *In novis domibus, siue quas de novo intrare contigerit, ollas plenas rebus diversis diis penatibus, quos STETEWALDIU vulgus appellat,*

sub terra in diversis angulis et quandoque fodiunt retro larem, vnde nec retro larem fundi quicquam permittent. Et de cibis suis illus quandoque proiciunt, ut habitantibus in domo propicientur (Klapper 36).

In the new homes, or in the houses where they have just moved in, they bury pots filled with various things in different corners and sometimes even behind the hearth for the household gods they call *stetewaldiu.*[80]

The parallel sense indicated in the penitentials of *cancellus* and *angulos* may allow for some clarification. The eleventh-century *Summarium Heinrici*[81] glosses *angulus* with *kancelum,* which is one of the meanings of *cancellus,* and with *uuinkil,* meaning "corner." According to the ancient Bavarian law code *Lex Baiuvariorum,* the term *uuinkil* first designates the extreme border of the field or house, then the four corners, the whole, in cases of taking legal possession of property.[82] We also know that in a new building, it was customary to place blessed branches and salt at the four corners of the home to protect it from evil spirits. The corner thus takes on a religious value in connection with a specific belief. The house was also afforded protection by the burial of objects such as nails (with the apotropaic virtue of iron) and plants (branches of hazel or mugwort) at its four corners.[83] In a letter from 1599, the Jesuit priest Petrus Culesius mentions a Latvian rite that clearly demonstrates the sacred value of the corner. At the end of a ceremony honoring the *Lares* and *Penates,* the father pours beer in one of the corners of the common room "to ensure that the Lares go back to the stove" (*laribus refocillandis*).[84]

It we compare this information with that gathered from the Siberian peoples, we will observe a similar notion: one of the corners of the house is dedicated to the house spirits. This is where people worship them and offer them sacrifices. The various meanings I have proposed for the two Latin terms under discussion reflect a reality that takes on several forms depending on the way the inhabitants keep their idols or what serves that function. Paul-Henri Stahl notes that in Romania, "The house has corners where people most often avoid sitting. They are marked out at the beginning of the construction: this is where the food intended for the dead is placed, where wheat and silver is placed and where the ground is sprinkled with the blood of the animal sacrifice, or where its head is buried."[85] The corners clearly represent a sacred space that permits communication with spirits and the dead. Christianity did not turn a blind eye to this matter and we have prayers that place the corners under the protection of the saints. Here is one to be recited before going to bed in order to protect the bedchamber:

In this room
There are four corners;
In each corner
There is an angel:
Saint Luke, Saint John,
Saint Mark, and Saint Matthew,
The four evangelists before God.
Glorious Saint Monica,
Mother of Saint Augustine,
My soul I entrust to you when I go to sleep.
Cross yourself, room, cross yourself bed,
So the evil spirit is driven off;
If by chance one remains,
Through the door he will leave.

Greece provides us with information that confirms what we found in northern Eurasia. Numerous accounts describe a household spirit called Stoicheio. Some are far from specific ("In every house lives a monster named Stoicheio"[86]), whereas others connect this individual to a corner ("In the impenetrable, dark corner of every home hides the Stoicheio of the house"[87]). Sometimes confused with a ghost or revenant, this entity is connected with the prosperity of the household and often takes the form of a serpent.*[88]

*It is also said to have the body of a snake, the head and paws of a cat, or that it is a winged monster with two heads, four eyes, and a bouquet of tails. The Stoicheio has the ability to shift its shape.

We can even take our investigation further afield: among the Aino of Japan, the rear, left corner of the square house is the seat of the domestic deity (*inao*) and among the Chuckee and Koryak of Siberia, the spirits (*yara-vairgit*) remain in the darkest corner of the house, from which they cannot, in fact, be separated.[89]

I must confess that discovering these kinships between such widespread places and time periods was a great surprise to me, which at the same time gave reinforcement to my approach and research method. When one is engaged with the job of detecting the traces of ancestral beliefs, it is essential to step out of the limited context of a country and an era. In my opinion, this is the sole means to come up with pertinent and acceptable conclusion.

Having reached the end of this general presentation of the house and some of the beliefs that are connected to its different sites and components—for I have had to make selections from an immense corpus of material—the reader now possesses a large number of clues that will let him or her accompany me further in our investigation. It is obvious that behind the elements involved—whether it is a corner, a beam, or the hearth—there are other things hiding, supernatural forces that are stimulated or neutralized by specific rites. These forces are embodied there, they have taken shape (human shape, most of the time), and they have been named, often based on their function.

By examining a large European area, we have noted an astonishing kinship between the various rites; constants are readily apparent behind the local variants. The dangerous spots are always the same: the openings of the house. The rites of circumambulation show that the notion of sacred enclosure is common to all the countries mentioned here. The means of protection are similar and are based on a similar vision of the world. But if we accept that people always react in the same way to the stimuli of the world around them, regardless of latitude, is this so surprising? The geographical situation explains why a horse head is used here and a seal's head is used there, maple here and birch there. Beyond all the differences, which are actually quite superficial, we find the same spirit, the same *Weltanschauung* everywhere.

The differences between the rites concerning the various buildings are minimal. Whether it concerns a cow shed, stable, sheepfold, or barn, the protections implemented are almost identical and located in the same parts of the building, walls, roofs, openings, ground, and foundations. The offerings to the supernatural forces are concentrated in the same places. It was commonly believed everywhere that a newly finished building was dangerous, and an animal was sent inside before a human being so that animal became the target of any misfortune or death.

In the first part of this book, I have described the settings and shown the sorts of rites that can only be explained by the presence of the household spirits. Now, in the second half, we will get to know them more fully!

PART TWO

The House Spirits

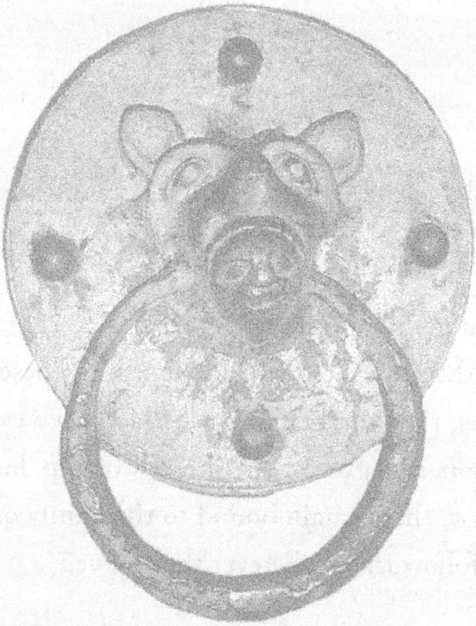

5

Domestic Spirits in Antiquity and the Middle Ages

What is a household spirit? Gustav Ränk has supplied the best answer to this question.

> The "household gods" are the minor deities on which the family's well-being and the success of the farm depends. These beings appear in various forms; they can be purely abstract; they can dwell in the house or outdoors in nature at the site of worship, hunting, or fishing. In every case, they remain bound to the family or to its specific members, and follow them wherever they move.[1]

Relying on northern European beliefs, Gustav Ränk only takes into consideration benevolent spirits. These spirits do not form a homogenous whole and can be divided into two groups: the first consists of the deities of men and their economic activities; the second those of women. In the latter case, this group has a medical function.* These deities were

*Especially for menstruation, birth, and illnesses affecting infants and livestock.

inherited; the son inherits that of his father and the daughter that of her mother. Only the paternal spirit plays a significant role. This distinction corresponds well with the patriarchal nature of the society in question, of course, but also with the sex attributed to the spirit, as we shall see.

In his study of the folk traditions of Ångermanland, Lauri Honko provides an important clarification: "Every hut has its spirit; wherever there is a heated room (a hearth) there is a spirit."[2] Since the fire is a symbol of habitation, this means that certain spirits prefer to live in houses, which earns them their description as domestic in contrast to those we find in nature, which are commonly called land spirits, spirits of place, or local deities.

ANTIQUITY

In antiquity, the domestic gods were under the jurisdiction of the familial cult. The Greeks believed Zeus was the father and protector of the house; once the farm has been surrounded by an enclosure, he was named Herkeios and his altar stood in the yard inside that enclosed space. He was also called Ktesios, "the Acquirer," because he gave out wealth and protected the reserves. As offerings he was given food-filled pitchers in a rite called *panspermia,* which indicates he was given seeds of all sorts. Zeus Melichios, which is to say the "Good, the Favorable One," had a serpentine form. He brought riches and was depicted on a throne holding a horn of plenty. Zeus Soter, "the Savior" received the first and last offering at feasts.[3] He was also nicknamed *Agathos Daimon,* "the good demon." He was offered pure wine at the end of the meal and he, too, was a serpent. A meal was prepared for the Dioscuri, the sons of Zeus, and foods were offered them; they, too, were depicted as serpents that guarded the house. It is noteworthy how frequently reptiles appear as part of the beliefs concerning domestic gods.

We also encounter several deities among the Romans. First we have the *Lar familiaris,* who was not a domestic god originally and whose worship evolved from the rural cult of the *compita* in which the *Lares* were venerated as protectors and guardians of the lands (*agri custodies*) surrounding the house. The hearth became the site where they were worshipped, as opposed to the fields where they initially received their sacrifices. The *Lar familiaris* received a portion of the meals with which he was traditionally associated. At family feasts he was offered wreaths, wine, incense, fruits, cakes, and honey, and, when a death occurred, a lamb.[4] This deity was connected to the entire family and its fate.[5] The sanctuary of all the household gods was the *Lararium* that housed their effigies, and two snakes were often painted on its walls.

Next we have Hestia, the goddess of the hearth, to whom wine was offered at the beginning and end of the meal. She corresponds with Vesta,[6] the personification of the hearth that is her headquarters; her altar is the centerpiece of the domestic cult overseen by the woman who prepares the offering (*far pium*) for her, which is cast into the fire.[7] During the meal a plate with the food intended for her was set by the fire.[8] Vesta was linked with the Penates, the generic name for all household gods worshipped near the hearth.[9] They were offered foods that were tossed into the flames or set out on a plate;[10] if a piece fell onto the floor, it was picked up, set on the table, then cast into the fire.[11] All of these rites refer to a fire cult whose existence is clearly confirmed among the Indo-Europeans.

Finally, we have the deities who watch over openings and the threshold: Limentinus and Limentina, Forculus, and Forcula.

Plautus provides us a good reflection of the beliefs of his time in his play entitled *Aulularia*.*A dead ancestor left his heir a considerable fortune buried beneath the hearth, but the heir's son gave scarcely any thought to the dead man and stopped leaving offerings of food. The tutelary ancestor left him, and he fell into poverty. Only the daughter faithfully continued to attend to the elder, each day bringing him the traditional offering of wine, incense, and so forth. This incorporation of a dead person into a place spirit is something that should be kept firmly in mind, as we shall see it again more than once in the later centuries.

Christianity fought these cults with all its might and in 392 a decree of Emperor Theodosius banned them,[12] but they continued to live on, mainly in the rural areas of the Roman colonies. The names of the deities

*[The Pot of Gold —*Trans.*]

vanished but not their function, and it was these unspecified entities that henceforth stood guard over the hearth and the opening into the house. The offerings made to these supernatural beings endured, often in identical form, and we will encounter them repeatedly.

THE MIDDLE AGES

In the Middle Ages, there were no longer any true deities; they had become spirits, meaning entities upon whom the family's well-being depended, as well as the success of their farming activities. I shall draw a distinction between direct accounts (those that leave no doubt about the nature of the entity depicted) and indirect testimonies (for example, those of fictional literature in which house spirits became simple dwarves of ambiguous nature).

Direct Accounts

In 743, the *Indiculus superstitionum* alluded to figures made of dough (*de simulacro consparsa farina*) in which researchers have recognized the household spirits. While only rarely do we find accounts, these are quite revealing once one succeeds in distinguishing what lies hidden beneath the words of their authors, most of whom were writing in Latin. For example, Burchard, Bishop of Worms, condemns a propitiatory rite at the beginning of the eleventh century using the terms "faun" and "satyr," but the context clearly indicates that the creatures mentioned have nothing in common with the ancient Roman beings.

> You have made tiny silly bows and children's shoes and tossed them into your cellar or your attic for fauns and satyrs to play with there so they will bring you the goods of others and make you richer.[13]

An explanation of the cryptic phrase "bring you the goods of others" is provided several centuries later by legends that tell us a household spirit brings the fodder stolen from a neighbor to your animals. This can also be the milk of the neighbor's cows, and in Scandinavia we have a spirit called troll cat or milk hare (*trollkat, mjølkhare*).[14] Working for a witch, this spirit steals the milk of others and spits it back out into the troughs placed next to the door of the house.[15]

In his *Gesta Caroli Magni* (Deeds of Charlemagne), Notker the Stammerer (died 912) relates a curious story.

> In that time, a demon or spirit, who played tricks on people and teased them, was in the habit of entering the smithy and playing all night with his hammers and anvils. When the blacksmith sought to protect himself and his property with the sign of the cross of Salvation, the Hairy One (*pilosus*) told him: "Hey friend, if you don't stop me from haunting your smithy, place your pitcher over there and find it full everyday." The poor man, who feared physical suffering more than the loss of his eternal soul, followed his adversary's advice.[16]

The "Hairy One" (the name is a Latin expression for what was a local reality) stole wine from a miser to fill the smith's pitcher. By comparing Notker's story with more recent texts, we see that this involves the conclusion of a contract between a spirit and a man. In fact, it is quite common for the household spirit to steal the property of others (fodder or food, for example), to give to the person he has adopted. Thus the Latvian *pukys* steals money, butter, wheat, and so forth from the neighbors and gives them to his master.[17]

In the eleventh century, Thietmar of Merseburg (died 1018) admonished the inhabitants of the Delitzsch region near Leipzig for worshipping their house spirits.[18] In the thirteenth century, William of Auvergne noted in his treatise *De Universo* (On the Universe), written between 1231–1235, that "evil spirits sometimes indulge in their games in the stables, carrying candles whose wax drops onto the manes and necks of the horses, and the manes of these horses are carefully braided."[19] Hiding behind this Christian interpretation (which demonizes the intruders), we find the spirits connected to these animals, and who either care for them or pester them.

In the Germanic countries, the domestic spirit generally hides behind the generic name of dwarf, which is the equivalent of the "pygmy" found in Latin texts. The term "dwarf" encompasses myriad characters, notably the *schrat* that glosses prior to 1000 CE gave as the equivalent of fauns, satyrs, hairy ones, sylvan ones, and other catchall terms. In 1460, Michael Beheim noted: "Many people believe that every house has its own Schrat that will make the fortune and enhance the prestige of whoever shows him honor," which is quite clear. And in 1482, a Latin-German dictionary translated *penates* with *schrat.* In the thirteenth century, Gervase of Tilbury recorded the following.

> Just as nature produces certain marvels in the world of humans, so spirits perpetrate their jokes in human bodies made of air, which they put on with God's permission. For instance, England has certain demons (though I admit that I do not know whether I should call them demons, or mysterious ghosts of unknown origin), which the French call *neptunes,* and the English *portunes.* It belongs to their nature to take pleasure in the simplicity of happy peasants. When peasants stay up late at night for the sake of their domestic tasks, suddenly, though the doors are closed, they are there warming themselves at the first and eating little frogs which they bring out of their pockets and roast on the coals. They have an aged appearance, and a wrinkled face; they are very small in stature, measuring less than half a thumb, and they wear tiny rags sewn together. If there should be anything to be carried in the house or any heavy task to be done, they apply themselves quickly to the work, and accomplish it more quickly than it could be done by human means. It is a law of their nature that they can be useful but cannot do harm.[20]

This is the first medieval text that provides us with the physical description and customary garb of house spirits. The image would long endure. In the thirteenth century, a German fable, "The Little Schrat and the Polar Bear," recounted the following.

> A Norwegian accompanied by a bear stopped to spend the night at a peasant's house, but the dwelling was haunted by a sprite who measured barely three spans but had enormous strength and wore a red cap. He had the habit of turning everything, furniture and utensils, topsy-turvy. In the middle of the night, this sprite emerged from his hiding place, approached the oven to get warm, and spied the bear sleeping by the hearth. He decided to chase it away and a rough-and-tumble fight ensued. In the morning, the sprite came to the peasant and told him he was leaving and would not be back until the large cat left the house.[21]

Even in the nineteenth century it was related how grateful peasants would make new clothes for these ragged house spirits; this would cause them to disappear, which was not at all the outcome they were expecting. *The Zimmern Chronicle,* written around 1566–1567, tells us the following in this regard:

> A Freising weaver rewarded the gnome in his service by offering him a pair of shoes and a black blouse, which the other gratefully accepted. He later gave the gift of a red cap, which the other received reluctantly before leaving, never to return.

Here it is the color red that compels the spirit's disappearance, a theme that is widespread throughout the Germanic countries.

In his treatise *On the Universe,* William of Auvergne is the sole person to my knowledge to have preserved two names for house spirits, *joculatores* and *joculares,* meaning "pranksters." Their actions can be summed up as follows. The prankster prevents people from sleeping by hurling stones or by turning the bedding inside out. He plays tricks on people by stealing small light objects that are easily carried away, in plain sight and even from out of their very hands, and taking them elsewhere.[22] William also mentions the *faunus,* "who the common people call *fulet* in French," meaning "sprite," but which is a blend of information from various sources. He tells us that these "sprites" are idolatrous, and deceive and lead men astray. They are very silly and undoubtedly "the children of incubus demons," and bear horns![23]

Gerald of Wales (Giraldus Cambrensis, 1146–1223) similarly relates a remarkable event.

> In these parts of Pembroke, in our own time, unclean spirits have been in close communication with human beings. They are not visible, but their presence is felt all the same. First in the home of Stephen Wiriet, then, at a later date, in the house of William Not, they have been in the habit of manifesting themselves, throwing refuse all over the place, more keen perhaps to be a nuisance than to do any real harm. . . . In Stephen's house things were even more odd, for the spirit there was in the habit of arguing with humans. When they protested, and this they would often do in sport, he would upbraid them in public for every nasty little act they had committed from the day of their birth onwards. . . .
>
> If you ask me the cause and the explanation of an event of this sort, I do not know what to answer, except that it has often been the presage, as they call it, of a sudden change from poverty to wealth, or more often still from wealth to poverty and utter desolation. . . . It seems most remarkable to me that places cannot be cleansed of visitations of this sort by the sprinkling of holy water, which is in general use and could be applied liberally, or by high holy water, or by the performing of some other religious ceremony.[24]

This last remark clearly shows that this concerns something other than unclean spirits and "demons"! Gerald of Wales cites another very interesting case.

> At about this same time, in the province of Pembroke, which I have been describing to you, a third manifestation occurred, in the home of Elidyr of Stackpole. It took the form of a young man with red hair called Simon. This was a full incarnation, for he could be seen and touched. He removed the household keys from the man in charge of

> them, and with complete self-assurance, took on the job of steward. He administered the household with such foresight and attention to detail, or so it seemed, that in his hands everything prospered and nothing was ever lacking. Elidyr and his wife had only to think of something which they would like for their table or their day-to-day use, mentioning it perhaps to each other, but certainly not to Simon, and he would immediately procure it, without having been asked to do so. "You wanted this," he would say, "and I have got it for you." He knew all about their family finances and the money they were trying to save. . . . Whatever he made up his mind to do, whether it pleased his master and mistress or not . . . he would carry out immediately, brooking no opposition. He never went to church and no Christian word was ever heard on his lips. He never slept in the house, but reported for work each morning with amazing punctuality.
>
> Then by chance he was seen one night by some member of the family conversing with his fellow-demons by the water-mill and the pool. The next morning he was interviewed by his master and mistress. He was dismissed on the spot and he handed over the keys which he had held for forty days or more. When he left they questioned him closely and asked him who he really was. He said that he had been born to some rustic beldame in the same parish, fathered on her by an incubus who had appeared in the shape of her husband.[25]

This account has a wealth of details in its adulterated story insofar as it blends the theme of the incubus, a direct product of clerical learning, underscored by the color of Simon's hair and his complete lack of religious feelings, with that of fairies and domestic spirits. The essential elements are readily apparent, however. Simon contributes to the well-being of the household; his supernatural nature is evident from his knowledge of all its secrets. Gerald of Wales also shows us that house spirits are polymorphous, since the accounts describe little old white-haired men or a young man. The most recent beliefs confirm this point and tell us that the spirit is not restricted to a single shape; it can even assume that of an object or thing. Finally, we have the testimony of the chronicles attributed to the

Senones monk, Richerus, which involves a perfectly harmless house spirit that remained in a house in Epinal from the time of the Nativity to the Feast of John the Baptist.[26]

Around 1250, Konrad von Würzburg tells of a wooden kobold (*ein kobolt von buhse*) in one of his poems,[27] and another poet, known under the name of Der Meissner, mentions a mute kobold.[28] These two examples obviously refer to a doll or fetish, a material representation of the domestic spirit. At the end of the thirteenth century, Konrad von Haslau indicates one should never draw a *taterman*[29]—another name for the *genius domesticus* (house spirit)—on a table, while Hugo von Trimberg (circa 1300) states it should never be drawn on a wall. In both cases, the context indicates that the metaphor in which the word "kobold" appears refers to some dishonest action. A person has to dig through an enormous number of texts to unearth a few tidbits of information, which are all the more valuable since they attest to the existence of the belief outside of literature.

There are three medieval accounts that are particularly expressive because they reflect various facets of the beliefs that interest us here. The first comes from a certain Brother Rudolf, a Silesian clergyman who wrote a treatise on *The Dignity of the Priesthood* between 1236 and 1250. According to Rudolf:

1. These women walk around the fire with the newborn; another woman follows behind asking: "What are you carrying?" and the foolish woman answering: "A sleeping hare, lynx, and fox."
2. They steal the brush used to clean the fireplace and brush the child with it.
3. They never give fire from their home to anyone and thereby sin against God during a birth, and with many other things.
4. When they bring a child back to the house (no doubt after the baptism), they crush an egg on the threshold with a broom.
5. In the evening, the woman stands with her child behind the entrance door and calls to the wooden woman that we call *fauness,* so that her child will weep and hers will behave.

6. Using five stones, these women ask who their husband will be. They give a name to each stone and place it in the fire; once these have cooled down again, they throw them into water. They are convinced that the stone that makes a shrill whistling noise when it hits the water bears the name of the husband they will wed.
7. They also throw nettles that have been soaked in their urine into the fire, as well as pieces of bone, pieces of wood from a coffin, and a good many other things, in order to make their husbands burn with love for them like the objects in the fire.
8. Others that think themselves more learned in the diabolical arts make images of wax or dough or sometimes some other material having the shape of a man. They then sometimes toss them into the fire, or sometimes on top of an anthill, to punish their lovers.
9. In new buildings or those into which they are going to set up their households, they bury pots filled with various things in certain corners and sometimes behind the stove for the Penates gods that the common people call *Stetewaldiu* ["Masters of the premises"]. This is why they refuse to let people pour just anything there. From time to time, they cast a bit of food there so that these gods remain friendly toward the household.
10. On the day of the apostles Philip and James (May 1), they stick hawthorn branches on their roofs to ensure their livestock give a lot of milk, and they plant trees in front of the door to their house.
11. They will not enter a house via the door through which a dead body has been carried.

Thanks to Rudolf, it is immediately apparent what the important areas of the house are: the hearth with its accessories, the threshold, the door, the corners, the roof—in other words, the center of the house represented by the fire burning there, the openings, and the covering. Keep these elements firmly in mind, because they will turn up again and again in texts even as recent as the twentieth century!

The second account is taken from an inventory of beliefs recorded by Antonius of Florence (1389–1459):[30]

1. Have you committed the error of believing that when the fire crackles it was a sign that someone was dying?
2. Have you refused to give fire to be taken out of the house for fear of inviting misfortune?
3. Have you saved the log that was burned at Christmas and placed it in your garden, or have you used it to bless your corners and doors?
4. If, in order to discover what you wish to know, you must recite the Our Father while facing the window and plugging your ears, so that you might draw that knowledge from the first words to come from outside, which is a mortal sin.
5. Have you believed that something will happen or that it means something . . . if you sneeze when leaving your house?
6. Have you placed blessed olive branches, or a grain of wheat taken from a manger, on your hearth in order to learn if someone shall live or die?
7. Have you refused to give something away from your house or promised to give something, on the first day of the calends, believing that your worldly goods would diminish?
8. Have you blessed your door or hung something in front of your house during the calends of March?

Antonius confirms the importance of the sites mentioned earlier, but his remarks are mainly aimed at castigating practices relating to divination and protection. On the other hand, his list has the value of providing us with the exact dates for certain rites. They correspond precisely with those of classical antiquity as well as those of more recent vintage.

The last account is an anonymous fourteenth- or fifteenth-century treatise that has come down to us in an anonymous manuscript from Saint Florian Monastery:[31]

1. Before going to Christmas mass, some people take a handful of dirt from underneath the bench, and if they find something living in it, they will not die.
2. When they return home from church with the branches, they first

place them in the manger before placing them beneath the roof, to ensure the cows will return with no difficulty (to the barn).

3. They walk around their houses with the branches so that foxes will not eat their chickens.
4. If someone sits on a table during Twelve Days, there will be a lot of ice.
5. On the last night of Twelve Days they walk around their house with a round loaf and cheese, and eat it. There will be as many haystacks in the field as there were mouthfuls.
6. If someone dreams that the oven collapsed, the master of the house or his wife shall die.
7. If someone places his hands above the fire, no worm will enter his ear nor will his nails turn dark.
8. On Christmas night, the folk fill a nine-liter container with water and leave it until morning when they measure the water level. If it is lower, the person will be poor during the year, if it is the same, nothing will change, but if there is more water, the person will be wealthy.
9. If one walks all around the house carrying the chickens before bringing them inside, the fox will not carry them off.
10. When one is about to take the herd out to pasture, it is necessary to bury a piece of steel beneath the gate and have the animals cross through it. They will not be bewitched.
11. They toss some of the second crop and beaten oats onto the roof and leave it there over Twelve Days, They then give it to their animals as feed. The storks will not eat the grain and the beasts will be fertile.

This collection grants significant status to the well-being of the animals and to rites of circumambulation, but divination and omens are not entirely absent and, once again, the parts of the house that are mentioned confirm what we have seen earlier. The three accounts we have just considered therefore complete, and help to highlight, the main themes of the research I am presenting.

Like so many other creatures that once embellished life and brought hope, house spirits have vanished and with them the souls of our houses have fled, never to return. Homes have sunk into anonymity; building rituals have almost entirely disappeared; the meaning of ornaments are no longer known and moon, sun, stars, and crosses have disappeared from our modern facades.

Above: *Sun-wheel patterns in the timber framing on the Royal Oak Inn in Tenbury, England*. Below: *The entrance building at Stokesay Castle, Stropshire, England.*

Left: *House with stone lower story and timber-frame upper part with "man" pattern and cross, Limburg, Germany*

Below: *House with shutter cut-outs; the sigil, sometimes called the Celtic Rose, is composed of four "spark of life" patterns. Melbourn, Cambridgeshire, England.*

Deer skull with antlers on house, Andlau, France. Photo by Claude Lecouteux.

Magic square on the door to protect an old house from evil spirits, Grenoble, France

Magic Square below a sundial. Its function is now ornamental because people here have forgotten the purpose of such formulas, French Alps. Photo by Claude Lecouteux.

The "Hexenhausla" (witches' house), Nuremberg, Bavaria, Germany

Speer post with St. Andrew's Cross or "dag" sign, Ryedale, Yorkshire, England. The name "witch post" for those apotropaic internal house features originates only in the 1930s.

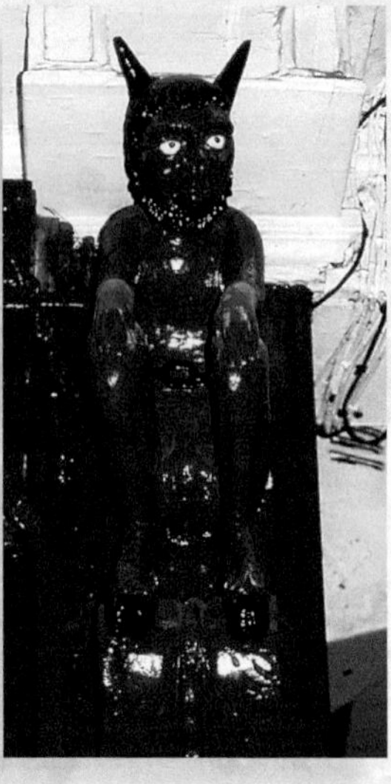

Above left: *Apotropaic mask on the gatehouse in the town wall, Rothenburg, Germany*

Above right: *Devil corbel on a medieval building, Stonegate, York, England*

Left: *Stone head above the entrance of a house, Heidelberg, Germany*

Left: *A stone-carved sprite from a medieval building, Wisbech, Cambridgeshire, England*

Geomantic mirror with the traditional eight winds/seasons sigils is placed above the door; made by Runestaff Crafts, Cambridge, England, 1990

Above left: *Eighteenth-century carving of the head of the martyred East Anglian king Edmund, patron saint of the city, Bury St. Edmunds, Suffolk, England*

Above right: *Traditional slate fireplace carved with apotropaic sigils in a house at Pentir, Snowdonia, Wales. On the mantel, glass vessels silvered with quicksilver (mercury) also have an apotropaic function.*

Middle left: Schratterlgatterl *placed to ward off bad luck and evil spirits, Karlsruhe, Baden, Germany*

Left: *Fairy loaves and fossilized sea urchins traditionally kept on the kitchen windowsill to ensure magically that there will never be a shortage of bread, Cambridgeshire, England*

Above left: *Pargetting (plaster stamped with carved wooden "press tools") with head pattern on the old post office at Great Waltham, Essex, England*

Above right: *Pargetting squares on a house outer wall at Great Dunmow, Essex, England*

Left: *Medieval timber-frame riverside houses in Strasbourg, France*

Below left: *Carved timber entrance to a barn with traditional sigils, including the Bauernhakenkreuz (Celtic Rose) and the date July 17, 1818, Hofgeismar, Germany*

Below: *Pargetted house wall at Great Waltham, Essex, England*

Above: *Timber-frame building constructed in 1946 to replace a building destroyed by bombing in World War II. The 1946 date shown in the gables is made of bottle ends, Norwich, Norfolk, England.*

Above right: *The early medieval sanctuary knocker on the west door of All Saints' Pavement Church in York, England, depicts an image reminiscent of the Fenris-Wolf swallowing Odin.*

Right: *Panel and binding-rope pattern pargetting on a house in Clare, Suffolk, England*

Below right: *Pargetting with various "press rolls" on a timber-frame wall in Saffron Walden, Essex, England*

Above left: *Foliated Head ("green man") in pargetted work on a house in Clare, Suffolk, England*

Above right: *Seventeenth-century pargetted image of the sun with two men in combat with sword and club above the yard entrance of the Old Sun Inn in Saffron Walden, Essex, England*

Left: *Romanesque binding-knot and other symbolic figures on the church at Scwäbisch Gmünd, Germany*

Below: *Pargetting wall sigil created from ribbed squares, Thaxted, Essex, England*

We should also take into consideration a marvelous thirteenth-century text, *Þáttr Þorvalds ens víðförla* (The Tale of Thorvald the Far-Traveled), whose information exactly matches that of the *Kristni saga* (Saga of the Christianization of Iceland) on this point.

> Around 981 or 982, Thorvald went with the Saxon bishop Fridrek to his father Kodran's house in Iceland. On his farm in Gilja he owned a stone to which he and his family brought offerings, believing that their helper spirit (*ármaðr*) lived in it. Kodran refused to be baptized as long as he did not know who was stronger, the bishop or the spirit. Fridrek sang some canticles over the stone, which exploded. Kodran then allowed himself to be baptized because the spirit had been defeated.

The story is more explicit and the details it presents give us a complete survey of the how the activity of a domestic spirit is represented.

> Kodran regarded the bishop as a seer (*spámaðr*) and retorted to his son that he already had one that was quite helpful: he predicted the future, protected his livestock, reminded him of what he needed to do and what he should watch over. He therefore held great confidence in him and had venerated him for a long time. Because the spirit advised Kodran not to convert, Thorvald suggested they see if the bishop could send it fleeing, after which his father would have no choice but to accept baptism. Kodran accepted the proposition. Fridrek sprinkled holy water on the stone, prayed, and sang canticles. That night the spirit appeared to Kodran in a dream, shaking with fear and full of reproaches. Fridrek was a cheat who sought to expel him from his home by pouring burning water on it; his children were weeping because of their injuries from the water. The bishop continued his operations the next day, and the spirit came back to see Kodran. His affable countenance and fine garb was no longer in evidence; he was draped in a frightful animal hide that was black and horrible to look upon. He begged Kodran to drive

> the strangers away, but Fridrek continued to sprinkle the stone with holy water, forcing the spirit to leave for a wilderness region. He then said: "Who will now protect your property as I have?" Kodran responded: "I honored you as a strong and useful god when I did not know the true God. Now that I have learned that you are unreliable and weak, it is right for us to part and for me to place myself under the protection of God who is better and stronger than you.[32]

The text speaks for itself, and the tutelary nature of the spirit is obvious. We have learned where he lives and the *Chronicle* of the Jesuits who converted Lithuania to Christianity noted a fact in the year 1600 that corroborates the two Scandinavian accounts. Speaking of the land's inhabitants, the anonymous author writes

> Elsewhere in the buildings [of the farm] large stones [*lapides non parvi*] are kept that are rooted in the ground and placed in such a way that their flat surface is on top and covered not with dirt but with straw. They are called *Deyves* [goddesses] and faithfully worshipped as protectors of the wheat and livestock.[33]

As it happens, the word *deyves* is the common name for supernatural beings, secondary deities similar to the domestic gods that protect every family and every farm. We find the same elements in this description as we do in Rome, where the altar of the goddess Ops Consuia, protector of grain, is buried in the ground and receives offerings.[34] The *Annals* of the Jesuits and the Roman traditions suggest that house spirits could well be the hypostases or avatars of ancient deities. This is a point we shall need to revisit.

In this way, through the stories of missionaries, we have a glimpse of something that matches the accounts of Burchard of Worms and Thietmar of Merseburg. We must therefore pay close attention to the cryptic statements in the ancient chronicles that cram into one hurried sentence a description of the worship of household gods, which they confuse with the worship of the major deities. All of this is just paganism, and the Church lumped it all together in one heap—it is up to us to sort it out! *Friðþjofs saga hins frœkna* (The Saga of Friðþjof the Bold) meanwhile informs us that the representations of domestic gods were warmed by the fire and dried with a cloth, which is something the Norwegians still did with the *Brödstainar* and the *Faksar* not so long ago.[35]

Indirect Testimonies

The romances of the Middle Ages were familiar with household spirits, although essentially in the form of dwarves. Since this is a generic term that was applied to all kinds of creatures of folk mythology, it is extremely difficult to unveil what it actually describes. By examining the texts and taking an inventory of these figures, such as Anne Martineau did for the dwarves of Arthurian literature,[36] it is possible to sort them into categories based on their status and their functions. This allows us to distinguish between at least three different families: the familiar spirits that have the role of educator, advisor, and protector of the hero, and who are veritable guardian angels; the localized spirits associated with specific places—bridge, tree, spring, chapel, boundary, and so forth; and finally, the house spirits, among whom the *genii catubuli* have best preserved their former character.

It is essentially thanks to two recurring motifs that we are able to trace the belief in domestic spirits in the medieval romances. The first is that of the servitor providing invaluable services to his master, providing him with everything he needs[37]; the second is the singular rapport the dwarves have with horses. Anne Martineau notes here: "The *corgie,* the sadly infamous works, whip of the dwarves, is incontestably a riding tool, one that is certainly often diverted from its normal purpose and used for evil ends." Taking a seventeenth-century play at its word, it would be the very emblem of stable sprites: "Do you see this sprite that holds a currycomb in one hand and a whip in the other?" This is a sprite that is only concerned with currying and grooming horses that have been neglected.[38]

Here is another example of the creatures we are studying that are all labeled dwarves. A fable by Marie de France informs us that the beings called by this name are naturally unsociable and shy, and detest being seen. Captured by a peasant, one dwarf is ready to grant him whatever he wants on the condition he does not show him to other people.[39] At first glance, and especially if one is not familiar with later traditions and those of Germany, it is impossible to discern a domestic spirit behind this "dwarf." However, its discretion, its fear of men, and its ability to grant wishes all smack of the *genius domesticus.*

As noted earlier, the household spirit is confused with the *spiritus familiaris* that takes the form of a man who suddenly appears out of nowhere to place himself in the service of a nobleman. This theme is mainly found in the *exempla* of clerical literature, but since the spirit-familiar is strictly labeled as a demon, it has gone unnoticed because researchers did not pay attention to certain details of the narratives. Here is a particularly revealing example, dating from the thirteenth century, of what we can find there.

> A demon assumed the appearance of a handsome young man and went to a knight to offer his services. The knight found this individual pleasing in both face and speech and gladly hired the young man, who entered his service immediately. He was so diligent, devoted, faithful, and pleasant, that the knight was in a state of constant amazement. Never did he mount or alight from his horse without finding his servant ready, holding the stirrup on bended knee. He proved to be forever discreet, careful, and cheerful. One day when riding together, they came to a large river. The knight looked around and spied several of his mortal enemies hot on his tail. He yelled to his servant, "We are lost! My enemies are pursuing us, the river bars our way; we cannot escape. They are going to kill or capture us." The other answered, "Milord, fear not! I know a ford. Follow me and we will get out of this predicament." The knight replied, "No one has ever forded this river," but he followed his servitor in the hope of escaping. After they crossed the river, their enemies remained on the other side saying in stupefaction, "Who ever heard of a ford in this river? Only the Devil could have helped him cross it," and they turned back, fear in their bellies.[40]

To treat the knight's wife when she fell ill, the servitor went to the mountains of Araby in an instant and returned with the milk of a lioness. The knight than asked him who he was.

> "Worry not, I am your servant." But because his master insisted, he eventually confessed: "I am a demon, one of those that fell from Heaven with Lucifer." The knight, in even greater astonishment, questioned him more closely: "If you are a devil by nature (*si natura diabolus es*), how is it you serve a man so faithfully?" The other answered him, "To be in the company of the sons of men is a great consolation for me," and when the knight stated, "I dare not continue availing myself of your services," he replied, "Be assured of one thing, if you keep me in your service, never will harm come to you by my doing." "I dare not," the knight responded, "but I will gladly give you what you ask as a wage even if it is half of all I own. No one has ever served me with such loyalty and efficiency. Thanks to you, I escaped death at the river's edge, thanks to you my wife's health was restored." The demon then said, "Since I can no longer remain in your company, I will demand only five sous." When he received them, he gave them back to the knight saying, "I beg you to buy a small bell with this sum that you will hang from the roof of that old ruined church so that at least on Sunday, Christians can be called to mass," and he vanished before his eyes.[41]

Since when do demons care about whether the faithful can attend Sunday mass? Since when do they devote all their efforts to doing good? The internal contradictions of this text are glaringly apparent! In fact, what we have here is a seemingly omniscient supernatural being—he knows the ford and a remedy for the ailing wife—and one who can go wherever he pleases in the blink of an eye. The most astonishing assertion, the one that should really tip us off, is that he finds consolation in the company of human beings (*magna est mihi consolatio esse cum filiis hominum*). Now quite often, folk traditions tell us that house spirits will do everything in their power to get inside a house, even changing themselves into harmless objects because they need to be brought into the house and are not always able to enter by will alone. Here, the spirit asks the knight to hire him as a manservant.

Clearly the belief in the existence of these mysterious individuals

De miniſterio dæmonum.

Spirits at work. Olaus Magnus, Historia de Gentibus Septentrionalibus *(Rome, 1555).*

became fodder for literature and the difficulty in identifying them primarily stems from their gradual conflation with dwarves in the strict sense, and even elves. It is therefore essential to have a reading grid that allows us to draw up an inventory of the primary features of household spirits is thus indispensable. Then, when we stumble across a particularly mischievous dwarf, it would be foolish to believe it was a simple imp. The same holds true when we encounter another one that brushes the manes of horses, curries the animals, or turns everything upside-down in the house. Let me repeat: "dwarf" and "imp" are generic terms in the Middle Ages. Nevertheless, the imp, a creature that originally had a close connection to water, received many features of the household spirit and stood in for that creature in postmedieval times.

In short, without succumbing to the error of making a contrary interpretation, which means projecting more recent elements back onto an older era, the mystery surrounding domestic spirits can only be clarified by evaluating the facts in the widest perspective and over the long term.

Again, this is the sole method for determining the realities of yesteryear when they concern folk mythology.

In the recent book by Bengt af Klintberg, *The Types of the Swedish Folk Legends,* one chapter deals with domestic spirits and confirms the results of our investigation.

> The Domestic Spirit is helpful and takes care of the livestock, feeds the cows, etc. He has a favorite animal and treats badly the others, and doesn't tolerate a horse of a certain color. He must have the right food, and when the farmer forgets butter in his porridge, he becomes furious and kills a cow or throws out all the hay in the barn. He punishes bad behavior by burning down the house or throwing a farmhand over the roof. The noise of the farmhands disturb him and he shows his anger by lifting a horse up to the hayloft.[42]

6

The Origin of House Spirits

SPIRITS AND GODS

Earlier we learned that there is a connection between certain spirits and the former deities of paganism. In some cases, the *genii domestici* seem to be hypostases of gods and goddesses of the type we find in classical antiquity, while in other cases, the material allows us to see that the creatures in question could be regarded as avatars or secularized forms of the gods. In the nineteenth century, Hersart de La Villemarqué noted:

> At the end of the pagan era, the household spirits seem to have dethroned the universal, public gods. Popular devotion, turning away from Teutates, Heusus, Belen, and several other inhabitants of the Celtic Olympus, preferred to shift its allegiance to local deities, who were less highly placed and therefore more accessible to humans.[1]

Lithuanian traditions are extremely revealing here. In ancient times, the hearth was sacred and the center of a familial worship dedicated to

Dimispatis. The *Jesuit Annals* note, in 1604, that the inhabitants of this land "have domestic gods (*deos domesticos*) that they call Dimispatis in their tongue and about which various opinions reign. Some say that he is the god of fire and that he protects the house from conflagrations, and they offer him a chicken. . . . Others maintain it is the family mother and they offer the mothers a pig." The spirits connected to the hearth and fire therefore definitely originate in the Dimispatis of this country.

The *barstucci* and the *aitvaras,* meanwhile, are considered as the servitors of Puscetus and compared to dwarves, but, as Jean Haudry notes, "contrastive analysis of the meanings of their names shows that the first are connected to earth and water, and the second to fire and air."[2]

If we also look at the mythological traditions that gave birth to the beliefs or influenced them (providing it was not the other way around), we see that each domain has its deity or deities. In Latvia, these deities are the Mothers, the Mother of the Forest, of the Wind, of the Night; and guardian spirits like the Laukasargai or Zemespatis, the master of the land, who look after the fields; and agrarian deities like Ceroklis, who protects the wheat, Useling (Using) who looks after horses, and Tensin who watches over pigs. An old Latvian man who was questioned by the Jesuits as to the number of gods that existed answered:

> There are different gods, depending on the variety of folk, places, and needs. We have one god that rules over the Heavens and another that reigns over the Earth; this latter, who is the greatest god on earth, has other lesser gods under his commands. We have a god who provides fish, and another who gives us game; we have a god for wheat, for the fields, for the gardens, for livestock; meaning the horses, cows, and other domestic animals. The sacrifices made to them are also different: some get larger offerings, others smaller, depending on the qualities of these gods, and all these offerings are made to certain trees and certain groves. These trees are said to be sacred. To the god of horses—who is called Deving Usching—everyone offers two coins and two loaves of bread, and throws a piece of lard for him into the fire. Moschel, the god of cows, is offered

> butter, milk, and cheese, and so forth, and if a cow falls ill, an offering is quickly given to the trees and it gets better. At certain times, the god of fields and wheat, Deving Cerklicing, receives in the grove the sacrifice of a black ox or chicken, or a black piglet, or so on, with several barrels of beer, a little more or less depending on custom, and this way the god Cerklicing gives them his help.[3]

This very rich account shows that there is no clear dividing line between gods and spirits; the nature of the offerings, and of the location for the sacrifices, show how the substitutions could have taken place. The example of how a person can obtain the healing of a sick animal is quite revealing.

In short, the whole of nature is populated by supernatural beings, every region is entrusted to the protection of deities or spirits, and we can imagine a line of development. The material needs of humans and their desire to protect themselves against life-threatening catastrophes—animal epidemics, weather-caused disasters, fires, and so forth—initially brought these entities first called gods into existence. When the mythology no longer corresponded with the social and religious development of a people, all that was retained was the function of these supernatural creatures. They therefore departed from the pantheon to take up residence with men, in the places that we have looked at earlier. The deities of the fruits of the earth found homes in barns and those of livestock moved into the buildings reserved for them. In some way, the deities settled down and became attached to specific dwellings. It is difficult to know to what extent ancestor worship played a role here, but there are indications that speak in favor of an interaction between the two spheres, that of the gods and that of the dead. These indications consist mainly in the offerings and sacrifices that fall on dates that are also those on which the gods and the dead are honored.[4] The matter of sacrificial meals organized among various European peoples during the winter months is worth exploring more deeply as these meals were often intended both for the good dead and spirits. I would like to point out one final indication of this transformation of gods into spirits: it is not uncommon to see that the *genius domesticus* does not live directly inside the house but rather in the garden, vineyard, or yard (or actually the hedge, which forms the boundary of the domestic space), the farm or residence, or even in a tree or stone that stands in the yard. Perhaps what we have here is the intermediary stage preceding the spirit's move into the heart of the house.

The lexical elements should also not be overlooked. A letter sent by Maeletius to Georg Sabinus, rector of Königsberg University, contains a list of deities among whom we find a certain Piluitus, a "god of wealth that the Latins called Plouton."[5] This Plouton is no stranger, he is the *Bilwiz* of German traditions, a being treated as a dwarf and sometimes considered to be a house spirit, and sometimes a wheat demon.[6] It so happens that Maeletius accords him the same status as the major deities like Patrimpas, Putscetus, and Antrimpas. Furthermore, he does not forget the Barstucci in his list, specifying that the Germans call them *erdmenle,* meaning "underground dwellers."[7] This is not exactly correct, since the folk traditions draw a distinction between the "Homunculus of the Earth" and the "Undergrounders" (*Underjördiske, Untererscbe,* etc.). Whatever the case may be, this example allows us to get an idea of the shifts that take place over the course of historical development.

Other advances are the result of lexical and semantic study. In the case of the *schrat,* which Michael Beheim presents as a fifteenth-century *genius catabuli* (spirit of the stable), it reveals the collusion between spirits and the dead. In the oldest glosses, schrat is translated as *larva* and *monstrum,* "dead one, revenant," and by *lares mali,* "evil *Lares.*" Beheim states, "Many folk believe that every house has a small schrat who makes the fortune and increases the prestige of whoever honors it," whereas his contemporary, Hans Vintler, maintained, "Many believe that the schrat is a small child, fast as the wind, and a soul in torment."[8]

The tangled nature of folk traditions does not permit us any foregone conclusions. However, the clues unearthed indicate that there is a logic behind the conflations and superimpositions, as well as a historical development in which mankind's supernatural creatures tends to become lumped together over time.

THE ORIGIN ACCORDING TO FOLK TRADITIONS

How does a home, whether a single dwelling or farm, acquire a spirit that will protect it? This question, which was repeatedly asked by the ethnologists who undertook the major studies of the first half of the twentieth century, was answered in a variety of ways by the peasants they interrogated. All of the answers were very intriguing in that they allowed a fundamental opinion to emerge, one that connected the spirit to a dead person.

The Various Traditions

Martti Haavio's research in Finland gives us a good overview of the basic explanations. The spirit is the one that lights the fire for the first time in the new house, who is the first to have arrived on the construction site and cleared it, or else the first inhabitant of the land who has died.[9] In Ångermanland and other regions on both shores of the Baltic Sea, this may be a topical spirit that has been tamed, so to speak, thanks to a building, sacrifice, or gift, an offering that represents in fact the purchase price of the land and thus the execution of a tacit contract between the man taking possession of it and the spirit.[10] The offering is placed beneath the threshold, beneath the floor, in a corner, between two specific beams, and so forth—whatever spot is believed to be where the spirit stays, who apparently retains his property and management rights, being the actual owner, whereas the new resident merely has usufruct of the premises. The spirit dwells wherever he pleases in the house, in one or more places where the farmer does not enjoy usufruct, and if someone sleeps there, he will wake them up and force them to move,[11] even going so far as to transform into a cat-shaped nightmare.

In the French Alps, the spirit is born from a rooster's egg hatched in the manure of a horse, or from a placenta that a cat has eaten. It is also said to be a wandering spirit that never received baptism, the souls of dead infants who were never baptized, but another explanation maintains that it can be purchased or obtained from the devil. "In order to obtain a little devil, you must proceed with a black chicken to the place where five paths cross, say a special prayer, and devote oneself to the devil for a year's time."[12] *Diablotin* (Little Devil) is only one of the many names of the spirit in the Isère region of France. The same thing is said in Latvia about the *pūkis:* one has to sell his soul to the devil or the double—the alter ego or external soul—of an evil individual.[13] In the Riga area, it is said to be obtainable in return for cold cash. The Alpine Servan buys, sells, or sends it, and the same notion is found in Germany where it is also said it must be ritually invited.

> A peasant once lived near a dike in Hattstedtermarsch (Schleswig-Holstein), a Frisian named Harro Harrsen. . . . He was a clever lad who knew how to get the most out of any situation. On seeing a cavity in an oak pillar, he told himself it would make a perfect lodging place for a little Niskepuk. When his house was built, for a trim beneath this hole he nailed a board as wide as his hand. On this he placed a bowl filled with liberally buttered gruel and softly called out, "Come here, kind Niskepuk!" They were not long in coming to examine the new building. They danced through the new home and one of them—three inches tall—remained, and settled in the hole in the pillar.[14]

Among the Sámi, a *háldi* spirit is often hereditary in some families, but it can also be purchased.[15]

Here is how the "birth" of a household spirit is described in Ångermanland: "When construction on a house is begun, a wooden cross is erected at which point the spirit is born; the cross is left standing until the walls are raised, and then it is pulled down and chopped into smaller pieces."[16] In Russia, every inhabited house has a spirit called *domovoj,* who is often the first person to have died there.

German traditions, extensively studied by Erika Lindig,[17] provide us with various details that we cannot afford to overlook. Often spirits seek to be hired by the master of the house exactly as would a farmhand or day worker, but mistrust from human beings sometimes obliges them to resort to a ruse. To enter the house, they change into a harmless object and wait by the edge of the road for someone to pick them up and carry them. This tradition therefore shows that a house cannot be entered without first having been invited or brought there. This clearly shows that the dwelling is a sacred space that stands securely against the intrusion of supernatural beings. We should be cautious here and refrain from assuming that this is an ancient notion; as I see it, it is instead evidence of the demonization of all these little spirits that have been stripped of some of their powers.

The spirit can also enter the house via the wood used to build it, the standard explanation for which is as follows. A spirit has been banished into a tree by a priest or sorcerer. When the tree is chopped down to be made into a beam, the spirit is still living there, and once the new building is finished it will begin a new life, this time as spirit of this construction.

Dwarf as housekeeper, Haslach (Germany), twentieth century (photograph by C. Lecouteux)

This tradition raises a problem that the current state of research leaves us unequipped to resolve, but that is worth noting. In Norse, the beam is called *áns* and *dvergr;* the first word refers to a god (i.e., one of the Aesir family) and the second means "dwarf." Did this wood used in building earn that name because it was allegedly the abode of a supernatural being, or simply because it was sacred, similar to the central beam that holds up the roof (*gusitora*), which the Goldi of the Amur River identify as the domestic spirit?[18]

The Spirits and the Dead

"The first dead inhabitant can change into a house spirit," notes Martti Haavio for Finland. Hans F. Feilberg confirms this for the Scandinavian countries, but Lauri Honko notes that this is never the case in Ångermanland.[19] Eugène Rolland cites a testimony from Finistère in Brittany that says: "The sprites of the stables are former farmhands. When still alive, they neglected the horses entrusted to them; after they died, they were condemned to take care of them."[20] Throughout my research I have been continually come across clues that imply a close connection between the domestic spirit and the dead man. Eventually, this caught my attention and posed new questions. Let's now examine some of the more significant traces.

Among the Wallachians, the *zimt* is the feast of the household gods—each hearth has one—and the ancestors. The house is cleaned, the table set, friends are invited, and the memory of the departed is also celebrated at this time. These deceased are invited to sit at the table where there are empty chairs reserved for them.[21]

In Bulgaria, at the Feast of the Dead, offerings are placed in the hearth while saying: "Rejoice, master of the house,"[22] In Germany, the souls of the dead intentionally remain close to the furnace, the habitual residence for spirits, while in Switzerland, traditions collected at the beginning of the twentieth century by Josef Müller in the canton of Uri, tell us that souls in torment stay, in front of, behind, or inside the stove.[23] The dead also live in the doors[24] and in the block of wood forming the lintel, and the following is asserted:

> Someone who knocks down an old house in the Schächental (Uri) and builds a new one, should never take the lintel block, which should have holes bored into it, otherwise the spirits and misfortune of the demolished house will enter the new one.[25]

In Estonia, Jacob Grimm informs us that "food for the dead is left on the floor of one room. The master of the house enters there late in the evening with a long torch and urges them to eat, calling them by name. Some time later, when he thinks they have eaten their fill, he commands them, while breaking his torch on the lintel, to return whence they came and to avoid stepping upon their robes while returning. If the harvest was poor, it was attributed to the poor hospitality shown the souls of the dead."[26] It so happens that this rite matches the one intended to propitiate the house spirits. Almost everywhere, the spirit behaves like a "white lady" (*banshee*) and heralds the death of the master of the house.[27] It is often confused with the rapping spirit (poltergeist) who is most often a dead person who reveals his or her presence by various noises.[28]

The sixteenth-century *Zimmern Chronicle* states, when speaking of *erdemenle* and *wichtenmendle:* "Many believe they are men who were once cursed and hope to find redemption through humans; this is why they work and behave so kindly in the homes of pious and honorable individuals."[29] In *German Legends,* the Grimm brothers write about a domestic brownie named Kurt Chimgen or Heinzchen.

> People think they are actual men beneath the features of small children clad in multicolored robes. If we can take some individuals at their word, some of these brownies have a knife stuck in their backs and others bear some other object, all have more-or-less hideous marks, depending on how they were previously slain and what the instrument of their demise was. I say slain, because they are considered to be the souls of those who have been murdered in the house.
>
> If sometimes the maidservant becomes curious to see her small valet, her Kurt Chimgen or Heinzchen, names that she gives the sprite . . . the spirit tells her when she may see him, but he rec-

ommends she carry a bucket of cold water with her at that time. Ordinarily she next sees him lying across a small cushion with a large cutlass stuck in his back. Some are so terrified by the sight they fall to the floor senseless. The sprite then gets up at once, pours the bucket of water over the woman's body and she comes back to her senses, but she no longer has any desire to see the sprite.[30]

The theme of death is repeated so often that researchers have accepted it as one of the roots of the belief in house spirits—the other being that of the genius loci—which would even represent "the collective soul" of a family[31] and is suggestive of ancestor worship. Leander Petzoldt notes in this regard, "the foundation of the representation of house spirits is to be sought for in the Manes, Lares, and Penates of the Romans, who were given offerings (food) in the corner of the fireplace. The hearth is dedicated to the ancestors whose good will must be attracted through sacrifices, and they exert a tutelary function over the household."[32] In favor of this deduction, the scholars emphasize that house spirits often possess the features of deceased individuals, they are by and large anthropomorphic, their nature is like that of humans, and they accept the same offerings and testimonies of respect as the deceased elders. Furthermore, both remain in the same parts of the house. When they have an animal form, it often corresponds with the depiction of the soul in the beliefs, to wit a snake or flying creature. Finally, it is worth noting that the spirits maintain precise relationships with infants: they come to rock them at night and feed them for example, and when they have the form of a snake, they eat from the same bowl as the little ones and play with them. We should further note that the Bulgarian *sajbija* is also a dead ancestor[33] and that the same notion can be found in Greece.[34]

The dead and spirits therefore allegedly linger in the same spots inside the house. In classical antiquity, the newborn was placed on the hearth to be presented to the ancestors and to the house spirits,[35] and the survival of this rite can be seen in the Mark, in Pomerania, and in the Lubeck region.

THE NAMES OF THE HOUSE SPIRITS

The spirits have an array of names depending on their country and place of residence. In the Middle Ages, the attestations are baffling because the majority of accounts come from clerics who distort everything by giving Latin equivalents for local names. All the names for the lesser ancient Roman deities can overlap with the figures of local belief, which hardly makes investigation easier, and it is only in context that one can see what is hiding behind the names that originate in another culture and which have been deformed by the Christian interpretation of things. We have seen that terms like *faunus, satyrus, portunus,* and *pilosus,* which for the ancient Romans designated deities of the fields and woodlands, were used as equivalents of domestic spirits in the works of Burchard of Worms and Gervase of Tilbury. In the secular literature, these same spirits were incorporated into dwarves most of the time, and even into nightmares. In the German-speaking regions during the Middle Ages, they were called *zwerc, schrat,* or *mâr.* Here again, we can only recognize them by their behavior since their manner of dress is simply that which is imputed to dwarves.

In the early Middle Ages, outside of what we find in a few isolated Latin texts, the available information is even more cursory. In Germany, Notker the German (950–1022), at monk at the Abbey of St. Gallen, translated *penates* and *Lares* with *ingoumo,* "something that can be spotted inside the house, that is owed respect," and *ingesid,* "cohabitants." These are not so much names as circumlocutions intended to convey the idea of a numinous power (*numinosum*). In the folk beliefs to which Notker refers, people refrain from uttering the name of the supernatural being for fear of causing it to appear. This is confirmed by another name, *wiht,* whose closest translation would be "creature"* and which was later used to form the term *Wichtelmännchen,* which designates dwarves and spirits. Collections of glosses prior to the year 1000 translate *genius* with "place god" (*stetigot*) or "domestic god" (*hûsgot*),[36] and even "Habitant" (*husing*), which we see again among the Latvians where Ûsins[37] is the guardian spirit of horses. In 1606, the *Jesuit Annals* speak of a *deo equo-*

*[The German term is equivalent to the archaic English word "wight." —*Trans.*]

rum, quem vocant Dewing Uschinge (a god of horses that is called Dewing Ushinge) and, according to Jacob Lange, writing in 1777, this god was gradually incorporated into Saint George (Saint Jürgen). Starting in the twelfth century, we begin seeing *kobold,* which means "the one who rules over the room," a creature who in the Old English glosses appears in the plural form *cofgodas,* "the gods of the room," with "room" either referring to all parts of the house (cellar, main room, and so forth), or else designating the stove, meaning the only heated room of ancient homes, the German *Stube.* Over time, the kobold supplanted all the other names, or else we come across vague terms such as *getwas,* "spirit, dwarf." In the thirteenth century, Rudolf of Silesia mentions the *stetewaldiu,* "he who rules over the place, he who leads the household," with the name therefore designating a function, and the thirteenth-century poet Konrad von Würzburg gives *taterman* as a synonym for kobold.

In the sixteenth century, house spirits were given the name of *sottrels* or *soteretz* in the Vosges region and were regarded as incubus demons seeking the carnal company of the women they followed.[38] In his discourse on specters that appeared in 1586, Pierre Le Loyer mentions several spirits that haunt houses, including the goblin.

> At time in private homes as well, one hears a noise and racket that the Rabbats, Brownies, or Spirit Sprites are making there. What they say about these sprites is no fable . . . for I would tell Lucian and his peers as incredulous as he, that they can find plenty of houses these Spirits or Goblins haunt and where they ceaselessly disturb the rest of those living there. For sometimes they move and overturn the utensils, the dishes, trestles, tables, plates, bowls, and sometimes they draw water from the well or cause the pulley to shriek, break the glasses, cause all manner of heavy objects to roll in small increments, cause the slates and tiles to fall from the roof, pretend sometimes to be a cat, sometimes a mouse, sometimes other animals . . . trample on people lying in their beds, draw the curtains or pull off the covers, and play a thousand pranks. And these Sprites cause no other nuisance or inconvenience to people except disturbing them,

> stepping on them, and preventing them from sleeping; for in the morning all the dishes that it seemed they were tossing about and breaking during the night can be found intact.[39]

The goblin, whose name we find for the first time in the *Life of Saint Taurinus* (eleventh century) appears here with every feature of the domestic spirits we will encounter several centuries later. He is a mischievous prankster, sows disorder, and behaves like a nightmare. In the Aubrac region, he is called a *drac.*

In the German-speaking regions, this kind of spirit is called a "Little Earthman" (*Erdmännleinn*), which is also the name for unspecified dwarves, and Count Froben Christopher of Zimmern's (died 1567) *Chronicle* calls these beings fallen angels whose transgressions were minor in comparison to those of Lucifer's companions: "They were given a *corpus solidum* [solid body] from the earth and are not ethereal like other spirits. . . . They have hopes of finding grace again and redemption," which explains why "they perform good deeds and visit honorable folk, and offer them help in their just, honorable business."[40] Johan Weier confirms their name: "Many individuals of the Lares and Larva family . . . are called 'Little Earthmen' by the common folk." He provides the following details.

> There are two kinds. Some are quite gentle, affable, and docile, which is why they are called, and rightly so, *Lares familiares,* which is to say small domestic spirits. They roam through houses, especially at night, and can be heard . . . as if they were quite busy, walking down the stairs, opening doors, lighting the fire, drawing water, cooking, and expediting everything connected to daily household duties, but they do none of this for real.[41]

The second kind consists of "wicked and violent [individuals] who disturb the household or at the very least give it a good fright." For the Jesuit professor of theology Petrus Thyraeus, they are homunculi (*homunciones*) and house spirits (*Lares domestici*), which men call *Jeannots*

(*Hensemenle*) and whom pagans customarily worshipped like idols.[42] It is interesting to note that Thyraeus thinks some spirits are only "human souls condemned to the torments of hell and others before being purified by the punishments of purgatory."[43] Opinions were split between an interpretation of spirits as devils—Luther's influence here is undeniable[44]—or as supernatural beings and the dead.

These opinions persisted into the seventeenth century and the Latin terms that repeatedly appear in the works of scholars like Johann Clodius and Johann Christoph Rudinger are *Lares domestici* and *Lares familiares,* although the latter name more properly refers to the spirit-familiar (*spiritus familiaris*) that was housed in a crystal flask or some other container.[45] Johannes Prätorius informs us that people believed these were the souls of people who had been murdered in the house.[46]

Folk traditions provide an enormous number of names, which can be divided into six types:

1. The creature remains vague and undefined; it is called "disturbing monster" (*Umg'hyri*), "ghost" (*Gespenst*), or "spook" (*Spuk*).
2. It is named after its physical appearance: Young (*Junge*), Little Fellow (*Kerlchen*), Little Man (*Männchen*), Little Woman (*Weiblein*), Dame (*Frau*), Maid (*Fräulein*); all terms referring to anthropomorphic creatures. We also have Tom Thumb (*Däumling*) and names with connotations of deformity (*Grieske, Schrättli*). But names referring to objects are also not uncommon, such as *puk* or *pug* (wood end), *butz* (plug of wood), and *poppele* (pottery shard). This tells us that these beings were initially amorphous but gradually given human features, and that they were certainly idols.
3. Their color is the determining factor and the names cited earlier are associated with the adjectives gray, white, red, or with the age attributed to the creature: it is elderly.
4. These beings can also owe their name to their place of residence or where they are active, such as Little Man of the Parsonage (*Pfarrmännel*) or Little Man of the Cellar (*Kellermännchen*), or

even their work: Little Man of the Fodder (*Futtermännchen*). It may also refer to their chief concern, such as Little Man of the Fire (*Feuermännchen*) or Little Man of the Stove (*Ofenmännchen*). In Scandinavia, the fire spirit is called Lokke and *aarevetti* (Hearth Spirit).

5. They are named on account of the way in which they manifest, with noise being the predominant feature in these names: Knocker (*Klopfer, Klopferle*), Noisemaker (*Schlapper*), Grumbler (*Rumpele*), and so forth.
6. Their dress plays an important role. One striking feature stands out and gives us: Little Cap or Little Hood (*Hütchen, Hödeken*), Boots (*Stiefel*), Green Robe (*Grünrock*), Blue Trousers (*Blauhösler*), and so forth. In some regions, one form takes precedence: in Saxony-Anhalt, it is that of the *monachus,* and those spirits quite simply called Monk, which brings to mind the Italian *Monaciello* (Little Monk).

The fact that half these spirits are male and that their names are often in the diminutive stands out, which is suggestive of the small stature of these individuals or is a connotation of familiarity and affection, something that is particularly evident in the human first names that make up about 5 percent of the appellations. These include Little Hans and Little Jack (*Hänschen, Jokele*), Bartel (the nickname for Bartholomew), and Chimeken[47] (Little Joachim).

Outside of these denominations, we encounter names that designate both the spirits and the dead. In Switzerland, for example, in the canton of Uri, *Umghyr,* "monster, revenant," and *Gspängst,* "ghost, spirit" are applied to all manner of supernatural manifestations inside the home. *Umghyr* corresponds to the northern German *Unhür,* which designates an evil dead individual who returns and who sometimes possesses the characteristics of a vampire. In the Valasian Alps, *Coqwergi* designates the domestic servant who is born from the egg of a rooster or black hen, which has been hatched by a man.

We are able to compare all this German-based material with that of other countries. In Russia, the domestic spirit is called *domovoj,* "the Master of the House," and Olga A. Cherepanova notes in regard to this country: "Another component of this fantastic universe is the depiction of transcendent beings who are the spirits and patrons of various places and domains. Their presence in the house and in the yard, in the fields, forests, and waters is proverbial for many inhabitants of the North even today."[48] The *domovoj* is especially protective of chickens and the Vot people have borrowed it in the form of the *domovikka* (*tomavoi, damavoi*). In Bulgaria, *stopan,* "the Protector," or *talasum,* "the Spirit of the House," designate the good spirit, while *sajbija,* meaning "Master of the Home," which is borrowed from Turkish, is only attested in the northwestern region of the country. Incidentally, we should note that *sajbija* also designates the man who has been buried in the house's foundation or a deceased family member who, because of his deeds, has left a good memory.[49]

In France, the folk traditions collected by ethnologists are equally as rich.[50] In the Alps we find the Servan, which comes from the Latin *sylvanus,* the Chaufaton, the Familiar, the Sprite (*follet, follaton, foulat*), the Farfollet, and the Matagot, whereas in the Pyrenees, Galtxagorri, Masmarro (who lives in the hearth), Osencame, and Sarricachau, "Isard's tooth," are charged with making sure that homes are run properly. In the Basque country, the spirit called Maide has even been Christianized into Saint Maide! The Lorraine *sotré* or *satré* is an ugly, deformed little man with cloven hooves. He helps at night with the domestic duties and loves to take care of children.

In Navarre, the house spirit's name means "Master of the Home" (Etxajuan) and among the Ossetians, Binat(i)xicau has the same meaning. We find Menos in Aragon and the Minairons in Catalonia. In contemporary Greece, the *töpakas,* meaning the "Protector of the Home, is etymologically related to *topos,* "site, place."

The Northern countries have a wealth of evidence for the belief in domestic spirits. Haltia is the most widespread name among the Finns and it means "the Master" (with the implied sense "of the place"),[51] and the Scandinavian Sámi, the northern reindeer herders, believe in the *háldi* (*hal'de,* deriving from *haltia*), who are anthropomorphic guardian spirits. In Ångermanland, we find many words composed with *haltia,*[52] such as

Huoneenhaltia, "the spirit of the living room." In Lithuania, according to a Jesuit account dating from 1604, Dimispatis is assigned to fire and protects the house from conflagrations (*domos ab igne custodit*),[53] whereas Gausas Mâte, "the Mother of Prosperity," oversees food, and there is evidence for various hearth spirits: the *pukys, aitvarai,* and *kaukai.* Estonia is mainly home to the *Majavaim,* "the Spirit of the House," the *Majahaldas,* "the Tutelary Spirit of the Dwelling," and the *Majahoidja,* "the Guardian of the Domicile." The Latvians worship a Master of the Dwelling (*Mâjas kungs*) who lives in the hearth. For its part, Scandinavia has five sets of names. The first set is based on *tomte,* "building terrain," which is combined with terms meaning "home, inhabitant, spirit"; the term also traveled into Finland.[54] The second set is formed from *tufte,* "place where a house shall be built," to which is added a determinant identical to those cited above or one meaning "guardian" (*vord*). The third set has *tun* for its base, which means "farm, settlement," and the fourth set, based on *gard,* has the same meaning.[55] The fifth and last set is based *rå,* "master, sovereign," alone or as part of a compound word. The Siberian Votyaks know the "Master of the Stable" (*gid-kuzo*), "Master of the Sauna" (*munt'so-kuzo*), and the "Man of the Grain Dryer" (*obin-murt*).[56]

We should also note that a house possesses one or several spirits. When there are many of them it most often involves a family, but this notion seems due to a conflation with dwarves. "Generally," it is said of the Puk in Schleswig-Holstein, "only one customarily lives in the house and people call it Nes Puk."[57] Another Frisian account provides us with the following:

> A poor peasant finally managed to finish building his house thanks to the gifts from his neighbor and to ensure his good fortune, he invited the Puki there. They soon arrived to inspect the new house, and danced about it until one of them, about three inches high, decided to stay there and chose a hole in the beam for his home.

I should stress, however, that every building on a farmstead has its own spirit, which is what gives rise to the plethora of names in a particular geographical area. The Latvians are familiar with the notion of whole families of domestic spirits and Andrejs Johansons cites the case of one family of Livonians who make offerings to the father and mother of the home as well as to their children.[58]

What essentially stands out from this presentation of the naming traditions relating to house spirits are the notions of master, guardian, and protector. The household spirit is first and foremost a tutelary spirit who is helpful and benevolent, and the majority of names reflect the anthropomorphic element. But what exactly does a house spirit look like? How does it manifest?

7

The Manifestations of Household Spirits

THE APPEARANCE OF THE SPIRITS

In his study of French traditions, Paul Sebillot points out that household spirits are most often members of the large family of elves and sprites there, and offers us the following summary.

> The shape of these tiny spirits is not described with any great precision: those of the peasants of the Berry region who claim to have seen the sprite, say that it was as large as a small rooster and also had a red cock's comb. Its eyes were fiery, and it had claws instead of fingernails. Its tail meanwhile sometimes resembled that of a rooster and sometimes that of a rat, and he used it like a whip to spur on his mount. In some parts of Upper Brittany, the Mait' Jean has goat legs, and he sometimes takes the form of an animal that is difficult to identify. The Sotré of the Vosges is a small, ugly fellow, who is deformed and has cloven hooves. The Soltrait of the Meuse region is a dwarf clad and coifed in red, while the Soltre of Lorraine wears a small red skullcap. . . . Not so long ago, the sprite of the Beauce region glided along the haystacks holding its lantern and, in the Jura

> Mountains, candelabra (in the local patois: *chandelottes*) could be seen moving back and forth in the stables frequented by sprites. It was not always known, however, where dwarves resided during those periods when no one saw them. In Upper Brittany, some spent their lives in attics, and a Servant from the Waldensian Alps stayed at the top of a ladder.[1]

These observations contain much information that can be found throughout Europe, and they point out more than one problem inherent to domestic spirits, starting with their form and appearance.

Anthropomorphism

When speaking of these beings, the notion of small creatures wearing a hood is inescapable because the image of the dwarf has supplanted that of these spirits, and a great amount of confusion holds sway in people's minds. Admittedly, the narrators and witnesses are not very clear, which also ensures that the appearance of house spirits varies considerably. This is certainly due to the fact that they imagined them in line with local considerations and their own education and life context.

Domestic spirits are not always visible and numerous elements indicate that we should not try to see them on pain of being punished or seeing them vanish. "If, by chance, you happen upon a sotré by surprise," it is said, "either in a stable or in a house, you should pretend not to see him and avoid speaking to him; otherwise complete commotion; he will get angry and his wrath is to be feared."[2] We know they are present, though, because we can hear them. "If the cows moo at night, it is because the Jüdel is playing with them," says a belief recorded by Jacob Grimm.[3] The mistress of the Italian household would say, "Be good for me" when she heard the Monaciello making noise.[4] They therefore produced acoustic manifestations—knocks, rapping noises, songs and moaning, laughter—each of which had its own meaning: some were evidence of their joy and others of their teasing nature or their displeasure and despair. They sometimes even had a prophetic value, frequently heralding an unlucky event. Among the Votyaks, when the "man of the house" or "master of the house" (*korkamurt, korka-kuzo*) appears in the form of the master of the house, this foretells misfortune,[5] and Lauri Honko notes that nothing can prevent the catastrophe, which may be a fire, death, theft, a setback, or the separation of those who had been close.[6]

To a great extent, the house spirit is anthropomorphic and appears in either the shape of a woman or man. In Ångermanland, for example, it is claimed that the female spirit brings misfortune and the male spirit brings happiness and prosperity: "One says that the house in which a male spirit lives is blessed, but if it is female, than misfortune dwells there; this is what the Elders tells us."[7] One possible explanation is that almost everywhere in Europe the female spirit has the features of a "White Lady" or deceased ancestor, often the female founder of a lineage. This trait can also be seen in Melusine and it seems to arise from a conflation with a family's tutelary deity. These creatures are small in size, sometimes even minuscule, and sometimes as large as an adult human, but the case is rare and essentially concerns female spirits. They are old, as confirmed by their gray hair and wrinkled skin, which is a sign of their science, knowledge, and wisdom. Among the Sámi, the *háldi* appears in the form of a tiny being who sometimes looks like a child and sometimes like an elderly person. In Estonia, where the spirit most often manifests with a noise (knocking, yelling, or rapping), he is said to be an old man with white hair and called "hearth-father of White-Hair" (*kodojezä-hiir-hius*), "family father" (*pereisa*), or "master of the house" (*maja-isa*). A loner, it generally remains invisible.[8]

These beings often have large heads or disproportionate limbs, and their bodies are squat and compact. Morphological details like this make them readily identifiable but sometimes prompt their being confused with changelings, which is to say an infant that has been replaced by supernatural beings.[9] In Norway, for example, Reidar Thomas Christiansen has recorded the following story.

> A spirit had been occupying the family hold for generations; no one remembered when he was born or arrived at the Lindheim Farm. He had never been heard to speak a word and people feared to do any-

thing to him or trigger his wrath. He had such a huge appetite that the inhabitants lived frugally from generation to generation. He was assumed not to be human and a test was implemented that is common in changeling stories: a little broth was put in a pot with a lot of spoons; they then waited to see the creature's reaction. In surprise it revealed its great age and betrayed itself saying: "When they burn my cabin of Guldhagen (Gold Mound), I shall die."[10]

What we are dealing with here, in fact, is a place spirit that moved into Lindheim but that, in contrast to the nature of true house spirits, did not summon prosperity to the home in which he dwelled.

Occasionally, they are missing a limb or other appendage: they can be headless or missing a leg or even an eye, like the Néton of the French Alps or the Ångermanian *tonttu.*[11] In Norway (Sørum, Rike), the domestic idol called Hernoss is depicted with a human head but no arms.

House spirits are clad in garments of olden times (*i gammaldags klær*), which are often blue (*av blår vadmel*) in Scandinavian traditions.[12] Other colors that have been indicated are red (the predominant color), green, gray, black, and white. The color is significant and suggests a connection to a specific event. In Schwerin, Germany, if the spirit shows up clad in red when he normally wears gray, this is a herald of war; if he appears in black, a death will follow. The texts therefore provide us with a relatively simple color code, but this is most often encountered among the spirits of the noble houses, and they are different from those of peasant homes in this regard. In Latvia, they sometimes wear a kaftan and smoke a pipe; female spirits, meanwhile, have hairy hands.[13]

These figures wear headgear in the form of a cap or hood, a feature they share with the dwarves of fairy tales and legend, and which explains their regional names based on words meaning "hat": *Hütchen, Timphut, Langhut.*[14] They wear a long robe or peasant's shirt, and on their feet they have stockings, shoes, or sabots. The descriptions of their footwear often correspond to the time period of the accounts but can sometimes reflect a much earlier era, because the spirits are frequently quite old.

Zoomorphism

The notions of a spirit in animal form[15] are undoubtedly much more archaic. They can be divided into three groups: domestic animals, insects, and reptiles. The first category includes cats, dogs, roosters, and hens; the second, beetles and bumblebees. The final category contains snakes, frogs, and toads; there is a linguistic reason for their being grouped together: during the Middle Ages and in Germanic folk traditions, these were all designated by one word, *unke,* which could even mean "dragon."

Among the Siberian Votes and Savakkos, the stable spirit took the form of a cat[16] but could also appear in the shape of a weasel or ermine. In fact, any animal living near the stables, whether a snake, lizard, frog, mouse, or skunk, is considered to be this spirit. In Russia, the *dvorovik,* the spirit that lives in the farmyard, can take the form of a snake with a rooster's head, and the *domovoj* sometimes takes the form of a black hare.[17] The *kotihaltia* of Ångermanland can be anthropomorphic or zoomorphic, it can appear in the guise of a woman or an old man. Every farm is different; in one he is a dog, and in another a serpent.[18] In Lithuania, the Laima of the Cows (*govju Laima*) lives under the sill of the stable door in the form of a black beetle,[19] and *Gausas mâte,* the "Mother of Prosperity" appears in the form of a mouse, a hen, and most often a toad. The Latvian *pūkis* takes the appearance of a bird, for example an owl, a salamander, and even a comet.[20] A Sámi story gives us a good glimpse of a spirit in the form of a cat.

> Once upon a time, there was a woman in Kvænland of whom it was said that when the cows came home and the lady of the house went to milk them, she found they had no milk. It went on like this everyday of the summer. Once the cold weather returned, the cows were kept in the house. Then, one time, the lady of the house went into the stable and saw something that looked like the reticulum—the cow's second stomach—hanging from one of the cow's udders. She picked up a piece of wood and approached it to strike it dead. It was a butter cat. She placed it on the fire and just at that very

moment the mistress of the neighboring farm fell ill, and in most vile fashion. She confessed to her neighbor that it was her butter cat who, during the summer, had milked the cows of the neighboring farm. This was how she had sold so much butter and became rich. She then gave this money to her neighbor and immediately felt her health restored.[21]

"Butter cat" is the name given to a particular spirit that enriches you with dairy products to someone else's detriment.

In the French Alps, the *farfollet* appears in the form of a calf, a dog, or a cat, and the *Matagot* like a red-and-white dog or a person.[22] In the Basque country, Galtxagorri appears in the guise of an insect or a human being, and Marmarro possesses a human or animal appearance.

Speaking of insects, we should note in particular the cricket, as it has become a proverbial figure. Isn't a good housewife referred to sometimes as the "cricket of the hearth"? In 1777, Jacob Lange gave the following definition in his *Latvian-German Dictionary:*

Zirzenu Nauda, the "money for the cricket," designates the few shillings that brides toss to someone, who it is I do not know.[23]

Almost everywhere in Europe we can find sayings like "A cricket in the living room brings good fortune" and "You must nurture a cricket in the house in order to have happiness in the home."[24] In the Baltic countries, people toss the milk teeth of their children behind the oven (*ceplis*) or on the stove (*aizkrâsne*), while shouting: "Cricket, take this tooth of bone and give me one of iron." The same rite is vouched for among the Swedes of Finland, who address Tomte or *Locke,* the fire spirit, the hearth spirit, when doing this. In Estonia, the teeth that had fallen out were dedicated to the cricket as well as to *virus-Kundra,* "the stove spirit," whereas in France, they were dedicated to the "little mouse." Incidentally, we ought to note that the cricket is almost always associated with fire, and in Estonia lives on or behind the stove.[25]

The snake also deserves specific mention as it is one of the most ancient forms for which we have evidence. Jan Lasicki (1534–1620) informs us:

> Furthermore, the Lithuanians and the Samogytians keep serpents in their houses, beneath the furnace or in the corner of the drying oven, where the table is. At certain times of the year, they honor them like gods (*serpentes fouent, quos numinis instar colentes*), inviting them to their tables with sacrificial prayers. Leaving their lairs, these reptiles climb upon the table with the help of a clean sheet and settle in. After having tasted a little of each dish, they then go back down into their holes. After they leave, the people gaily eat the dishes they tasted, hoping that the year will be a fortunate one (*sperant illo anno omnia prospere sibi euentura*). If, however, despite the prayers of those willing to make this sacrifice, the snakes do not appear and refuse to taste the dishes served there, they then believe great misfortune will strike that year (*credunt se anno illo subituros magnam calamitatem*).[26]

The practice also seems to be widespread in Russia inasmuch as a Western ambassador visiting Moscow during the sixteenth century noted the existence of snake worship.

> At the present time, there are still many idolaters in this region who nurture in their homes, like *penates gods* [my italics], snakes of a black and corpulent variety. . . . They are called "*giwoites*," and on the assigned day they will slither through the house to the food prepared for them. The entire family is present to watch them with fearful respect until they see they have eaten their fill and returned to their nests. And if the inhabitants experience some reversals of fortune, they believe it is because their domestic snake-god was given a poor reception or ill fed.[27]

In Greece, a snake lived in every house and still recently, the Stoicheio, which we discussed with respect to the corner, is often a two-headed serpent spirit. The Romans consecrated an altar to their spirit—an altar surrounded by a snake—and had reptiles in their room considered to be house spirits.[28] "At one time," people in Ångermanland say, "domestic serpents were kept in many places, the sauna, the corner between the stove and the wall, or beneath the floor, and men fed and worshipped them. . . . They caused no harm."[29] This snake is called *kartanomato* (farm serpent) and believed to be a manifestation of the house spirit. In 1592, Michael Herberer stopped at an inn where he saw children and snakes eating from the same bowl[30] and, in 1777, August Wilhelm Hupel indicates in his description of Livonia and Estonia: "The ancient custom, introduced even into numerous German homes, of keeping domestic snakes, feeding them milk, and giving them a home in the stables so the livestock will be happier, appears, it seems, to have stopped."[31] Old beliefs die hard, and Ernst Jünger describes exactly the same thing in his 1939 novel *On the Marble Cliffs*.[32] In Estonia, it was thought that snakes inhaled the "poison of the earth" (*maa viha*), protecting the house and its inhabitants, and encouraging farming. It was therefore called the "serpent of the master of the house" (*maja-taadi uss*).[33] Among the Czechs, the domestic serpent is called *hospodáricek*. The Slavs long worshipped the ancestor of the race in the form of a snake that was placed beneath the hearth or the threshold, but on the right side. In the eighteenth century, the Montenegrins carefully avoided hurting serpents they called "hearth guardians." In Belorussia and Poland, a viper was the object of worship and called the queen of snakes. If it settled in at the foot of the wall of a house, this was a good omen.[34] Around 1400, the *Consolation of the Soul,* a Swedish instructional treatise, forbid belief in domestic serpents (*Tomptorma*) and, in 1555, Olaus Magnus informs us that they were considered to be like Penates, playing with children in their cradles and even sleeping with them.[35] In Ödakrå, on the isle of Skåne, snakes nested in the stables and the milkmaid gave them milk so that the cows would become beautiful and fat. In Asarum, in Bleking (Sweden), if the milkmaid killed a snake, her most beautiful cow would die,[36] which clearly shows that this reptile was a domestic spirit assigned to the protection of animals. In Austria, a respectful fear was felt toward the domestic viper. Sometimes it is said that this snake wears a crown, but here we are entering the realm of the legends that enlivened the evenings of our ancestors.

The Household Spirit as Object

In her study of German traditions, Erika Lindig notes that spirits sometime adopt the guise of a doll called a Kobold, a statuette, a bale of hay, pieces of cloth, and wooden hangers.[37] Names like *Puk, Butz,* and *Poppele* etymologically reflect the notion of a doll and it is probably not too presumptuous to see domestic idols in these depictions, especially since in Saxony, the name for this spirit, *Gütel,* is a diminutive form of *Gott* (God). The ancient Christian laws of the Norwegian *Eidsivathings Kristenrett* (1152) state that no one should have in their homes "staffs or stakes" (*staf eða stalla*). In the Riga region, the *Pûkis* is a fetish that can be purchased, whereas in northern Russia, the guardian horse of the hearth takes the form of a carved block that holds up the stove's hearth, but among the Siberian peoples the spirit resembles a crude human silhouette. The object is set in a specific place and should not be moved, which could have harmful consequences because this would be an attack on its sanctity and to the sacredness it confers to the place it sits, which is equal in value to that of the altar in a church.

In Franconia, a saying about people who enjoy an unusual amount of good fortune and well-being, that "they own an Areile," refers to the mandrake (*Areile* being a distortion of the German word for mandrake, *Alraune*), which allows us to assume that this spirit was depicted in the form of this plant.[38] The parallel it establishes with other sayings such as "he has a *drac*" or "he owns an elf,"[39] to label those whose farming efforts and business matters go exceptionally well or to simply say he is lucky, leaves no doubt as to the underlying conception. We can detect the same thing in the Basque country, where it is said about those who are lucky: "The *Galtxagorriak* protect them." In short, the functions of the mandrake have often been incorporated into the duties of the house spirit, and the confusion goes back a long way, as in 1575 a man from Leipzig sent this plant to his brother who lived in Riga, with instructions on how to use it. He happened to use the terms *Alruniken** and *Ertmänneken*† as synonyms, whereas normally they designate two different realities.[40] In

*["Little mandrake" —*Trans.*]

†["Little earthman," a term similar to the *Erdmännleinn* and *Erdmännchen* mentioned earlier —*Trans.*]

Geneva, the Consistory summoned before it on several occasions people who secretly obtained mandrakes and kept them at home as "devil familiars." In 1682, two inhabitants of Magland (Upper Savoy) were accused of trying to buy "rare spirits" from the Genevans, said "spirits" which were meant to increase the yields from their property.

The Protean Spirits

The plethora of forms house spirits could adopt—of which the reader has now seen quite a few examples—reveals the attempt of humans to grasp the inexpressible and give an appearance to a reality that evades them. As a numinous power, the house spirit evades all form; the forms it does assume are based on local elements. Most of the time, these are beliefs connected to animals or even plants or minerals invested with powers and with independent existences. In France, the *sotré* can even adopt the appearance of a whirlwind that carries off everything that crosses its path. In the archaic mind-set, an incident had to be connected to an animal or thing before it was given an interpretation smacking of the supernatural. It is quite difficult to push this hypothesis further, as the old accounts lack precision and all we can latch on to is the visible tip of the iceberg.

Some spirits are characterized by their ability to metamorphose, and here the forms are limitless. They range from animals of every sort to objects, from clouds to light, from priest to hunter or blood-spattered child, and so forth. Furthermore, there is one figure that appropriates the entire constellation of aforementioned features, or nearly so. One name for this protean spirit, *Hinzelmann,* has been infamous in the German-speaking world since the eighteenth century, when an anonymous compilation devoted to it was published.[41]

THE NATURE OF THE SPIRITS

The scrutiny and classification of an immense but repetitious corpus makes it possible to trace the primary character traits of house spirits. Lily Weiser notes that they do not care for strangers[42] and Tor Åge Bringsværd provides us with a fine example from Norway.

> There was a spirit (*tunkall*) in Tengesdal, in the Hylsfjord region, that lived in the home. When strangers came to the farm and tried to sleep there, they were tossed out into the hallway as soon as they lay down.[43]

Spirits detest filth and messiness, and cannot stand the sound of bells (a way of emphasizing they belong to the pagan world). They are wrathful and vindictive, and will not hesitate to slay the best cow or keep the misbehaving servant girl dancing until she dies. The Votyaks believe that the wrathful spirit transforms into a nightmare.[44] The Chemisses of Finland report identical behavior from such spirits, in addition to making a loud racket and substituting children.[45] In the French Alps, the Servan and the Chaufaton also behave like nightmares if one has the misfortune to linger in the spaces that belong to them.

> A land owner of La-Chapelle-de-Merlas owned magic books thanks to which he was able to procure a servant. . . . There was a domestic in his house that slept on straw as all domestics did then. One day, he complained to his master that he was unable to sleep in peace. Every night, just as he fell asleep, he was rudely awakened by someone stealing his covers. He never saw anything but all his efforts to keep his covers were futile; something kept uncovering him. Suspecting that his servant was the guilty party, the master told his valet: "This evening, place a bowl full of millet seed close by; if the bowl is overturned, say: 'Very well, pick up all the seeds now, otherwise you will get what's coming to you.'" Things came to pass in exactly that way. The bowl was overturned and the valet ordered the servant to collect the seeds. All the seeds were back in the bowl the next day, but the domestic was never again a target for the servant's malice.[46]

In the Upper Aude Valley, the Follet can assume the appearance of air or wind to attack girls. The Ångermanland *tonttu* "enriches the farm on which he lives and with the master with whom he feels friendship. If he becomes angered, he destroys the crops, impoverishes the owner, or takes off."[47] The Swedish *tomte* can degenerate this way into *bese,* sometimes a wealth fetish but more often an animal possessed by evil forces, and become a malevolent creature called a *tomtebese.*[48] The spirit's actions are a reflection of a human's behavior: if someone behaves poorly, he will do the same; if one behaves properly and if one bestows a blessing on him, he will cause no harm.[49] If one forgets the offerings or if one destroys his sanctuary, then the livestock die or a misfortune strikes the household. Here is a revealing account from Bulgaria.

> Bojno's daughter recounted her dream, but no one in the house believed her and refused to grant the wish of the *namestnik.* The household spirit, whose feelings were hurt, became quite vexed and death carried off the entire household except for the girl, whose life was spared. The people died in their beds, the cattle and horses in their stables, and the sheep in their sheepfold. Bojno's prosperous house went downhill. A week later, Bojno's son returned home after a prolonged absence and fell to the ground senseless when his sister informed him of what had happened. While he was unconscious, the *namestnik* appeared to him and consoled him telling him to prepare the customary feast. Everything in the house would then be tripled and three times more beautiful than before. Once he had returned to his senses, the son summoned three women, his closest relatives, and entrusted them with the charge of preparing the feast for the house spirit (*stopanova gozba*).* The next day, before dawn, an unknown stranger arrived and led the boy through three villages before marrying him to the most beautiful girl of the fourth one. When the young husband returned home with his new bride, he found the farm filled with sheep, the dark stables full of cattle and horses, the deep granaries overflowing with grain and white wheat, the barrels of the cellar filled with sparkling wine and strong brandy, and baskets crammed with butter and cheese and chests packed to the brim with gold coins. The stranger vanished. A year later, the couple had twins, a boy and a girl, as beautiful as the stars. . . .[50]

*Still called *namestnikova trapezaa,* "feast of the household spirit."

The household spirit becomes restless and makes noise when the farm's inhabitants violate a standard of behavior, and calms down when everything is restored to order. He therefore shares some of the traits of the rapping spirit but is distinguishable because the poltergeist makes noise out of its own malice for no reason, and is an intruder akin to ghosts.[51]

In her study of the *sotré,* Sylvia Mougin has gathered together everything that has been said about it, and this deserves attention because it demonstrates to us the extraordinary kinship of all these beings.

> The sotré takes care of horses, currying and grooming them. If he is seized with a sudden urge to take a little ride, he braids the mane of his horse, the better to hang on with, and the horse will be found the next day exhausted and sweaty. He also takes an interest in the welfare of the cows and gives them fresh bedding, he helps perform domestic chores at night, and above all, loves to take care of children. He will kidnap them on occasion and conceal them in some part of the house, or come at night to sit heavily upon their chests, which makes him a source of dread to all mothers who protect their young by covering them with red garments or by painting their cradles that same color. One of my informants in the Vosges, who is now deceased, told me how when he was still a child his mother would advise him to take off his scarf before going to bed, lest the sotré strangle him while he slept. Nightmares are attributed to the sotré. Like many of his cohorts, he is extremely sensitive and cannot tolerate crude behavior, and, before leaving the house where he has been ill-treated, will tangle up the distaffs or break the dishes. One means of preventing him from entering a room is to place a small basket filled with cinders in his path. The sotré will never fail to knock it over and is inevitably compelled to gather the cinders together one by one before leaving the house, to which he will never return.[52]

The fundamental characteristic of the household spirit is its helpful nature. It helps men and will take their place when they are absent. The Alpine Matagot protects the large estates, overseeing the goods and the servants; the Basque Mamarroak helps people perform their daily tasks and protects the family with whom it lives. The Minairons of Aragon and Catalonia provide wealth but can also transform into destructive spirits. Near Luchon, women who are going away entrust their children to the *Sédètes,* the house fairies, for short periods. In certain places, the female house spirit is considered in effect to be a fairy who performs the chores of men, feeds children, spins, keeps busy in the stable, and cares for the cows of those who give them a little milk. In any event, this is what the documents gathered by Charles Joisten in the Alps tell us.

The second character trait that distinguishes domestic spirits from other similar beings is their taste for pranks and jokes—although admittedly these are not always in the best of taste. Ronsard was aware of their misdeeds as early as the sixteenth century.[53]

Upon our stomachs, they probe and prod,
At night they move benches, tables, and stools,
Locked doors, gates, cabinets, beds, chairs, step ladders,
Or count our treasures, or crash against the ground
Sometimes a sword and sometimes a glass:
However in the morning nothing broken can be found
Nor any furniture moved from its normal place.

The Menos of Upper Aragon and the Bearnaise Truffandec are malicious pranksters. Thousands of stories tell how they hide or move objects, and tie animals together—in short, how they play all kinds of tricks and burst out laughing when they see the discomfited expressions on human faces. What's more, this laughter has become the stuff of proverbs: in Germany, people say "laughing like kobolds," and in England, "laughing like pixies."[54] The disappearance of small objects is blamed on Osencame, a spirit-familiar of the Béarnaise homes of the Atlantic Pyrenees. He moves these things out of malice.

For example, they were believed throughout the whole of Europe to be the ones responsible for tangling and braiding horses' manes;[55] this was even how the inhabitants of a farm knew they were sheltering a spirit. Here is how George Sand characterizes the sprite in rustic legends.

> There are good ones and bad ones. The ones who groom the horses in the stable, and whose whips and calls to the horses can be heard by the stable hands, just like those who gallop the horses over the pastures at night, and who mess up their manes to make stirrups for themselves (because they are too small to stay on the animal's rump and always have to sit astride the neck) are fairly good children who flee at the approach of a human. Their malice consists entirely in causing mares to abort whose manes have been cut when it was their pleasure to braid and knot them for their own use. The sprites' favorite mounts are called "buckled horses" and these animals were once valued as the best and most spirited.[56]

Sand thus provides us with the reason for tangled manes in popular belief. The former names given these plaits reflect their attribution to supernatural beings. In German-speaking areas, they are called "dwarf braids" (*wichtelzopf*), or "elf braids" or "nightmare braids" (*Alpzopf, Drutenzopf*), which are again found in the Netherlands as *mahrenlocke* and *elfklatte, marelok* in Denmark, and in England as "elflocks." In Shakespeare's day, the verb "to elf" meant "to mat,"[57] and in Norway, the terms *nisse-plaits* or *tusse-plaits* were used, both of which were coined from two names for spirits. In France, there is evidence for the same belief with regard to the Breton Courriquets, the Lorraine sotrés, the Familiarak of Navarre, the Catalan and Aragon Familions as well as for many other individuals of this same world.[58]

In reality, the phenomenon results from a disease of the mane commonly called "Polish plait" (*plica polonica or coma caesarea*), which causes the hair of the mane to become tangled and matted. One of the oldest accounts is that of William of Auvergne (1180–1249), who lists the deeds and gestures of diabolical spirits.

> Evil spirits indulge themselves in other mystifications . . . sometimes in the stables, as well . . . the manes of the horses are meticulously braided (*comae ipsorum diligenter tricatae*).[59]

Two opposing explanations are given for these braids: either the spirit takes care of the horses and looks after their health, or else he detests them and displays his hatred in this fashion.[60] In Czechoslovakia around 1600, the following practice was recommended in order to prevent the house spirit (*hospodáricek*) from bothering the livestock.

> During the first quarter of the new moon, take blackthorn branches and make a small studded arrow and a doll, and hang this at the stable door. The spirit will play with it and leave the livestock alone.[61]

We can note in passing that in the beliefs of northern Russia, the *domovoj,* a house spirit we will return to later, hurls himself at night on the woman he loves and braids her hair. An account from the Vologda region[62] even indicates that a farmyard spirit (*dvorovoj dux*) formed the habit of visiting an old maid, sleeping with her, braiding her hair, and forbidding her from letting her hair down. One day, a widower came to ask her hand in marriage and the spirit strangled him.

With varying degrees of frequency, all the countries of Europe commonly share the characteristics of spirits we have just examined here. The divergences are so minimal that it is staggering to observe their close kinship. While in certain regions the similarities can easily be explained as borrowings from neighbors, in the greatest number of cases, this is impossible. The belief therefore clearly reflects the anthropological structures of the imaginal realm.

THEIR PLACES OF RESIDENCE

To clearly identify the favorite places domestic spirits prefer to stay, we can rely on the offerings made to them, since these are not left just anywhere or at random.

One of the most revealing signs of the belief in house spirits is obviously the set of rites lumping offerings or sacrifices together, which can take place on a daily basis or on certain dates. These propitiatory actions are attested from one end of Europe to the other and form a tradition whose traces can still be detected in some regions where development has lagged behind that of our industrial society, most often because these lands are isolated and their economy has largely remained rural.

De ſuperſtitioſa cultura Lituanorum paganorum.

The Lithuanians worship a house spirit in the form of a snake. Olaus Magnus, Historia de Gentibus Septentrionalibus *(Rome, 1555).*

In 1695, Christian Kelch notes in his *History of Latvia:*

> I have even known people who have certain spots in their house where, when they are cooking, they spill a little beer and milk, and toss a little of all their food. When they have made their offerings to the earth, they have also shown me various springs in which they have always cast something as a sacrifice when asking for rain.[63]

What we have here is a kind of summary of what we can find everywhere. In Latvia, on Christmas night, the elders place a pig's head, bread, and beer in the *riija* (barn) for the "Master of the house" (*Mâjas kungs*), and these offerings remain there until January 1.[64] In Estonia, "people cast away a little piece of bread from the freshly cut loaf; a few drops are carefully spilled from a full goblet onto the ground: this is an offering to the invisible spirit." When the peasants of this country "slaughter an animal, even a simple chicken, they place a piece of it behind the stable as an offering," Jacob Grimm informs us.[65] In Latvia, the chimney hook is rubbed with a little of the food that has been prepared: it is intended for the *pûkis* (*drac*).[66] A legend from this same country reports the following: "A landholder fed his pûkis this way and experienced much good fortune. One day, a maidservant alone at the farm forgot to spill several drops on the chimney hook. The pûkis avenged himself by setting fire to the house. The landholder, who was visiting his neighbors, spotted the fire and rushed home, where he tossed the old cart wheel in which the pûkis resided onto the roof. The fire went out." Food scraps, cream, flour, religious cakes, and money were offered on Christmas and on King's Day (Tyrol), on the feast day of Saint Thomas and Christmas (Austria), as well as on Easter and during Lent.

Elsewhere, a bottle of brandy, bread, and salt would be placed in a corner of the farmhouse, especially on the eve of Saint George's feast day.[67] In Sweden, food for the *tomte* was placed in the stove or the oven; in Galicia, the oven had to be greased every Sunday. Maide, the nocturnal spirit of the Basque country, entered houses through the chimney in search of the offerings the lady of the house had left in the hearth before Gaueko, "He of the Night" (in other words, the entity that ruled over the nocturnal hours), arrived to take possession of his domains. In the Isère region of France, when wine was drawn, it was necessary to leave a little in the bowl for Servan. This is what was said about the *follet* (sprite) in France: every time a loaf of bread was sliced, a mouthful had to be placed under the table, otherwise someone would be slapped. In a story from Pierre Dubois's anthology, it says that "it was possible to spare the farm from the *iouton's* misdeeds; every evening it is necessary to place a bowl of thick cream on the outside edge of the window, which had been picked up by the 'torn pocket,' a kind of wooden slotted spoon. It was important that no one watch over the bowl. From time to time, a *rotie* (a small slab of butter) would be offered in the same manner."[68] Another account confirms the extraordinary kinship shared by all the European accounts on domestic spirits.

> At Poutin farm near Planches-en-Montagne, the farmer's daughter was distracted on this particular evening, She forgot to prepare the iouton's bowl of milk as was her custom before going to bed. When he arrived in the middle of the night and noticed this oversight, he became violently mad out of irritation or jealousy. He climbed into the attic, picked up the sacks of dried peas, and began turning them upside down and tossing their contents in all directions causing a ruckus that woke up all the folk in the house. The young children were weeping in terror. The mother and father quickly grasped what was going on and begged, "Have pity on us, kind iouton. We love you. We did not do this on purpose."
>
> But he refused to listen to a word and furiously continued rolling the peas over the floor and down the stairs. The young girl then stepped in, "I love you very much, iouton, but I was so tired. I was falling asleep on my feet and I thought I had already prepared your bowl of milk before I went to bed, as I do every day, as you know. But I promise you, I will never ever forget again." Only then would he listen and go away.
>
> Another time, a cowherd inadvertently drank the iouton's bowl of milk. Woe on him! When he woke up the next morning he had a fine surprise: not a single cow was in the barn; he found them all on the roof.[69]

The offerings can be divided into four categories: those made when moving into a house; those made at the time of a marriage, birth, or acquisition; those representing a tribute paid to a spirit or as a mark of respect to him; and, finally, those we do not know if they were addressed directly to the spirit, because they are essentially defensive measures.

The sacrifice on the threshold falls into the first category. In Lithuania, "once upon a time, people who were moving out of a house took two roosters, one young and one old. They slew the old rooster on the sill of the stable so the cows would prosper," a rite also attested in Russia.[70] The second category includes all those that could be called rites of aggregation and even rites of passage: circumambulation of the hearth, oven, or stove with the throwing of coins or food by the new bride; the placement of an offering on the threshold; and so forth.[71] In thirteenth-century Silesia, following the birth of a child, women would smash eggs on the doorsill.[72] The notion of a rite of passage is especially apparent in the beliefs connected with the sauna in northern and eastern Europe. In Estonia, a separate building is used as a dwelling and sanctuary for births, marriages, and funeral rites. People give birth there, and the dying are placed there. The "sauna spirits" (*sauna-vaimud*) live there, the "mother" and "father" of the sauna (*sauna-ema, sauna-isa*) who are the recipients of regular offerings. In Russia, the bannik, an unclean spirit, stays in the bath cabin. If it burns down, it will be rebuilt and a plucked chicken is buried beneath the sill to placate the spirit. Its throat is not cut, but it has been smothered; people then leave the bath walking backward.[73]

The third category concerns behavior. In Ångermanland, the genie is greeted morning and evening when entering the living room, whose response is a creaking sound. Often people sign themselves at the same time, sometimes while saying: "May my house be blessed as well as its spirit."[74]

In the final category, we find all the apotropaic rituals intended to prevent misfortune from striking the home, a glimpse of which was provided earlier. The accounts do not explicitly say that the sacrifices are performed to earn the spirit's favor, but we can deduce this from their nature and the place where they are performed. In the nineteenth century, in the Russian region of Kostroma, the head of a rooster would be cut off at the doorsill to the drying house or the bathing cabin, and its blood was spread around its four corners in order drive away any evil spirits seeking refuge there.[75] In Estonia, when the livestock were taken out to pasture for the first time in the new year, eggs would be buried beneath the doorsill over which they would cross in order to banish all ills.[76] It seems clear that these rites aim to encourage a spirit to perform its tutelary duty. Sacrifice falls into the context of a tacit contract; the individual expects his offering to be matched.

In all these rites, what stands out is that the domestic spirit receives a portion of the household's food as an offering. It is regarded as a family member and treated as such. It has a marked preference for dairy products, a feature it shares with fairies who often perform the same duties as it does, even if they do not remain in the house and only stop there during the Twelve Days or on other dates (Ember Days, All Saints' Day, and so on). The marks of veneration and respect shown one's spirit are expressed in the indispensible rituals, for if they are omitted, catastrophes are sure to follow because the spirit is rather strict when it comes to its prerogatives and never hesitates to seek revenge for even the slightest offense, which is also one way of remembering that its cohabitation with human beings is based on a pact.[77]

Spirits will not stay just anywhere. Certain parts of the house are reserved for them, either because they have personally claimed them or because people imagine the spirits are in their homes. When the taboos concerning certain places are examined, and when we inventory the list of places where offerings are made, it becomes readily that there is a widespread unity among the European traditions. Furthermore, these places correspond precisely to those that are the focus of the remarkable set of beliefs and rites described in the first part of this book.

Generally speaking, it can be said that the house spirits' living quarters are a direct reflection of its sphere of activity. We therefore find them in the cellar, the common room, the attic (where people say a gap must always be left open so the spirit can come and go as it pleases), the barn, and the stables. Depending on the culture, it can also reside in the immediate proximity of the house, meaning in the yard or garden. This is why the Estonians of Kraasna keep a small sanctuary in the corner of the garden, beneath or near a stone, where they worship the "father of the garden" (*aia-jezä*) in order to obtain good fortune and prosperity for the house and the family.[78] They believe that the spirit of the house (*majavaim*) or tutelary spirit of the home (*majahaldas, majahoidja*), which simultaneously bears the features of a genius loci (those of a fire spirit and hearth spirit as well as its function, and those of an ancestor) dwells beneath the doorsill, in the hearth, behind the stove, under the roof, in the attic, and so forth, yet nonetheless make offerings outside, under a tree or stone.[79] This detail suggests that a distinction must sometimes be made between the home of the supernatural spirit and the spot where his gifts are placed. We shall return to this topic later. This apparent confusion is undoubtedly caused by the plethora of specialized spirits. In Russia, the *domovoj* stays in the house, the *dvorovik* in the farmyard, and the *bannik* in the bathing cabin that it sometimes shares with the *domovoj* as in the nineteenth century when young Russian girls would go to the baths to try to predict if they would marry. If the *domovoj* touched them with his hairy hand, they would make a happy marriage in accordance with the common saying: "If a hairy hand taps you on the buttocks, you shall wed a rich *mujik* [peasant]."[80] The same thing can be found in the Scandinavian and Baltic countries. In Latvia, an area surrounded by a hedge, and the corner of the garden where offerings were made, were the preferred living quarters of the house spirit.[81]

The fire—fireplace, stove, oven—the house center, domestic altar, and symbol of the *ignis communio* (communal fire), is the primary residence of the house spirit, and we are certainly dealing with the vestiges of fire and even ancestor worship, as it was the case among many different peoples that the dead, and especially children (Russia, Tyrol), were buried beneath the hearth.[82] In Brittany a cat would be walled up alive in this spot when the house was built, and we know that the spirit often assumes feline form. Among the ancient Kamtchadal (Itelmen) people, the spirit stays behind the hearth.[83] Among the Christian Samoyeds, the images of the saints of the Orthodox Church have replaced the domestic idols and are kept behind the hearth, where the former worship was celebrated.[84] In Sweden, the food for the spirit (*tomte*) is placed behind the stove or oven, which must be greased every Sunday.[85] In Swabia, this is residence of the "Little Oven Man" (*Ofenmännchen*); in Brittany, the evening prayer was made kneeling in front of the fireplace.

The threshold is second in importance. In 1739, near Volmar (Valmiera),

Latvia, the peasant Pilatz Behrtul learned from an old seer how to worship a domestic deity (*elka dievs*).

> After looking vainly from one end of the threshold to the other, he finally drew near a stone near the door and said that Elka Deews was there. Heeding the teaching of the Elders, every year, for more than nine years, Behrtul spilled beer there as well as three spoonfuls of soup and three mouthfuls of meat. He also sacrificed a chicken there on Saint Michael's Day in 1738, so that his horses would remain healthy.[86]

In this same country, restrictive rites connected with the threshold are explained by the presence of a deity called Laima: sweepings should not be swept out of the house over the sill otherwise "they would be cast in Laima's eyes." Wood should not be chopped here either as this could "blind Laima in one eye" or "decapitate her."[87] It so happens that the word *laima* also means "happiness, success, prosperity, destiny." Cutting branches on the sill will cause her to flee and the *drac* will then set fire to the house. The space beneath the door (*padurve*) must be carefully swept as well as beneath the sill (*paslieksne*) because this is the way used by Laima to enter the living room.[88] The Laima of cows (*govju Laima*) lives beneath the stable threshold in the form of a black beetle.

In short, the rituals observed betray the existence of a supernatural being and our ancestors saw proof of this by the presence of any kind of animal or by hearing a particular noise.

The spirit can also live in the ground beneath the floor and a widespread legend attests to this belief. In Norway, a spirit appeared to a peasant in dream and told him why his cow was dead: "I killed it because the way you built your cowshed makes the manure fall on the middle of my table."[89] Similar stories can be found elsewhere.

Some places are forbidden to humans because the spirit reserves them for his own use. According to a well-known scenario, he informs whoever has the misfortune of sleeping there of this by appearing to them in a dream, or by actually waking the sleeper up and tormenting him until he complies.[90] Sometimes he hurls himself on the intruder, which explains why in numerous Slavic, Baltic, and Germanic tongues, the name for nightmare is also the name of the house spirit. In France, the Chaufaton and the Servan behave in the same way. Erika Lindig cites the following story for Germany.

> In a farm next to Stiefenhofen, a spirit appeared in a most distinctive fashion. Nothing was seen in the house during day or night, but if someone tried to sleep on the oven bench between six o'clock in the evening and three o'clock in the morning, the spirit would not stand for it and the person would be unceremoniously tossed to the floor.[91]

What emerges from all these accounts is that every house possesses a demonic spot that could any number of places: a hole in the roof beam, a dark corner under the stairs or in the attic, a room (which the Germans call the *Geisterstübel,* the "spirit's little room"), the hearth, the threshold, and so forth. Sometimes the entire building belongs to the spirit after nightfall, as is the case with the sauna and bathing cabin. This is one of the reasons that the house spirit has been demonized. In Estonia, some accounts say that an "old pagan" (*vanapagan*) or an "evil spirit" (*kuri vaim*) lives in every house. Others mention a "domestic ghost" (*kodu tont*), a black cat that lurks behind the stove.[92] Occasionally Saint Anthony (Tonn, Toniss) has replaced the spirit; he takes the form of a wax doll clad in rags that is secretly kept in a bushel basket. The evil spirit is also given the devil's features and called *tontti,* in other words, kobold. The *Votes of Kattila* say that it haunts and attacks the animals and that nothing good can be expected of it. In this case it has been merged with a poltergeist.[93] The demonization accounts call for the intervention of a priest whose power is revealed to be superior to that of the spirit.

> There was an old farm in Krasnoje Selo. The spirit there was turning everything upside down. From the stove he even threw cow manure and old shoes at the priest summoned to calm him, as was in his power to do. The priest's prayers and blessings settled him down.[94]

It is clear that in this Russian anecdote the priest performed an exorcism ritual, which cannot help but bring to mind the previously mentioned *Kristni saga* (Saga of the Christianization of Iceland). The demonization of house spirits was a general rule and in Sweden it was said that the *Nisse* would gradually take possession of the body of the farmer he served. In Norway, it was claimed that a *Nisse* said it had acquired seven souls on the farm and was only waiting for one more—it had been living there for three generations.

Three French documents from the beginning of the seventeenth century show domestic spirits being expelled from their places of residence. Around 1665, a sprite was haunting the home of Pierre Critan in Thônes (Upper Savoy); it was exorcised by Saint François de Sales. When the first reformed Bernardins settled in Rumilly (Upper Savoy), they found a mob of pixies living in the house that had been placed at their disposal, but the exorcisms by the Oratorian, R. P. Billet, put them to flight. After the churchmen left, they retook possession of the premises.[95] In 1615, in the house of a Lord of the Dauphiné near Valence (Drôme), a brownie was playing a thousand tricks. The Bishop of Valence went there, accompanied by priests, to bless the house and perform exorcisms.

> A no less remarkable thing was told, the Commander said, about a spirit that was said to have done several very strange things in the house of a Lord of the Dauphiné, not far from Valence.
>
> One day a flask of rose water was broken by a stone, and, although it was at the feet of the Maiden of the house, the water that was in it nonetheless was all carried aloft and spilt upon her head. Those who tell you this, says a jurisconsult who was also present, are telling the truth, about which I am highly informed, having in fact been brought to the scene and told by several eyewitnesses about what had taken place.
>
> This spirit was a brownie who manifested at the beginning of the year 1615. He paid his respects to the holy days of Sunday and the Festivals, on which he never made noise or molested anyone. Several times he was seen throwing things with such force that it

seemed they should knock the people they hit senseless; however, none of the targets were ever injured, except very mildly when they vexed it is some way. Ordinarily it was quite friendly; several bouquets had been made in anticipation of a baptism the following day, and it wished to make its own. It spent the night before loading the tapestry with cabbage leaves it had taken from the garden, and, for even greater effect, it filled the vases on the buffet with them.

A certain person, whose identity I will not reveal, had come there wearing a beautiful long beard. As he was conversing with the others in the room, this spirit brought from another corner of the house where a Potter was polishing the crockery a tin of polish, and so covered the face to which this fine beard was attached with it, he had the devil's own time getting it cleaned off again.

Here is something you will appreciate. Several clergymen had come to the house to pray and perform other duties of their profession against this spirit. When the dinner hour came they were placed at the head of the table with the others below. As if to flatter them, this Brownie begged their forgiveness for the meat on their board and replaced their plates with others of metal scraps and shot and so many other such things it was only with the greatest difficulty that they could eat their meal. On similar occasions he could often be heard laughing, and three days before he vanished he was heard playing the fife, beating the drum, and singing some very melodious tunes, not that he uttered any recognizable words. A Huguenot, after requesting and receiving from him anything that he wished for in the household, asked again to be given a brace of pistols; instead of giving the pistols, he filled his soul with such dread that he left the house greatly bewildered. What seems more remarkable is that he often placed several things in sealed rooms, and none could say how they had been introduced there.

Some opening, the clergymen say, must have been there, for such penetration is reserved to God alone; but demons are subtle, and through a sudden local movement they deceive (obfuscate) the eyes of spectators, just like those performing feats of sleight of hand, and undoubtedly this Brownie did likewise.

"I believe him," said the Jurisconsult, and resuming his remarks eventually concluded that after Monsieur of Valence was requested to come there with some kind of remedy, he did so accompanied by six or seven priests to bless the house. They perfumed it with incense in all its rooms and spoke the exorcisms of the church, after which nothing was heard there ever again.[96]

8

The Purveyor Spirits

THE PECUNIARY *DRAC*, THE LITTLE MONEY MAN, AND THE ALF

Whatever its name—*drac* (compare German *Drache*, "dragon"), *little money man, alf, latanic, kaubuk,* or *pūkis*[1]—there is a particular spirit, sometimes confused with the personified mandrake, which is is distinguished from the other spirits by its specialty: it has a connection to money and brings fortune to the home in which it has elected to live.[2] *Drac* is a generic term applied in the Germanic regions to an often demonized igneous phenomenon (hence its name *Teufel*, "devil") which is also conflated with elves—it is referred to as both an Alf and a kobold. Depending on the country and the region, it simply means "spirit" and is given a connection with a certain number of the products of the soil. This is why we can find the *drac* of wheat, semolina, barley, and, in Lusatia, that of grains (*zitny smij*) and milk (*mlokowy smij*). In Lusatia, we also find the pecuniary *drac* (*penezny smij*), who ensures that its master will never want for money. In France, this spirit is called Matagot and there, too, it is likened to the mandrake.

When it flies though the air and enters the house via the chimney or a hole in the roof, it looks like a long pole on fire, but it can also be depicted as a little man wearing a red vest—hence its name of Rôdjackte in Pomerania. His igneous character clearly emerges from his names in Lower Saxony such as "Burning Tail" (*Gluhschwanz, Glûswanz*), which suggests a trail of fire, and "Red Iron" (*Glûbolt*). In Westphalia, names coined from the word *Brand,* "fire," reflect similar notions. The idea is hardly new and can be found in a witch trial that took place in Coburg in 1611. Sometimes the *drac* resembles a simple ball of fire or a flaming star. This connection with flames explains why in some places it is attributed the same form as the devil[3] or a sorcerer, and why he is regularly accorded the fireplace as a residence, or the back of the stove (which in Germany bears the significant name of *Hölle,* "hell").

Its other local attributes are like those of common house spirits. Depending upon the load it is carrying to its master, the *drac* often assumes an animal shape—chicken, rooster, lizard—and various colors. If it sparkles, it is silver; if it is dark or gray, he is transporting vermin; if it is golden, it is gold or wheat; and so on. Incidentally, the mention of vermin clearly indicates that the spirit's intentions are not always good, and the Silesian accounts confirm this. For the Latvians, it is a fetish that can be purchased.

Most of the time, this spirit is obtained by signing a contract with the devil, but it is also said that it is born of a yolkless egg. It begins life by starting trouble in the stables and barns before flying away to start its life as a *drac.* When an egg like this is found, it should be thrown over the house so that it breaks. In Latvia, it is believed to be the outer soul, meaning the double (*alter ego*) of an evil man—a sorcerer or magician.[4]

The nature of the *drac* is ambiguous because he enriches his owner at the expense of the neighbors from whom he steals the goods he brings back. This is expressed in sayings such as those we encountered earlier.[5] Therefore, at the same time as it is desirable to have one, the *drac* is also feared. Of course, this ambiguity is connected with its identification with the devil and his retinue, or with sorcerers and other magicians. Witch trials since the sixteenth century have instructed us that the owners of *dracs* are individuals versed in magic and the occult arts. In popular tradition, however, this individual is often a pastor. This is hardly surprising, because since the Middle Ages, clergymen (who gradually supplanted the local healers) have often been seen as magicians.

Like all the other house spirits, the *drac* needs to receive offerings, but they are more thought of as a salary for its activity, which shows that its relationship with the household is not identical to that maintained with the standard spirits. It therefore receives cakes, meat, milk, and millet broth that are placed in the fireplace or on the stove, and it should be noted that cooked foods are predominant. If this is overlooked, its vengeance is terrible and in accordance with its fundamental nature: it sets fire to the house! But if a person is unhappy with its services, it can be punished, which, in Mecklenburg, takes the form of a good flogging.

Ultimately, the pecuniary *drac* is a rather troublesome companion, so people sometimes try to get rid of it. These measures coincide with the rites we looked at in the first part of the book: sweeping the entire house, giving away all nonessentials to the poor and to the Church so that it will be easy to rebuild the building after the *drac* has set fire to it, performing a circumambulation of the house, plugging the chimney, and, to prevent it from stealing the wheat, the sheaves should be stacked in a cross in the four corners of the barn.[6]

While money just represents a facet of the *drac*'s activities (since it is also a purveyor of grains and so forth), the "Little Money Man" (*Geldmännlein*)[7] specializes in one thing alone, as its name clearly indicates. It can either help you amass a fortune or increase what you already possess. It is not surprising, then, that it too was confused with the mandrake in people's minds. From at least the sixteenth century on, this marvelous, mythical plant is called the "Little Man of the Gallows" (*Galgenmännchen*) in folk traditions, firstly because it vaguely resembles a human body, and secondly because it is reputedly born from the urine of hanged men and grows beneath those sinister-looking constructions.[8] Its English name, mandrake, refers both to its humanlike appearance and to the "drake" (*drac*). Our "Little Money Man" is also called the "Little Man of the Hedge" (*Heckemännchen*) and the "Money Shitter" or "Money Breeder" (*Geldschîsser, Geldbrüter).* As always, the names vary according to region. This is why we can find *Heckemännchen* in Saxony and Thuringia, *Geldschîsser* in Bavaria, *Alraunel* in Lower Austria, and so forth. We should note that the money it procures is not said to be stolen from someone else. In fact, the increase in one's fortune is entirely magical and is triggered by the very nature of this creature.

The "Little Money Man" (Geldschîsser). Photograph by C. Lecouteux.

This particular spirit looks like a little gray man, whose eyes are sometimes light colored. Occasionally it can be seen wearing a red cap and a green jacket. It can also take on animal shapes—a consistent trait of these spirits—such as that of a frog or toad, owl, or beetle. Its confusion with the mandrake (for which it seems to be a direct projection or emanation) determines most of the information we have been able to collect about this spirit. It can be found at a crossroads at midnight by digging under a cluster of three hazel trees; it can also be purchased. It is most often kept

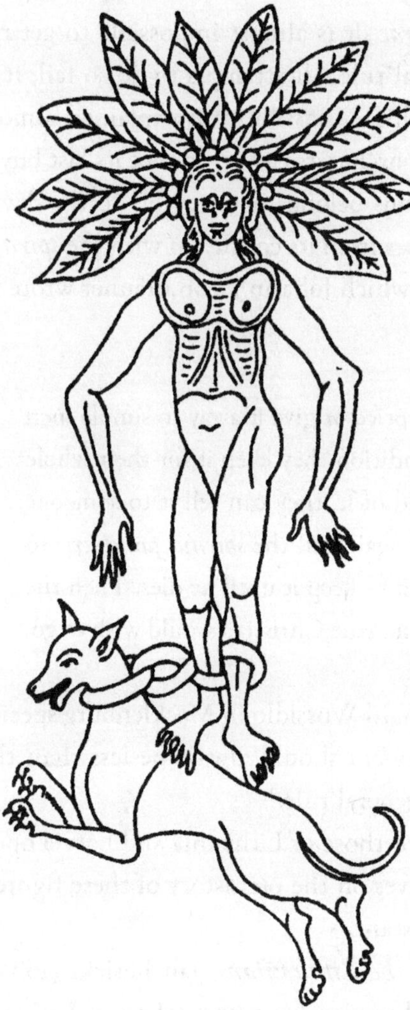

Mandrake (Alraun, Geldmännlein, Galgenmännlein). England, thirteenth century.

in a chest or box stored in a closed room or attached to the center beam of the common room. When the *Geldmännchen* is free, it prefers to stay in the attic or a dark corner of the house, or even on the manure pile.

As payment for its services, freshly baked little loaves of bread and milk are set out for it, sometimes also with sweets and a glass of wine. All these foodstuffs are placed in the attic. It is also cared for exactly like the mandrake. In the western Alps, it must be bathed everyday in a spoon and given food to eat from one's own plate. In other regions, it is offered fine clothes.

In contrast to the pecuniary *drac,* it is almost impossible to get rid of a Little Money Man. As a general rule, all attempts to do so fail; it is even resistant to death and fire. This impossibility is explained almost everywhere as follows: its first two purchasers can sell it, but its last buyer is obliged to keep it, and his soul thus belongs irretrievably to the devil. This characteristic undoubtedly arises from its confusion with the *spiritus familiaris,* the spirit-familiar, about which Johann Jacob Bräuner wrote in 1773:

> Its owners sell it for a ridiculous price or give it away to simple men who are far from God . . . on condition they keep it for their whole life or else, if they want to get rid of it, they can sell it to someone else. The second owner can then again sell the *spiritus familiaris* to a third person who will be obliged to keep it until he dies. Then the devil will carry him off to a place no true Christian would wish to go.

The traditions collected by Richard Wossidlo in Mecklenburg specify that the sale price of the *Geldmännlein* should always be less than the purchase price, half that price as a general rule.[9]

Comparison of these beliefs with those of Lithuania and Latvia open up particularly interesting perspectives on the prehistory of these figures, so we shall linger here for a brief instant.

In his treatise on *The Gods of the Lithuanians,* Jan Lasicki (1534–1620; he wrote under the Latinized version his name, Johannis Lasicius) mentions the Barstucci, which he glosses with *erdmännlein*—one of the names of house spirits, as we have seen. They are the servitors of the god Putscetus, deity of the *lucus* (sacred grove) and the sacred trees that men beg to have sent to them "believing they will be richer with these Barstucci living in their home."[10] Studies by scholars have shown that these individuals refer to two families of different, although related, creatures: the *kaukai* (singular: *kaukas*), and the *aitvaras,* who in contrast to the kaukai only appears singly—a valuable clue showing they are indeed different entities. In 1837, Wilhelm von Tetau and Jodocus Temme provided a glimpse of the Barstucci, based on ancient sources.

> The Barstucci are tiny *Erdmännchen* who bring much good fortune or harm, depending on whether their mood is good or bad. Great efforts are made to befriend them. A table, properly covered with a cloth, is set in the barn in the evening, with bread, cheese, butter, and beer. They are then invited to come eat. If nothing remains on the table the next morning, there is much rejoicing and hope that the household will prosper. If, by contrast, the food remains untouched over the night, people are distressed and believe that the Barstucci have left and will cause problems. This superstition is particularly widespread in Samie.[11]

By collating all the collected information, we can create a description of these creatures.

The kaukai are bearded, chthonic creatures who are anthropomorphic and benevolent. They enter the house in the form of a harmless object that a person finds on his path and brings home, or else something that he finds already in the home. The inhabitant of the house makes a contract with the kaukas who has chosen to live near him and offers it appropriate clothing, which is one of the elements of the pact binding the household to the spirit. In return, the kaukas brings natural products of a wondrous sort: several grains transform into several bushels of wheat, one sheaf is enough to fill a barn, and so forth. If the man does not respect the tacit agreement, the kaukas will become angry and will seek revenge by setting fire to the house. Here is a peculiar thing that has not been seen elsewhere in the beliefs under consideration: the kaukas dies in this fire. Sometimes the fire can be dispelled.

> According to a Latvian story, the *drac* is fed in the following manner. Every time food was cooked, it was necessary to spill a few drops on the chimney hook from which the pot was hanging; this would satisfy the *drac*. One day, a servant girl alone in the house forgot to do this and the *drac* avenged this slight by setting fire to the house. The owner, who was visiting with his neighbors, spied the

fire, rushed home, and threw the old cart wheel, in which the *drac* lived, onto the roof. The fire went out immediately.[12]

The *aitvaras,* called *pūkys* in some regions of Lithuania and *pūkis* in Latvia, is an aerial and more often zoomorphic creature, whether it is good or evil. When it travels through the air, it takes the form of a red poker, a trail of fire, or a shooting star, which makes it similar to the Hungarian *lidrac.*[13] It is born when a man urinates in the moonlight and, once he goes back home, has sexual relations with his wife. It can be bought like a lump of coal and it is hard to get rid of. Algirdas J. Greimas cites the following events.

> This is the retelling of a misfortune which happens to one farmer, who returning home finds "under the wild pear tree" "a little black chick, drenched and trembling from the cold" and, feeling pity for it, brings it home. The chick soon manifests as an *aitvaras*: he started to carry off the potatoes, grain, coins. The farmer, a God-fearing man, doesn't know how "to rid himself of the aitvaras." Meanwhile, "people would see how at night a glowing pillar would descend behind the farmer's hut and started to gossip that keeps the devil." The entire community finally decides that the man must move from the house, leaving the aitvaras in it. Then he "sold everything, crops, animals, whatever he could do without, and bought himself a place a mile away and moved there. When he was hauling the last wagonload and there was nothing left in the cottage, he set fire to all four corners of the cottage: Burn, you rascal; I will get my money back later for the field."[14]

Like the spirit-familiar, the *aitvaras* obeys its owner and it is the master of the money that comes back (*pareitinai*). The German traditions call this money *Heckethaler,* which literally means "hedge thalers" (with the hedge reflecting the notion of the marvelous and the supernatural, for it is a place where spirits dwell). The enclosing hedge is where witches get the broomstick that serves them as a mount and from which they get one of their names: "hedge riders" (Middle High German *zûnrîte,* Norse *túnriðr*). These characteristics show that the *aitvaras* is the equivalent of the pecuniary *drac* with whom it shares a pronounced igneous nature, not only in its appearance but also by the goods it brings, which have always gone through fire; for example, the foods it provides have always been cooked. This connection with fire is also present in Latvian traditions: people smeared a little of all the food they cooked on the chimney hook for the *pūkis*.[15] Lastly, we should note that *aitvaras* also means "plique" ("Polish plait"), the disease we discussed earlier, which makes this spirit similar to those household spirits that snarl the manes of horses.

Based on this identification, it turns out that the *kaukas* should correspond to the Little Money Man, but careful reading of the data reveals that things are not always so simple. As the *kaukas* and the *aitvaras* possess the traits of both *Geldmännlein* and *Gelddrache,* we can envision both hypotheses. On the one hand, it may involve the origin of a single entity, which over the course of historical evolution gradually grew apart to the point that there were two different figures. Speaking in favor of this hypothesis is the fact that Lasicius speaks of the *Barstucci* and not of *kaukas* and *aitvaras,* which emerged in more recent traditons. On the other hand, however, they may always have been distinct entities.

The heterogeneous nature of purveyor spirits appears elsewhere, and whether in Lithuania (with the *pykis, aitvaras,* and *kaukas*), Latvia (with the *pūkis*), Germany (with the *Geldmännchen* and the *Gelddrache*), and Sweden (with *bjära* and *bese*), we are facing the same information and the same syncretism, which is remarkable considering we are dealing with different peoples. The question of a common origin therefore arises, even if we cannot answer it given the current state of research (for we would also need to examine the Celtic traditions, where we find beings bearing the same name: the *puk,* the *poca,* and the *phooka*).

THE DUTIES OF HOUSE SPIRITS

The farm's prosperity depends on the house spirit. A house without a spirit is cursed, for the spirit is identified with happiness and good fortune. When failure or misfortune are inexplicable, the belief arises that an evil spirit is on the premises or the house spirit is absent.[16] The saying in the Scandinavian countries that "the *tomte* brings it to the farm" (*tomten drager till gården*), meaning that the farm prospers, reveals this fundamental notion. The belief has even given birth to a particular spirit: the pecuniary *drac* that we examined above.

Throughout all of Europe, the spirit supervises the behavior, mores, customs, life, and actions of the home's inhabitants. If order is not

Illustration by Gustav Olms for a book of fairy tales published in 1930.

maintained, it will punish the household or the guilty party. It will be alarmed and irritated by swearing, quarreling, card playing, whistling, and fighting. It will then make noise to display its disapproval or criticism. It looks after the cleanliness of the house and will, for example, cause a skin disease or a fire if someone spits or throws trash into the fire.[17] It is therefore an upholder and defender of morals. In this sense, its behavior matches that of ghosts. In the Basque country, Gripet or Gripetsa steps in to console an abandoned child as compensation for the absence of the mother; this spirit will punish a family member for absentmindedness or encourage an individual to be patient. The spirit does not permit a corpse to be left alone in the common room. It oversees the relations of the domestic community and does not hesitate to punish any deviation. When transgression occurs, it first delivers a warning. If that goes unheeded and the spirit is ignored, it then leaves, which brings misfortune down upon the house.[18] It is therefore invested with one aspect of the master of the house's duties: the ethics of the household.

If it is treated well, it is essentially a tutelary being, and among the Livonian people, for example, if it is not well fed, it will call down lighting to strike the house.[19] In Germany and Scandinavia, it performs practically all the domestic chores and takes care of the livestock. In a word, its activity is the same as that of people and its function is to be a supernatural assistant to the master of the house.

The spirit's second essential duty is therefore to protect the house against any and all attack—both human and supernatural. It counters curses and opposes the neighbor's house spirits that come to steal goods to enrich the master of the domus where they have chosen to live. It especially prevents the intrusion of all kinds of indeterminate spirits, which the Germans call an *Alp,* a generic name that includes dwarves and demons, as well as nightmares (seen as the work of a distinct entity, the *Mahr*) and ghosts. The foreign spirits are intruders that may come from another neighboring farm and if they succeed in gaining entry, they have to be expelled. Alas, sometimes they are stronger than the host spirit and their eviction requires a complicated ritual:

> One day a foreign spirit entered our house. My mother took a black rooster and sat over the fire tongs while holding it in her hands; my oldest sister took a pocketful of birch, and a candle she placed in the lantern, then hid it so no one in the village would see the light. Before leaving the common room, they bowed three times to God and said a prayer; they then walked around the farm three times counter-sunwise and recited the *voskrosnei malitsa* (Praise for the Resurrection of Our Lord). Four of us remained inside the common room praying to God: my younger sister, two of my brothers, and me. We then heard running in the hall, and the noise was so loud one would have said there were one hundred runners, and the two doors to the hall flew open. This was how the foreign spirit left the farm and our undertaking succeeded. Sometimes it does not leave until one has sowed around the farm three times.[20]

Other more disparate duties can be added to these two functions—duties that could be described as prophetic, such as announcing with its tears the death of one of the inhabitans[21] (if the farmer dies, the spirit mourns or leaves), or an event, generally unlucky, such as a fire. Here again, we see the spirit's role as an advisor: when necessary, the spirit reveals itself and tells you what you should do.[22]

Independent of the fact that some spirits are attached to the places that house domestic animals (barns, stables, and so forth), one of their essential tasks is to protect and care for the animals. When Jacob Grimm notes that "many houses and stables will not endure white livestock: it dies or is crushed,"[23] this refers to a belief attested in Sweden, Norway, Denmark, Germany, Estonia, and in Russia among the Vepsians and Mordvins.[24] Paul Sébillot notes that the brownies of Normandy are so solicitous they even lead the horses to drink; in the Beauce, Franche-Comté, and so forth, they curry them, care for them, and feed them. In Upper Brittany, the horses start whinnying when the Mait' Jean brings them their food. The Fouletot of Franche-Comté will even steal to provide its favorite animal with the best hay of the area if its master has none in his hayloft, and in Normandy, the brownie steals the best oats for its favorites. Horned animals are subject to the same solicitude. The Sotres of the Vosges region take care of the livestock, changing their bedding and giving cows the most appetizing fodder. The Follet of the French-speaking region of Switzerland (Romandy) steals the freshest blades of grass from others for his favorite cow. In Lower Brittany, Teuz-ar-pouliet, the prankster of the marsh, took care of animals and even churned milk.[25]

The stable spirit would take care of the horses if it liked their color—there is no good or bad color in itself; everything depends on each stable. If the spirit was dissatisfied, it would tease and worry the horses, which would be found later covered with sweat. To discover the suitable color, people turned to soothsayers, sorcerers, or cartomancers. The cleanliness of the horse is a sign that the spirit is taking care of it; it will also comb and braid its mane.[26] This belief accounts for a ritual recorded by Francis Conte: when adding a new horse to the herd, the Russian peasant asks the *domovoj:* "Little father domovoj, I have bought a new horse; if his coat does not please you, wait until summer (or winter), I will sell him."[27] We should note that this kind of behavior also pertains to cows, but the number of accounts is far fewer, which raises a problem.

Within the corpus of material that tells us about the relationship between spirits and animals, the horse holds the predominant place for an unknown reason. There are several conceivable theories, although unfortunately none of them is certain. One primary explanation would be the role of the horse in the domestic economy: as a draft animal that can provide both transportation and labor, it holds the greatest value. A second explanation is undoubtedly more in tune with the reality of the beliefs. In European folk religions, horses have always possessed a religious value and are reputedly connected to the world of the spirits and the dead. They are the ones who bring souls into the beyond—in the role of psychopomp—and the Celtic and Germanic peoples sacrificed them to their gods. Buried in the ground, their skulls offered protection to places. The horse belongs to two worlds, the world of men and the spirit world—and this, in my opinion, is the key to its obsessive presence in the stories of domestic spirits. Studies are underway,[28] led by Marc-André Wagner, my student, but we still must wait a while before the results are in.

Another point we should not overlook is that of the relationship between the house spirit and the rooster. Firstly, this is because this gallinaceous creature figures in magical rituals of protection (he allegedly puts spirits to flight); secondly, he is one of the most regularly sacrificed animals; and, finally, he has a connection to the horse. The Finns and the Estonians keep a rooster in their stables to protect horses from the ill-defined, evil spirit known as the Alp and from curses, or else they bury one in the stable to ensure that their livestock will prosper. In this case, the rooster should be black and buried beneath the door posts on Saint George's day.[29] It is also placed in the hayrack used by the horses and it should be the same color as the horses. The problem is that in Sweden and Denmark, the dog takes the place of the rooster, and the stories may be summarized as follows. A peasant's horses were not prospering in their new stable and were found shivering every morning soaked in sweat. A "man in the know" (an expression generally designating a magician or sorcerer) advised burying a dog in the stable alive, and everything returned to normal.

Just to complicate matters a bit more, folk traditions tell us that the rooster can transform into a kobold when slaughtered at the age of nine years, but this information remains an exception.[30] We should also note that the rooster is just one of the many forms taken on by the house spirit; it is very common, for example, in Franconia.[31] In Russia, a rooster carries away the body of the *domovoj* when it dies.[32]

The reader can see that many shadowy areas remain. Studies need to be conducted on each animal to see how and why they were connected with the house spirit; to determine if there are notable differences between the various peoples of Europe; and to see if anything can be discerned that resembles the vestiges of an ancient cult dedicated to a major or minor deity, who was depicted in the form of a specific animal. These projects do not fall under the scope of our current concerns because I am primarily attempting to present a global overview of these spirits and to point out the questions and problems that are still unresolved, in the hope that other investigators will take up these leads.

House spirits from a painting by Goya

9

Haunted Houses

How I love to see the decay
of these old ruined castles
Against which the mutinous years
Have deployed their insolence . . .
Retreating there are demonic sprites
Who with malicious frolics
Deceive our senses and torture us.

UNKNOWN AUTHOR

At this point in our investigation, it might be helpful to introduce the problem of certain haunted houses because, even though the contemporary interpretations attributed these manifestations to the devil, the implications of the stories collected raise more questions than answers. Clearly, we should not allow ourselves to be deceived by the assertions of Satanism in these texts because, when the reports are sifted through critically, it quickly becomes apparent that there is something hidden between the lines. To convince the reader, all that is needed is the presentation of several texts in parallel, which have been selected from a vast body of work that covers almost a millennium.

In the story about the Rumilly brownies (seventeenth century), we are told how a group of reformed Bernadins moved into a house that was left at their disposal. I will insert subtitles throughout in italics to provide a better evaluation of the events.

The State of the House

As this House had not been inhabited for some time, a vast quantity of rubbish had collected on all sides, so much that two Sisters went there every day to remove it. Little accustomed to this labor as they were, they found it provided them a sure field for exercising their Patience and their Humility. "This was," Sister Louise said with much insight, "the first exercise of our Sisters in Rumilly. So must it be, O my Lord, that to render ourselves your worthy servants, our first concern and our first Occupation is to cleanse our Souls of their spiritual stains. Or rather, it is You, O Lord, who should cleanse this inner House with the purity of your precious Blood."

The Brownies and Their Activity

There was not merely material Filth to remove from this same Place; there were yet Unclean Spirits to drive away to make it habitable for these pure Virgins. A horde of brownies had made themselves its Masters and had almost transformed it into a Hell, by the confused noises that they excited both day and night and by the capricious Ravages they perpetrated on all sides. Sometimes they overturned all the Dishes, and sometimes they threw all the Books on the ground. Then they cleaned it up so promptly, that it was almost impossible to perceive, and these books they would open by turning their pages with an unimaginable speed. Other times they would walk about with a heavy tread in the House, as if in a great urgency. At other times they threw so many stones in various places that the former Residents there were in mortal dread. How could the presence of guests so malign and so formidable not force them to abandon a dwelling so taxing and so dangerous to their lives?

Excommunication of the Brownies

What an affront that the Daughters, naturally so shy, would dare succeed them and take their place? They nonetheless did not cause the slightest difficulty after Father Billet, at their request, gave this House his Benediction. But he was not peacefully left to do so as these invisible Troublemakers, upset to find themselves compelled by his Conjurations to move out, caused as much aggravation as they could by the horrible Racket they made, and by the tumultuous Quantity of stones they threw in one Room while he was blessing another. It was inevitable their rage would acquiesce to the power of the Exorcisms. They were driven from this House almost as they had been driven from Heaven; at least they never returned as long as the nuns still lived there.

I say as long as they lived there because as soon as they had left to dwell in the other House, about which I shall speak in good time, this infernal troop seeing their former abode emptied of these Angels of the earth, whose Presence was as formidable and intolerable to them as that of the Angels of Paradise, they returned to make it their home and began at the same time causing the same disorders.[1]

It is worth comparing this story to the one told by Johann of Winterthur in the *Chronicle* he began compiling around 1340.

In 1307 a woman of Walenstadt died. She arose from her funeral bier and spoke of numerous people that were in the beyond and stated that she had almost been damned because of a sin she had dared not confess, but that Saint Francis had saved her. He had restored her to life so she could confess and then, purified, find rest. She then lay back down and died. In the dead woman's house, an evil spirit manifested because the Franciscans had stolen a soul away from him. It terrified the inhabitants and its manifestations stopped when the house was given to the Franciscans. From then on the building served to house the lesser brethren who collected alms.[2]

In the case of the Bernardins, we are not told why the house was abandoned and comparing it with John of Winterthur's text and other similar more recent cases allows us to presume it was haunted. In both texts, the activity of the spirits ceased once members of the church inhabited the premises. There is a trail worth following here, because it shows us how the dead transformed into spirits, then into sprites or brownies, and eventually into devils. The following story offers evidence for one of the stages of this transformation.

> A man of Buschweiler died and was about to be taken for burial, and his coffin was already waiting in front of the house. The neighbors went to pick it up to carry it to the cemetery. All of a sudden the coffin lid raised up, the dead man appeared and, laughing, began speaking in patois. The coffin was nonetheless placed in the consecrated earth but the spirit still since that time began raging in the house making it uninhabitable. Two Capuchin brothers were summoned and they banished the spirit to a grove located on the Kirrweiler road, called the Kissel. This grove has since been cut down then and its ground is currently under cultivation. People can still hear the spirit mocking the people who work the fields, and sometimes it hurls stones at passersby.[3]

In the seventeenth century, brownies lived in Kernosy Castle, about which the teachers "knew all the stories since childhood,"[4] told them by their governesses, and Paul Sébillot tells how in 1880, when his gardener wished to light a fire in a room of the Chateau of Saudraie in the Brittany region of the Côtes d'Armor, "all the chairs began dancing, knocking him on his back and beating him until he fled."[5]

Generally, people abandon haunted houses. In 1551, in Vevey (Switzerland), a *tschauteret* (sprite) lived behind the Villeneuve and entered the Boillet Tower where he performed all kinds of mischief and made a loud racket. After some deliberations, the village council therefore ordered all the exits from the tower walled up to prevent this spirit from going in and out.[6]

Collin de Plancy recorded a very interesting legend, the events of which took place in the Yorkshire area more than a century ago. A boggart entered a farmer's home and, once he got settled in, disputed with the farmer over who had the right to live there. He could not stand children and was always grabbing their buttered bread or bowls of milk from them, he tormented the farmer and his wife, and generally terrorized everyone. When everyone was in bed, they could hear the noise of someone in the stairway wearing wooden shoes who was loudly walking up and down. The earthenware and tin plates were found broken or scattered across the kitchen floor, and sometimes an enormous weight pressed down upon the sleeping children. The farmer decided to leave his house, loaded all he owned onto a cart, and left. On his way, he met a neighbor to whom he explained the reasons for his departure when, at that very moment, he heard a voice that indicated the boggart was away on a trip. They therefore retuned home and henceforth lived in better understanding with this spirit.[7] As can easily be seen, this story commingles the notions of the wicked house spirit and the poltergeist.

Let's now compare these stories with more recent accounts. In the middle of the nineteenth century, the Cideville Presbytery in the region of Seine-Maritime enjoyed a flurry of renown following the conviction and imprisonment of a sorcerer.[8] He was prey to a number of manifestations, which included the following: tiles broke; objects sailed in all directions; tables toppled over or traveled about; chairs clustered together and remained floating in the air; dogs were tossed toward the ceiling; knives, brushes, and prayer books flew out one window and flew back in the opposite one; the shovels and poker left the hearth and advanced into the room of their own volition; enormous desks crashed together and broke; and a black hand was seen coming down the chimney. The prayers of the clergymen who had come to help the parish priest were unsuccessful in stopping the "evil spells." If we dispense with our prejudices and compare these events with those of earlier centuries, what we see here are the actions of a wrathful house spirit, a spirit who has been largely demonized in the form of a black hand emerging from the chimney. The sequel to this report provides another interpretation of the facts. The principal actor was a shepherd seeking revenge for the conviction of the sorcerer. However, no explanation of the way he went about it was put forward; moreover, when summoned and interrogated, the shepherd revealed he did not act alone and was aided by four companions. We do not know who they were or where they came from. Clues point the reader in the direction of witchcraft: the person responsible was in fact a shepherd who was sometimes invisible and sometimes appeared in the form of a green flame that gave off a reeking smoke. This is an easy explanation but it does not stand up to analysis. As in other stories involving the supernatural, the witnesses unconsciously fall back on their own interpretative framework, one which is the product of their personal knowledge and education.[9]

This allows us to formulate a hypothesis with regard to the stories about haunted houses: every era has interpreted the facts in accordance with then-prevalent beliefs. During the Middle Ages and the Renaissance, the notion of the house spirit was still quite alive, and the authorship for evil tricks was attributed to sprites and brownies. By the nineteenth century, spirits and brownies had fallen into the realm of legends and fairy tales, at least in large part depending on the region, so the last resort was another explanation: witchcraft and the devil. There is good reason to reexamine all the stories about haunted houses and compare them* to discover how ancestral beliefs continue on in different guises. This is something that requires a simultaneous analysis of poltergeist stories. Such a study offers us some very interesting material: in modern times, these events are attributed to someone living in the house, generally a person of the female gender regarded as a medium or as hysterical. The proof is forthcoming after consultation with an occultist or other "expert" who advises that the suspected individual be removed from the house. Once this is done, the strange manifestations cease.[10] The manifestations include pieces of furniture dancing around the room, flying stones, moving objects—the police files are full of reports of such incidents! But explanations remain rare and the hauntings that affect some houses retain a large part of their mystery. Speculating a bit, we could undoubtedly

*[See *The Secret History of Poltergeists and Haunted Houses* by this same author. —*Trans.*]

claim that household spirits have not vanished entirely and have simply adapted to modern times. This is more reassuring than thinking we are confronted with diabolical phenomena! In the final analysis, our ancestors have bequeathed to us a code for living with spirits and we need only apply it, to prevent it from becoming obsolete. Then calm will be restored to our homes.

Once Upon a Time . . .

Having reached the end of this study—the sole aims of which are to rescue from oblivion this set of beliefs, traditions, and ancestral rites centered on the house, and to attempt to identify the mental world that gave them birth—a certain number of elements commonly shared by all European peoples have come to light.

First of all, the fundamental notion of the sacred nature of the house, a microcosm that is reconstituted by the human being who has an obvious need for shelter, a place where he or she can feel safe, protected from the hostile and malevolent forces that emanate from other human beings—both the living and the dead—as well as from supernatural beings. These forces are often quite clearly embodied in the offspring of folk mythology, who have been granted all kinds of forms and a dreadful nature. Fear—which has some of it roots in the unknown, or, more precisely, ignorance—has played a major role in the construction of domestic beliefs. It is fair to say that every unusual event and all manner of catastrophes and misfortunes have inspired a desire for explanation that became condensed in the idea of the existence of visible and invisible creatures that manifested in such a way and could even attack you. People's reactions were simple and classic: they tried to protect themselves by implementing rites intended to defend the house's weak points—its openings—and to win the good graces or neutrality of some of these supernatural beings. These rites, which were initially prophylactic and apotropaic, later (or simultaneously) became propitiatory, and offerings were made at the spots where the spirits who had assumed a tutelary role in the home were believed to stay. Thus, just like with the other cases I studied in my research on land spirits, human beings created an interior sacred space meant to serve as a rampart against the demon world. An examination of the rites, and especially those relating to the creation of a sanctuary inside the *domus,* makes it possible to state that a veritable form of worship was established—one with its own ceremonies and with specific dates for offerings. This was obviously intended to revitalize the sacred dimension and to express respect for the terms of the tacit contract established with the tutelary spirit.

It so happens that this spirit is a complex figure with a long history, of which we can grasp only the culmination. Its form in the Middle Ages has already been subject to numerous influences and has, at the very least, a threefold origin. It incorporates the features of the good ancestors who have been raised to the rank of spirits—place spirits—who, thanks to the appropriate procedures, have become household spirits, as well as the features of those spirits who reside in materials such as wood and stone. Over the course of its development, the house spirit has become commingled with creatures called dwarves, fairies, and spirit-familiars, hence the difficulty in finding it in the ancient texts. We should note, however, that these influences and borrowings have not been unilateral and that fairies also owe some of their distinctive features to these spirits. Subsequent to its adoption into literature, whether romance or fairy tale, it has been mythicized and cut off from living belief to become a kind of literary convention as well as a highly stereotyped image: that of a tiny bearded man with a red cap and old-fashioned clothes. The figure I have depicted here is the product of an interplay between the scholarly, literary, folkloric, and oral data, and the world of belief.

The house spirit therefore falls primarily under the jurisdiction of folk religion; he was part of our ancestors' mental structures and embodied a transcendent element that people could turn to in need. It corrected adverse situations, redressed inequalities, and provided valuable assistance. In short, its existence offered reassurance because it gave physical expression to happiness and to the order without which nothing could prosper.

Its religious dimension arises from its moralistic and conservative nature, and it was sometimes claimed that its behavior was only a reflection of that of the household. As people once said: "Good spirits come to nice people." The notion of moral and social order seems to me to be a fundamental element of the history of this spirit. This is why wicked spirits, those who sow disorder in the home, seem to have another origin that should be sought in the realm of dwarves (using the word in its generic sense), sprites (for their mischievous and joke-playing nature), and evil spirits that nothing could tame. Here, too, the problem is complex, since it could also be a case where a foreign house spirit is harming you so that its own master may prosper.

All that remains is for me to make a sad observation. Like so many other creatures that once embellished life and brought hope, house spirits have vanished and with them the souls of our houses have fled, never to return. Homes have sunk into anonymity; building rituals have almost entirely disappeared; prefabricated industrial materials have replaced the quest for and attentive selection of materials that were wrought with love; the meaning of ornaments are no longer known and moon, sun, stars, and crosses have disappeared from our facades; radiators have replaced the hearth and stove; our corners have become little more than dust collectors; and there is no longer anything concealed beneath our thresholds. We have been transformed into rootless wanderers with no fire or place to call our own. The individual no longer has any attachment to a house that has been passed down for generations. In losing all of this, we have lost a piece of ourselves, one of our most solid anchors, and like dead leaves carried by the wind, we settle one day here, and the next day there, driven by the whims of our professions, but we no longer bring the embers from our hearths with us, and the surviving spirits weep in abandoned houses.

APPENDIX 1

Sayings and Beliefs

Below, the reader will find a selection of sayings and beliefs concerning the house and its inhabitants. The frequency of omens will leap out and the reader will see the veritable monopoly held by the many recommendations aimed at ensuring happiness, health, and protection. The references in parentheses refer to the bibliography. I have drawn from the collection of Johann Georg Schmidt[1] (eighteenth century) in particular as it is so rich and allows comparisons to be made with the beliefs of other countries.

1. A house without a spirit is cursed (Honko, 174).
2. To keep a cat or dog from getting out, make them walk around the *hearth* three times then rub them against its wall (Schmidt, II, 63)!
3. You should not throw out the hot water when *sweeping* the common room; otherwise a quarrel will ensue (Schmidt, VI, 12).
4. It is not a good idea to *sweep* the house after sunset. This runs the risk of sweeping away, along with the dust, the souls of the dead who often obtain permission to return to their former homes at this time (Le Braz, 268).
5. In the Breton area of the Côtes-du-Nord, it is still believed today that the souls of the dead often return to their former residence

at this time, and one risks sweeping them out with the dust: if the wind brings them back, one should take special pains to avoid expelling them a second time. Those who fail to heed these instructions will be vulnerable to being awakened at any time by dead souls (Paul Sébillot, *Folklore de France,* vol. 1, 136).

6. The threshold must be *swept* thoroughly so that *laime* (happiness or good fortune) can enter (Johansons, 147).
7. Whoever has dough in the kneading trough should not *sweep* the room before taking it out; otherwise the bread will be swept away as well (Schmidt, I, 33).
8. As long as the corpse has not been removed from the mortuary house, the floor should not be swept or the furniture dusted, nor should any dust or sweepings be thrown away, for fear of also evicting the soul of the dead person and drawing his vengeance down on your head (Le Braz, 153).
9. Many houses and stables cannot bear *white livestock,* who will die or be crushed (Schmidt, V, 3).
10. When carpenters cut the *wood* for a new construction, the building will burn down if sparks fly from the first blow of the ax (Schmidt, V, 94).
11. When a man you love tries to leave the house, he can be kept there by brandishing the *chimney hook* around his head three times (Johansons, 134).
12. You should remain with your guest so he cannot steal the *chimney hook* (Johansons, 133).
13. When the *drac* brings back eggs, butter, cheese, and lard to people who scorn him, yell the name of our Savior several times and it will let everything fall (Grimm, no. 520).
14. If you wash your money in pure water that has had salt and bread thrown into it, the *drac* and evil folk will be unable to carry it away (Schmidt).
15. Whoever *enters* a new dwelling must begin by throwing a living thing like a cat or dog inside, because whoever enters first dies first (Grimm, no. 499).

16. You should never *enter* a newly built house for the first time without having some kind of domestic animal go in before you, be it a dog, chicken, or cat (Le Braz, 96).
17. The bride should not *move in* when the moon is waning; whosoever moves in when it is raining will be rich (Grimm, no. 498).
18. When the young couple returns from the church, they should allow a black chicken to go before them into their house; all misfortune will fall upon it (Schmidt, IV, 90).
19. Whoever *enters* a new home or dwelling for the first time and sleeps there, whatever he dreams of that evening will come true (Schmidt, II, 30).
20. One must *move in* during the new moon; this will cause food to increase (Schmidt, III, 55).
21. When taking an infant to church to be baptized, he should be taken outside the home through the *window!* This will make him healthier and he will live longer (Schmidt, III, 85).
22. For people who have lost children, while carrying the newborn they should have the infant baptized not by the door but by the *window* (Grimm, no. 843).
23. When a person dies, the *windows* of the house should be opened so that the soul can leave (Schmidt, III, 3).
24. As long as the dead person has not been laid in the coffin, one of the openings of the house must remain unclosed, unless there is one of those gaps in the door called a cat hole or a pane is missing from the window frame, as is frequently the case even among the well-to-do. If this is not done, it is said that the soul of the dead person will roam around the house until he causes the death of another family member (Le Braz, 159).
25. You should never leave the house empty during the *burial,* otherwise the dead person, whose remains you believe are accompanying to the cemetery, will remain there to guard it (Le Braz, 175).
26. A woman in labor should never look out the *window;* else the first animal-drawn vehicle that passes will carry off her happiness (Grimm, no. 782).

27. It is not good to let a stranger carry fire or light outside of the house, for this is how food will leave it as well (Schmidt, I, 97).
28. The tutelary spirit of our huts keeps watch on the *fire* (Johansons, 126).
29. The *fire* never goes out in a house where the cat, dog, and rooster are black (Grimm, no. 1056).
30. When *fire* is burning in the hearth, lightning will not strike the house (Schmidt, II, 34).
31. When *fire* crackles in the stove, a quarrel will follow (Schmidt, IV, 45).
32. The new maid should immediately look through the *stove* hole; in this way she will quickly become acclimated (Schmidt, I, 98).
33. If many chickens, ducks, pigs, and so forth are dying one after another, light the fire in your *oven* and cast an animal of each species inside: the witch will die as they die (Grimm, no. 569).
34. If someone steals something from you, attach a horseshoe found by chance at the place where the *fire* always is burning: you will get it back (Schmidt, III, 35).
35. There is a spirit living in every hut; when there is only one *stove* (meaning only one heated room), the spirit will stay in it (Honko, 167).
36. When a *candle* goes out by itself in the house, one of its inhabitants will die (Schmidt, IV, 48).
37. At night, a *candle* should never be stuck in upside down on the candleholder; if a thief comes in, no one in the house will wake up (Schmidt, II, 74).
38. The corpse being taken out of the house should be placed on the *sill* three times; once the corpse has been taken away, the gate should be closed and three piles of salt placed in the deceased's room. They should then be swept up and both broom and sweepings tossed into a field (Grimm, no. 846).
39. When the house is finished, no one who lives there should dare enter first. Whoever does shall be the first to *die* (Honko, 199).
40. Whoever begins a construction will *die* shortly thereafter (Schmidt, V, 58).

41. When the peasant dies on his farm, the spirit either mourns or leaves (Honko, 221).
42. If someone [on his or her deathbed] is unable to *die,* then three tiles should be pulled off the roof (Grimm, no. 721).
43. There where a life has just been *born,* another should be sacrificed in thanks, otherwise the *mâju gars* will be furious because it has been neglected and will soon carry off the child's spirit (Johansons, 185).
44. If a mole pushes up the dirt inside the house or if the cricket sings, someone is going to *die;* it is the same when the chicken crows or the owl hoots (Grimm, no. 555).
45. When entering the common room, do not look back when going through the *doorframe* (Grimm, no. 360).
46. The spirits are granted the space between the *doors;* they should therefore never be slammed, or they will be harmed (Grimm, no. 892).
47. When an infant is taken out of the house, the top half of a double *door* should not be closed, otherwise he will not grow any bigger (Grimm, no. 345).
48. Whoever makes off with the measure used to measure a dead man and presses it at night against the entry *door* can rob the inhabitants without waking them (Grimm, no. 849).
49. Whoever places a wheel above the *main door* will enjoy good fortune in the home (Schmidt, IV, 30).
50. If you draw crosses on the *doors* before Walpurgis Night, witches cannot harm you (Schmidt, I, 93).
51. If a stranger looks into the common room through its *door* on a Monday, the man will beat his wife (Schmidt, I, 15).
52. If a serving maid wishes to learn whether she will have her position for a long time, she should turn her back to the *door* on Christmas night and toss the shoe off her foot over her head; if the tip is pointed toward the door, she should leave; if it is the heel, she will stay (Schmidt II, 5).
53. An elder planted in front of the stable *door* will avert evil spells (Grimm, no. 169).

54. When you place a broom upside down behind the *entry door,* no witch can enter (Grimm, no. 1007).
55. In the spring, when it is time to let the livestock out, they bury axes, hatchets, saws, and other iron objects in front of the stable *door,* which can then be no longer bewitched (Grimm, no. 516).
56. Serviceberry branches, which are still called "dragon tree," hung over the house and the entry *door* of the stable on Saint Walpurgis night prevent the flying *drac* from entering (Grimm, no. 971).
57. He who is visited by the *mar* (the nightmare), a large woman with thick tresses, should pierce a hole in the bottom of the *door* and stick as many hog bristles as needed to plug it up. He can then sleep peacefully and promise a gift to the *mar* if she comes; she will leave and return the next day in human form, seeking the present (Grimm, no. 878).
58. Writing *Nicaise* in chalk on the *door* on that saint's feast day will drive mice away (Schmidt, II, 81).
59. If one draws a pentacle on the *door,* witches have to stay away (Grimm, no. 644).
60. Whoever trips over the *sill* when leaving should immediately turn around; otherwise misfortune will befall him (Grimm, no. 895).
61. If someone chops twigs on the *doorsill,* the *drac* will carry *laime* (happiness) off and set fire to the house (Johansons, 147).
62. If when leaving early in the morning, you touch the *threshold* with your right foot, you will have good fortune all day long (Schmidt, IV, 81).
63. Light should not be cast beneath the *table* where people are sitting; otherwise a quarrel will break out (Schmidt, I, 48).
64. Nothing should be left on the *table* before going to bed; otherwise the eldest or the last born will be unable to sleep (Grimm, no. 1004).
65. Nothing should be left on the *table* overnight; otherwise the angels will not protect us (Grimm, no. 572).
66. When someone on their deathbed cannot pass over, the *table* should be put in a new place or a shingle on the roof turned over (Schmidt, VI, 37).

67. Whoever is planning to leave on a journey should wait for the *table* to be cleared; otherwise the travel will be difficult (Grimm, no. 442).
68. Houseleeks planted on the *roof* avert lightning (Schmidt, I, 61).
69. If the stork builds its nest on the *roof* or chimney, the master of the house will have long life and wealth (Schmidt, II, 15).
70. You should not put the grill and *trivet* on the fire without putting something on it; the woman who does this shall gain a wrinkle (Schmidt, II, 18).
71. When the *trivet* is left on the fire, poor souls are in torment (Le Braz, 267).
72. Shards that break off from the slabs of the floor of the *common room* indicate that a visitor is coming (Schmidt, I, 73).
73. If magpies are squawking in the *yard* or on the *roof*, if the embers of the fire fly behind it, it means guests are arriving (Grimm, no. 889).
74. A swarm of bees that alights on a house means fire (Schmidt, II, 68).
75. Whoever harms a domestic viper, or simply looks at one, shall die in the coming year (Schmidt, II, 51).
76. Swallow nests and cricket nests are a blessing on the house (Schmidt, V, 39).
77. The calls of cranes around the house means a corpse, even if only the cadaver of an animal (Grimm, no. 496).

APPENDIX 2

The Alf

In his collection of East Prussian legends, Erich Pohl has provided an excellent summary of common traditions regarding the *alf,* another name for the *drac.*

> When a pauper in East Prussia suddenly becomes rich in an inexplicable way, he is quickly suspected of owning an *alf.* More rarely, people talk of *dracs* and, in Masuria, the people call it *Lataniec* and *Kaubuk* in their dialects.
>
> In their house, the farmer and his wife have the *alf* in the form of an animal, a chicken, a gray goose, or a bird resembling an owl. . . . It is also simply called "the *alf* bird." More rarely, it is described as a black cat or a calf. As a flying animal, the *alf* spends most of its time in a large cask in the attic. But he also stays in the stable, the barn, in the peephole near the chimney, or in the chimney itself. It is also said that he takes his own room so that no one can enter except the master of the house. In one case, the room must even be carpeted with dirt. The *alf* should be fed milk, scrambled eggs, prunes, or birch flour broth by his owner.

The *alf* is also depicted as an igneous phenomenon with no definite shape that travels through the air, resembling a broom on fire or a pole. In the stories spread about it, most often it is the flying *alf,* but others focus on the zoomorphic *alf,* which is either a quadruped or a bird, but these depictions overlap with one another. Sometimes it is alluded to when someone says the chicken is flying like a tail of fire. An *alf* flying through the air in the shape of a pole will change into an animal in the house, a winged creature, and when it leaves at night it will resume its earlier appearance. . . .

The *alf* helps you in the house or procures wealth for you, or does both simultaneously. It cooks lunch while the farmer is in the fields, throws hay to the people who feed the livestock, and thereby allows the beasts to prosper and butter not to sour; in short, he causes all activity to move forward. It primarily increases the wealth of the home. It is even said to shit gold. It steals all kinds of valuable goods and brings them to its owner, especially cereal grain. Because the *alf* steals this from granaries, people draw the sign of the cross on them to protect them. At planting time, the *alf* even brought one peasant's seeds to the other's home and, during harvest time, did the same with the sheaves. It stole eggs from strangers' henhouses and brought them to the peasant to whom it was devoted. When the *alf* traveling through the air is red in color, it is bringing money; when it is blue, it is grain. He enters his owner's house through the chimney. When someone seeing it crossing through the air calls out the *alf,* it forces it to let go of his burden. But this individual must quickly find a roof to shelter under, otherwise the *alf* will pour lice down upon him.

In many legends, the *alf* is a being who needs to live with people. In the form of a chicken half-dead from the cold, it allows himself to be brought inside the house by a merciful man and will faithfully serve him its entire life. If the man dies, it seeks refuge with the man's relatives and continues serving them. If an *alf* is upset with its owner because he feeds it poorly or is trying to get rid of it, it will cause as much harm as the aid it once provided. It will carry off all the riches it brought to the house and even set it on fire, which can also happen when feeding the *alf* with burning fodder.

Many stories underscore the *alf*'s diabolical side. A pact is concluded with the devil for a certain period of time, and it goes off with the man's soul. In those houses that own an *alf,* there are often hauntings following the owner's death. It is even claimed that the Freemasons have an *alf.*[1]

APPENDIX 3

A Brief Summa

In a theatrical production staged on July 12, 1696, by the Italian actors of the Hotel de Bourgogne, titled *Les Bains de la Porte Saint Bernard,* the powerful magician Arlequin names the spirits and summons them to appear.

Troublemakers of the universe,
Who find great delight
In turning all upside down;
Spirits inclined to malice,
Who by peerless means
To blind others, will poke out your eye;
You who by a role steeped in deception
Will introduce yourself as guide to those passing by
And lead them to the precipice.
Brownies, Lemures, Sprites,
Pans Eegipans, Hamadryads,
Lares, Wood Nymphs, Dryads,
Goatfoot Gods, Pixie Spirits,
Who I have under my control,
Leave the inanimate bodies,

In which you are held prisoner,
And by the effort of my power
Whose effects are wonderful
Come out and show yourself![1]

Then all the furniture in the room changes into brownies and one of them named Cochemard* "takes great delight in attaching himself to those who sleep on their backs." To a certain extent, the invocation provides the summa of all the beings of folk mythology who were still sufficiently known during this time as to be recognizable.

*["Nightmare" —*Trans.*]

Notes

FOREWORD

1. Patlagean, "L'Histoire de l'imaginaire," 249–69.
2. Delavigne, "Sur la piste des êtres de la basse mythologie," 31–40.
3. See, for example, Grambo, "The Lord of Forest and Mountain Game in the More Recent Folk Traditions of Norway," 35–52.

CHAPTER I. THE HOUSE AND ITS CONSTRUCTION

1. Honko, *Geisterglaube in Ingermanland,* 189.
2. Grimm, *Deutsche Mythologie,* vol. 3, no. 98.
3. Rantasalo, *Der Ackerbau in der Volksaberglauben der Finnen und Esten mit entsprechenden Gerbräuchen der Germanen verglichen,* 6 and 12.
4. Ibid., 14.
5. Ibid., 13.
6. Sverdrup, "Die Hausurnen und die Heiligkeit des Hauses," *Avhandliger utgitt av Det Norske Videnskaps-Akademi i Oslo II. Hist. Filos. Klasse,* 1939, No. 1, 10.
7. Honko, *Geisterglaube,* 189.
8. Ibid.
9. Ibid., 190.
10. Ibid.
11. Ibid., 191.
12. Johansons, *Der Schirmherr des Hofes im Volksglauben der Letten,* 54ff.

13. Ibid., 58.
14. Rantasalo, *Der Ackerbau,* 15ff.
15. Honko, *Geisterglaube,* 197.
16. Johansons, *Der Schirmherr,* 58.
17. Ibid., 60.
18. Ibid., 68.
19. Strömbäck, *Die Wahl des Kirchenbauplatzes in der Sage und im Volksglauben mit besonderer Rücksicht auf Schweden,* 37ff.
20. Cf. Forêt, "Les Concepts géomantiques des trois capitals Qing," in Flora Blanchon, *Aménager l'espace Asie* II, Paris, 1993, 122–38, with maps and blueprints.
21. Müllenhoff, *Sagen, Märchen und Lieder aus Schleswig-Holstein,* 299.
22. Conte, *L'Héritage païen de la Russie,* 260.
23. Cf. Taloş, *Meşterul Manole.*
24. Johansons, *Der Schirmherr,* 64.
25. Honko, *Geisterglaube,* 194–96.
26. Sébillot, *Le Folklore de France,* vol. 4, 88ff.
27. Anne-Hélène Delavigne provided photos that depict this clearly; they were taken in Agia Marina, around twenty-five miles northeast of Athens in January 1998!
28. Johansons, *Der Schirmherr,* 55.
29. Sjövall, *Om byggnadsoffer och besläktade bruk hos greker och romare,* 55.
30. Sverdrup, "Die Hausurnen," 9 and 21.
31. Lecouteux, *L'Allemand du Moyen Age,* 116–18.
32. Ronsard, *Songs and Sonnets of Pierre de Ronsard,* 97.
33. Ovid, *Metamorphoses,* VIII.
34. Wundt, *Mythes und Religion,* 165ff.
35. Sartori, *Sitte und Brauch,* vol. 2, 165.
36. Conte, *L'Héritage païen de la Russie,* 106.
37. Honko, *Geisterglaube,* 196.
38. Grimm, *Deutsche Mythologie,* vol. 3, no. 1000.
39. Ibid., vol. 3, no. 778.
40. Lindig, *Hausgeister,* 74ff.
41. Conte, *L'Héritage païen,* 249.
42. Mélétinskij, "La Poétique historique du folklore narrative," 616.
43. Leroy, *Montaillou, village Occitan de 1294 à 1324,* 612ff.
44. Johansons, *Der Schirmherr,* 117ff.
45. Laisnel de la Salle, *Croyances et légendes,* vol. 2, 186ff.

46. Grimm, *Deutsche Mythologie,* vol. 3, no. 499.
47. Honko, *Geisterglaube,* 199.
48. Sébillot, *Le Folklore de France,* vol. 4, 97.
49. Thiers, *Traité des superstitions,* 117.
50. Grimm, *Deutsche Mythologie,* vol. 3, no. 429.
51. Bächtold-Stäubli, *Handwörterbuch des deutschen Aberglaubens,* 8: 1199 ff.
52. Wuttke, *Der Aberglaube der Gegenwart,* 59, § 67; 61, § 71.
53. Honko, *Geisterglaube,* 197.
54. Ibid., 197ff.
55. Bächtold-Stäubli, *Handwörterbuch,* 8: 1199ff.
56. Honko, *Geisterglaube,* 202.
57. Paulson, "Die Hausgeister," 142.
58. Honko, *Geisterglaube,* 175.
59. Conte, *L'Héritage païen,* 258.
60. Ibid.
61. Ibid., 257.
62. Coomaraswamy, *Traditional Art and Symbolism,* 504.

CHAPTER 2. THE BUILDING

1. Tatiana A. Bernstam, "Le conte dans la vie et dans la culture de la paysannerie slave orientale," *Ethnologie française* 1996/4, 619–27, at 621.
2. Pliny, *Natural History,* 30, 32.
3. Ertlé, *Sorciers, Magiciens et Enchanteurs de nos terroirs,* 370.
4. Grimm, *Deutsche Rechtsaltertümer,* vol. 2, 505.
5. *Egils saga skallagrímssonar,* chap. 58; *Eyrbyggja saga,* chaps. 33 and 60.
6. Ertlé, *Sorciers, Magiciens et Enchanteurs,* 306.
7. Simon, *Tiez, Le Paysan Breton et sa maison* II.
8. Johansons, *Der Schirmherr,* 63.
9. Ibid., 64.
10. Ibid., 66.
11. Grimm, *Deutsche Mythologie,* vol. 3, no. 1110.
12. Olive, "La Salutation au soleil," 1–25.
13. Grimm, *Deutsche Rechtsaltertümer,* vol. 2, 329.
14. Conte, *L'Héritage païen,* 162.
15. Communication of July 15, 1999, from Astrid Guillaume, accompanied by some photographs.

16. *Grettis saga* and *Flóamanna saga*; cf. Lecouteux, *Return of the Dead,* 85–86, 97–100.
17. Burchard of Worms, *Decretum* X, 14; XIX, 5, 95.
18. Thiers, *Traité des superstitions,* 159.
19. Rolland, *Faune populaire de la France,* vol. 6, 103.
20. Bächtold-Stäubli, *Handwörterbuch,* 8: 357.
21. Ibid., 8: 1500.
22. Ibid., 7: 1091.
23. Ibid., 7: 1688.
24. Ibid., 7: 1358.
25. Ibid., 7: 1672, 1675.
26. Grimm, *Deutsche Mythologie,* vol. 3, no. 789.
27. *Les Évangiles des Quenouilles,* line 2209ff.
28. Ibid., 1846ff.
29. Ibid., 536 ff; 1726ff.
30. Grimm, *Deutsche Mythologie,* vol. 3, no. 889.
31. Lecouteux, *Witches, Werewolves, and Fairies,* 166ff.
32. Thiers, *Traité des superstitions,* 147.
33. Ibid., 144.
34. Paulson, "Die Hausgeister," 129.
35. Grimm, *Deutsche Mythologie,* vol. 3, no. 1020.
36. Ertlé, *Sorciers, Magiciens et Enchanteurs,* 366.
37. Rantasalo, *DerAckerbau,* 61.
38. Olive, "La Salutation au soleil," 7.
39. Schilling, "Les Lares grundiles." They were also buried beneath the canopy of the house, in which case they were called *subgrundarii.*
40. Wirth, "Von Bauernhaus und Hof in Anhalt," 117.
41. Berlioz, "Pélerinages et Pélerins," 188.
42. Grimm, *Deutsche Mythologie,* vol. 3, no. 77.
43. Conte, *L'Héritage païen,* 179.
44. Kabakova, "Adam et Eve dans la literature des Slaves de l'Est," 228ff.
45. De Marliave, *Petit dictionnaire de mythologie basque et pyrénéenne.*
46. Taloş, *Petit dictionnaire de mythologie populaire roumaine.*
47. Grimm, *Deutsche Mythologie,* vol. 3, no. 849.
48. Thiers, *Traité des superstitions,* 114.
49. Wirth, "Von Bauernhaus," 134.
50. Grimm, *Deutsche Mythologie,* vol. 3, no. 971.
51. Conte, *L'Héritage païen,* 179.

52. Magnus, *Historia de gentibus septentrionalibus,* 19, 48.
53. Grimm, *Deutsche Mythologie,* vol. 3, no. 307.
54. Marliave, *Petit dictionnaire de mythologie.*

CHAPTER 3. THE OPENINGS OF THE HOUSE

1. Von Schwerin, "Leges Saxonum und Lex Thurinforum," 3, 4.
2. Pliny, *Natural History,* XXVIII, 135.
3. Arnobius, *Adversus nationes,* III, 25.
4. Paulson, "Die Hausgeister und ihre idole in Norderasien," 127.
5. *Postes attingui iubentes*; Pliny, *Natural History,* IXXX, 30.
6. Plutarch and Lucan, *Quaestio Rom,* 31.
7. Dioscorides, *De materia medica,* II, 73.
8. Ovid, *Fastes* VI, verses 130ff. and 166.
9. Pliny, *Natural History,* XV, 39; Ovid, *Tristes,* elegy I, 39.
10. Pliny, *Natural History,* XXIV, 72.
11. Eis, *Medizinische Fachprosa des späten Mittelalters und der frühen Neuzeit,* 20.
12. Apuleius, *Metamorphoses,* I, 11–14. Citation from *The Golden Ass,* trans. by P. G. Walsh, 14.
13. Vintler, *Bluome der tugent,* verse 105.
14. Alice Joisten, "Croyances su diable," 34ff.
15. Schönwerth, *Aus der Oberpfalz. Sitten und Sagen,* 3, 200.
16. Grimm, *Deutsche Mythologie,* vol. 3, no. 1007.
17. Ibid., vol. 3, no. 644.
18. Pliny, *Natural History,* XXVIII, 157.
19. Ibid., XXVIII, 85.
20. Bächtold-Stäubli, *Handwörterbuch,* 1: 143ff.
21. Grimm, *Deutsche Mythologie,* vol. 3, no. 169.
22. Ibid., vol. 3, no. 516.
23. Wirth, "Von Bauernhaus," 134.
24. *Malleus maleficarum,* II, 2, 7.
25. Eis, *Medizinische Fachprosa,* 263.
26. Bächtold-Stäubli, *Handwörterbuch,* 1: 136.
27. Raudvere, *Föreställningar om maran i nordisk folktro,* 150.
28. Bächtold-Stäubli, *Handwörterbuch,* 1: 136.
29. Le Quellec, *La Vendée mythologique et legendaire,* 95.
30. Vorreux, *Un symbole franciscain: le Tau. Histoire, théologie et iconographie,* 26ff.

31. Happ, *Kommentar zum zweiten Buch von Wolframs Willehalm,* 224.
32. *Tav que postem nota test crux que fugat hostem.*
33. Martino, *Italie de Sud et Magie,* 27ff.
34. Liebrecht, *Zur Volkskunde,* 311.
35. Grimm, *Deutsche Mythologie,* vol. 3, no. 971.
36. Thiers, *Traité des superstitions,* 268.
37. Bächtold-Stäubli, *Handwörterbuch,* 1: 145.
38. Schmidt, *Die gestriegelte Rockenphilosophie,* vol. 2, 81.
39. *Flóamanna saga,* chap. 22; *Eiriks saga rauða,* chap. 6.
40. *The Saga of Snorri the Godi* [= *Eyrbyggja Saga*] (chap. 33 and chap. 60) and *Egil's Saga* (chap. 58) are early confirmations of this practice that survived in Scotland into the nineteenth century.
41. Johansons, *Der Schirmherr,* 144.
42. Grimm and Grimm, *Deutsche Sagen,* 209.
43. Grimm, *Deutsche Rechtsaltertümer.*
44. Grimm, *Deutsche Mythologie,* vol. 3, no. 389.
45. Thiers, *Traité des superstitions,* 150.
46. *Distaff Gospels,* l. 260ff.
47. Grimm, *Deutsche Rechtsaltertümer.*
48. Johansons, *Der Schirmherr,* 143.
49. Ibid.
50. Ibid., 142.
51. Ibid., 148.
52. Ibid., 143.
53. Pliny, *Natural History,* XXVI, 67.
54. Thiers, *Traité des superstitions,* 114, 143.
55. Bächtold-Stäubli, *Handwörterbuch,* 1: 136.
56. *Romanus Büchlein* (Venice: n.d.), consists of 48 pages bound in parchment with no indications on the plates or the back. The place of publication is false; it was done to deceive the censor. The extremely rare copy is located in the Sorbonne University Library, Paris IV, (Centre Malesherbes). Translated by Lecouteux in *Le livre des Grimoires,* 224–247.
57. Ibid.
58. Johansons, *Der Schirmherr,* 144.
59. Grimm, *Deutsche Mythologie,* vol. 3, no. 486.
60. Ibid., vol. 3, no. 38.
61. Ibid., vol. 3, no. 1101.
62. Pliny, *Natural History,* IXXX, 83.

63. Grimm, *Deutsche Mythologie,* vol. 3, no. 782.
64. Ibid., vol. 3, no. 443.
65. Schmidt, *Die gestriegelte Rockenphilosophie,* vol. 3, 85.
66. Thiers, *Traité des superstitions,* 114.
67. Grimm and Grimm, *Deutsche Sagen,* 209.
68. Johansons, *Der Schirmherr,* 144.
69. Briggs, *A Dictionary of British Folk-Tales in the English Language Incorporating the F. J. Norton Collection,* vol. 1, part B, 382.
70. Grimm, *Deutsche Mythologie,* vol. 3, no. 61.
71. Tubach, *Indes exemplaires,* no. 978.
72. Merceron, "Recherches sur le symbolism cosmique de la toiture et métaphysique de la cheminée et de la toiture," 7.
73. Conte, *L'Héritage païen,* 210ff.
74. Cf. Vinogradova, "Les croyances au demon dans la structure du calendrier populaire," 739.
75. Grimm, *Deutsche Mythologie,* vol. 3, no. 524.
76. Ibid., vol. 3, no. 38.
77. Ertlé, *Sorciers, Magiciens et Enchanteurs,* 13.
78. Delpech, "Légendes généalogiques et mythologie porcine," 270, footnote 85.
79. Schmidt, *Die Gestriegelte Rocken-philosophie,* vol. 2, 15.

CHAPTER 4.
THE HOUSE INTERIOR

1. Grimm, *Deutsche Mythologie,* vol. 3, no. 777.
2. Schmidt, *Die Gestriegelte Rocken-philosophie,* vol. 3, 35.
3. Robertson, *Selected Highland Folktales,* 24.
4. Bächtold-Stäubli, *Handwörterbuch,* 6: 1191.
5. Grimm, *Deutsche Mythologie,* vol. 3, no. 526.
6. Ibid., vol. 3, no. 126.
7. Olive, "La Salutation au soleil," 9.
8. Grimm, *Deutsche Mythologie,* vol. 3, no. 1056.
9. Olive, "La Salutation au soleil," 12.
10. *Distaff Gospels,* 11. 578 ff.; 1753 ff.; 710 ff.
11. Schulz, "Il vaut mieux souffrir du froid maintenant. . . ," 33.
12. Johansons, *Der Schirmherr,* 75.
13. *Les Ethiopiques d'Héliodore,* 6, 14.
14. Mazalova, "La Médicine populaire dans les villages de la Russie du Nord," 673.

15. Bächtold-Stäubli, *Handwörterbuch,* 6: 1189.
16. Abry and Joisten, *Êtres fantastiques des Alpes,* 38ff.
17. Grimm, *Deutsche Mythologie,* vol. 3, no. 777.
18. Schmidt, *Die Gestriegelte Rocken-philosophie,* vol. 2, 63.
19. Bächtold-Stäubli, *Handwörterbuch,* 6: 1195.
20. Ibid., 6: 1192.
21. Thiers, *Traité des superstitions,* 115.
22. Grimm, *Deutsche Mythologie,* vol. 2, 975; vol. 3, 406, nos. 10, 14; 408.
23. Bächtold-Stäubli, *Handwörterbuch,* 6: 1197.
24. Mazalova, "La Médecine populaire," 674.
25. Bächtold-Stäubli, *Handwörterbuch,* 6: 1194.
26. Ibid., 6: 1194.
27. Mazalova, "La Médecine populaire," 672.
28. Grimm, *Deutsche Mythologie,* vol. 3, no. 569.
29. Cf. Joisten, "Croyances au diable et à la sorcellerie dans la vallée du Freissinières," 40.
30. Pliny, *Natural History,* XVIII, 267.
31. Bächtold-Stäubli, *Handwörterbuch,* 6: 1198.
32. Le Braz, *La Légende de la mort chez les Bretons armoricains,* 1982.
33. Bächtold-Stäubli, *Handwörterbuch,* 6: 1196.
34. Grimm, *Deutsche Mythologie,* vol. 3, no. 322.
35. Bächtold-Stäubli, *Handwörterbuch,* 6: 1271.
36. Ibid., 6: 1272.
37. Bächtold-Stäubli, *Handwörterbuch,* 6: 1272.
38. Johansons, *Der Schirmherr,* 140.
39. Ibid., 125.
40. Ibid., 135.
41. Ibid., 127.
42. Merceron, "Recherches sur le symbolisme," 3.
43. Bächtold-Stäubli, *Handwörterbuch,* 4: 1275.
44. Ibid., 4: 1274.
45. Cf. Conte; Merceron; and Johansons, *Der Schirmherr,* 120–42.
46. Thiers, *Traité des superstitions,* 116, 141.
47. Johansons, *Der Schirmherr,* 135.
48. Ibid., 134.
49. Ibid., 135.
50. Bächtold-Stäubli, *Handwörterbuch,* 4: 1277.

51. Grimm, *Deutsche Mythologie,* vol. 2, 992ff.
52. Johansons, *Der Schirmherr,* 136.
53. Ibid., 138.
54. Ibid., 126.
55. Thiers, *Traité des superstitions,* 145.
56. Liebrecht, *Des Gervasius von Tilbury Otia imperialia,* 245.
57. Laisnel de la Salle, *Croyances et Légendes du Cœur de la France,* vol. 2, 11.
58. Bächtold-Stäubli, *Handwörterbuch,* 4: 1271ff.
59. Olive, "La Salutation au soleil," 10.
60. Merceron, "Recherches sur le symbolisme."
61. Johansons, *Der Schirmherr,* 135.
62. Duvernoy, *Le Recueil d'inquisition de Jacques Fournier, évêque de Pamiers* (1318–1325), vol. 1, 137, 551.
63. Duvernoy, *Le Recueil,* vol. 1, 135, 545.
64. See the entry "trépied" in Le Quellec, *La Vendée mythologique,* 413.
65. *Distaff Gospels,* ll. 1714ff.
66. Schmidt, *Die Gestriegelte Rocken-philosophie,* vol. 2, 18.
67. *Les Évangiles des Quenouilles,* ll. 530ff., 552ff.
68. Bächtold-Stäubli, *Handwörterbuch,* 6: 1203.
69. Ibid., 6: 1201.
70. Ibid., 6: 1199.
71. Jeay, *Les Évangiles,* 11. 550ff.; 1722ff.
72. Sverdrup, "Die Hausurnen," 23; cf. also Zell, Bauer.
73. Abraham, "Les Pierres oubliées de la maison bretonne," 21.
74. Paulson, "Die Hausgeister," 126ff.
75. Ibid., 136.
76. Wasserschleben, *Die Bußordnungen der abendländischen Kirche,* cited (W); Schmitz, *Die Bußbücher und die Bußdiziplin der Kirche,* cited (S); Kottje, *Die Bußbücher Halitgars von Cambrai und des Hrabanus Maurus,* cited (K).
77. Grubmüller and Schnell, et al., eds., *Vocabularius ex quo,* 22–26; Bremer, ed., *Vocabularius optimus,* 28–29. The oldest manuscript dates from 1328–1330. Schmidt, ed., *Liber ordinis rerum,* 2.
78. Sverdrup, "Die Hausurnen," 19.
79. Cf. Weiser, "Germanische Hausgeister und Kobolde," 1–23; Birkeli, *Huskult og hinsidighetstro,* 84–87; in Bø and Berg, *Faksar og kyrkjerestar,* 43–76, Olav Bø believes that the *faksar* are the vestiges of sculpted figures pulled out of churches destroyed during the Reformation (1538) that gradually became regarded as

domestic deities. This is a possibility, but the *faksar* could have replaced older representations. Whatever the case may be, even Olav Bø's theory reveals the need people once had for household gods.

80. Klapper, "Deutscher Volksglaube in Schlesien in ältester Zeit," 36.
81. Hildebrandt, ed., *Summarium Heinrici,* vol. 2, 83; vol. 2, 10, 221; vol. I, 226, 240; vol. 2, 177 and 416.
82. *Lex Baiuvariorum,* tit. 16: *de venditionibus,* 17.
83. Cf. the entries in Bächtold-Stäubli, *Handwörterbuch,* for "Ecke" (2: 544–50) and "Hausgeister" (1: 1568ff).
84. Johansons, *Der Schirmherr,* 82ff. Other examples of rites connected to corners on pages 64–66; cf. also Honko, *Geisterglaube,* 180, 233.
85. Stahl, "L'Organisation magique du territoire villageois roumain," 157.
86. Karagiannis-Moser, *Le Bestiaire de la chanson populaire grecque moderne,* 322.
87. Ibid., 322.
88. Ibid., 326ff. and 329.
89. Paulson, "Die Hausgeister," 125ff.

CHAPTER 5. DOMESTIC SPIRITS IN ANTIQUITY AND THE MIDDLE AGES

1. Paulson, "Die Hausgeister," 124.
2. Honko, *Geisterglaube,* 167.
3. Cf. Sjövall, *Zeus im altgriechischen Hauskult.*
4. Cicero, *Leges,* 2:55.
5. Plautus, *Aulularia,* prologue, 2–5.
6. Cicero, *De natura deorum,* 2:67.
7. Silius Italicus, *La guerre punique,* vol. 2.
8. Ovid, *Fastes,* 6, 310.
9. Servius, *Aen,* 2, 514.
10. Ibid., 1, 730.
11. Pliny, *Natural History,* 28, 27.
12. *Theodosian Code* 16, 10, 12.
13. Burchard of Worms, 140, col. 106.
14. Grambo, *Svart Katt over veien,* 86–89, 212.
15. Cf. Wall, *Tjuvmjölkande väsen* I: äldre nordisk tradition; II: yngre nordisk tradition.

16. Haefele, ed., *Notkeri Balbuli Gesta Karoli Magni imperatoris,* 1:23.
17. Johansons, *Der Schirmherr,* 121. The idea can be found throughout the whole of Europe.
18. Thietmar of Merseburg, Chronicle VII, 69.
19. William of Auvergne, *De universo,* vol. I, 1066.
20. Gervase of Tilbury, *Otia Imperialia,* bk. III, sec. 61. Translation by Banks and Binns, pages 65–67.
21. Edited by Hagen in *Gesamtabenteuer,* vol. III, 257ff.
22. William of Auvergne, *De universo,* vol. I, 1030: *"alias res leves & facile translatibiles auferunt de oculis hominum, etiam de manibus ipsorum, & tranferunt eos ad alia loca."*
23. William of Auvergne, *De universo,* vol. I, 852, 1019, and 1029.
24. Cambrensis, *Itinerarium Cambriae* I, 12; *Giraldi Cambrensis Opera,* 97–99; English translation from *The Journey through Wales and the Description of Wales,* 151–52, slightly amended.
25. Cambrensis, *The Journey through Wales,* 154–55.
26. Richard, *Traditions populaires, Croyances superstitieuses, Usages et coutumes de l'ancienne Lorraine.*
27. Schröder, *Kleinere Dichtungen Konrads von Würzburg,* vol. 3, no. 32, v. 211.
28. Hagen, *Minnesinger,* vol. 3/1, 108.
29. We know this, thanks to Hugo von Trimberg, who in *Der Renner* (v. 10318 and 10884) gives the two names as synonyms (BLVSt, 247–48).
30. Cf. Lecouteux, *Mondes parallèles: l'univers des croyances du Moyen Age,* 113–18.
31. Cited by Grimm, *Deutsche Mythologie,* vol. 3.
32. Kahle, ed., *Kristni saga, Þattr đorvalds ens viđförla, Þattr Isleifs biskups Gizurarsonar Hungrvaka,* chap. 1.
33. *Annuae litterae Societatis Jesu,* 550.
34. Cf. Ziegler and Sontheimer, *Der Kleine Pauly: Lexikon der Antike,* vol. 4, col. 318ff., with bibliography.
35. Weiser, "Germanische Hausgeister," 13.
36. Martineau, *Les Nains dans la littérature arthurienne française du Moyen Age,* 1998.
37. For more on the feeding aspect, cf. Martineau, *Les Nains,* 375ff.
38. Ibid., 431ff.
39. "De nano et rustico," in Marie de France, *Die Fabeln.*
40. Strange, *Caesarii Heisterbacensis Dialogus miraculorum,* V, 36.
41. Ibid., V, 36.
42. Klintberg, *The Types of the Swedish Folk Legends,* 150–67.

CHAPTER 6. THE ORIGIN OF HOUSE SPIRITS

1. "Myrdinn ou l'enchanteur Merlin," cited by Laisnel de la Salle, *Croyances et Légendes du Coeur de la France,* vol. 2, 111.
2. Jouet, *Religion et Mythologie des Baltes,* 130.
3. Cited by Gieysztor, "Les Divinités lettones," in Grimal, *Mythologie des peuples lointains ou barbares,* 105.
4. Cf. Eliade, *Patterns in Comparative Culture,* 351–53. The dead have always been given a connection to germination and fertility.
5. *Piluitum, deum divitiarum, quem latini Plutum vocant.* Cited from Jouet, *Religion et Mythologie,* 66.
6. Lecouteux, "Der Bilwiz: Überlegungen zur Entstehungs-und Entwicklungsgeschicte," 238–50.
7. *Barstuccas, quos Germani erdmenlen, hoc est subterraneos, vocant.*
8. Cf. Lecouteux, *Les Nains et les Elfes au Moyen Age,* 182–84.
9. Haavio, *Soumalaiset kodinhaltiat,* 39–71.
10. Ibid., 194.
11. Ibid., 235ff.
12. Account collected in Isère in 1960; cf. Abry and Joisten, "Croyance au diable," 69. There is a good overview of domestic spirits on pages 59–90.
13. Johansons, *Der Schirmherr,* 121.
14. Cited by Lindig, *Hausgeister,* 78.
15. Labba, *Anta: Mémoires d'un Lapon,* 473.
16. Honko, *Geisterglaube,* 194.
17. For the following, see Lindig, *Hausgeister,* 74–79.
18. Paulson, "Die Hausgeister," 129.
19. Honko, *Geisterglaube,* 193.
20. Rolland, *Faune populaire de la France,* vol. 4, 199.
21. Cf. Schott and Schott, *Contes roumains,* 258.
22. Bächtold-Stäubli, *Handwörterbuch,* 4: 1271.
23. Müller, *Sagen aus Uri,* nos. 997; 998; 1059.
24. Ibid., nos. 1021; 1162 C and D, but other spirits can be found there as well, see nos. 1021; 1044 A; 1087.
25. Müller, *Sagen aus Uri,* no. 1162G.
26. Grimm, *Deutsche Mythologie,* vol. 3, no. 42.
27. For Franconia, see Linhart, *Hausgeister,* 370ff, 382, 400ff.
28. Cf. Lecouteux, "Ces bruits de l'au-delà," 113–24.

29. Barack, *Zimmersche Chronik,* vol. 4, 228.
30. Grimm and Grimm, *Deutsche Sagen,* 116, 126ff. (no. 75).
31. The state of the research is presented in Lindig, *Hausgeister,* 154ff.
32. Petzoldt, *Kleines Lexikon der Dämonen und der Elementargeister,* 91.
33. Arnaudov, "Der Familienschutzgeist im Volksglauben der Bulgaren," 131. See also Rabuzzi, "Some Notes on the Household Spirit in Norway," 97. Rabuzzi has no hesitation in asserting that "the *gardvord,* personifying the *rudkall* or *stamfader* could serve as a rallying point, a symbol of the collective."
34. Arnaudov, "Der Familienschutzgeist," 132.
35. Dieterich, *Mutter Erde,* 9ff.; other traces among the Reginon of Prüm and Burchard of Worms, cf. Grimm, *Deutsche Mythologie,* vol. 3, 410.
36. Steinmeyer and Sievers, *Die althochdeutschen Glossen,* vol. II, 468, 18 passim; 361, 4 passim.
37. Johansons, *Der Schirmherr,* 201–07.
38. This led to an erroneous etymology that sees *sottrel* of the verb *saltare* (to jump), whereas the term comes from the Latin *satyrus.*
39. *Discours des spectres,* IV, 18; cited in Walter, *Le Bel Inconnu de Renaut de Beaujeu,* 205.
40. Barack, *Zimmerische Chronik,* vol. 4, 132.
41. Weyer, *De praestigiis demonum,* 63.
42. Thyraeus, *Loca infesta, hoc est, de infestis, ob molestantes daemoniorum et defunctorum hominum spiritus,* 327–43.
43. Thyraeus, *Loca infesta,* 17.
44. Luther, "Tischreden," in *D. Martin Luthers Werke,* vol. 3, 634ff.
45. Ibid., 63.
46. Prätorius, *Anthropodermus Plutonicus,* 314ff.
47. For more on this famous German figure, see Temme, *Die Volkssagen von Pommern und Rügen,* no. 214.
48. Cherepanova, "La Profondeur de la mémoire," 156.
49. Cf. Arnaudov, "Der Familienschutzgeist," 127–37. For more on the *stopan,* see also Johansons, *Der Schirmherr,* 89ff.
50. Cf. Lecouteux, *Nos bons voisins les lutins,* 21–24.
51. Christiansen, "Gårdvette og markavette," 137–60, 140ff.
52. *Kotihaltia, Talonhaltia, Tuvanhaltia,* for example.
53. Cf. Johansons, *Der Schirmherr,* 127.
54. Cf. *riihtonttu* and *tontti. Riihija,* or *rehi etelurehi,* designates all the rooms of the homestead under one roof and placed under the tutelage of a Protector

(*rehehaldjas*), often demonized into a ghost (*rehetont*) and a black devil (*must*); cf. Paulson, "Die Hausgeister," 107ff.

55. *Tomtegubbe, tomtekall, tomtevette; tuftebonde, tuftevette; tunkall, tunvord; gardbo, gardsbonde, gardsrå, gårdbo, gårdbonisse, gardvord.* For more on this last figure, see the fine short essay by Bringsværd, *Phantoms and Fairies from Norwegian Folklore,* 89ff.
56. Paulson, "Die Hausgeister," 144.
57. Lindig, *Hausgeister,* 49.
58. Johansons, *Der Schirmherr,* 158 and 171.

CHAPTER 7.
THE MANIFESTATIONS OF HOUSEHOLD SPIRITS

1. Sébillot, *Le Folklore de France,* vol. 3, 114.
2. Ertlé, *Sorciers, Magiciens et Enchanteurs,* 157ff.
3. Grimm, *Deutsche Mythologie,* no. 454.
4. Sverdrup, "Die Hausurnen," 21.
5. Paulson, "Die Hausgeister," 143.
6. Honko, *Geisterglaube,* 207–11.
7. Ibid., 171.
8. Paulson, "Die Hausgeister," 100ff.
9. Cf. Doulet, *Les Changelins.*
10. Christiansen, *Folktales of Norway,* 92ff.
11. Honko, *Geisterglaube,* 170.
12. Christiansen, "Gårdvette," 145 ff.
13. Honko, *Geisterglaube,* 362, 360, 323. Other accounts concerning their appearance appear on: 223 ff., 268, 323, 354, and 370 (dog).
14. Weiser, "Germanische Hausgeister," 2.
15. For more details see Linhart, *Hausgeister,* 130–41.
16. Honko, *Geisterglaube,* 264.
17. Conte, *L'Héritage païen,* 203.
18. Honko, *Geisterglaube,* 164 and 169.
19. Johansons, "Das Heimchen und der lettische Hausgeist," 127–32, at 145.
20. Johansons, *Der Schirmherr,* 124.
21. Labba, *Anta: mémoires d'un Lapon,* 533ff.
22. Abry and Joisten, *Êtres fantastiques.*
23. Johansons, *Der Schirmherr,* 130ff.

24. Ibid., 117–19.
25. Paulson, "Hausgeister," 102.
26. Lasicius, *Die diis Samagitarum libellus,* 48.
27. Herberstein, *Moscovie du XVIe siècle vue par un ambassadeur occidental,* 210.
28. Pliny, *Natural History,* XXVIIII, 72.
29. Honko, *Geisterglaube,* 184ff, 228.
30. Sverdrup, "Die Hausurnen," 30.
31. Paulson, "Die Hausgeister," 102.
32. Jünger, *Auf den Marmorklippen,* 254–56. I would like to thank Marc-André Wagner for pointing this passage out to me.
33. Conte, *L'Héritage païen,* 214ff.
34. Magnus, *Historia de gentibus septentrionalibus,* XXI, 48 (776).
35. Sverdrup, "Die Hausurnen," 28.
36. Lindig, *Hausgeister,* 69.
37. Cf. Linhart, *Hausgeister,* 158.
38. Ibid., 213; 265.
39. Johansons, *Der Schirmherr,* 209ff.
40. Cf. Joisten, "Quelques attestations de récits légendaires antérieurs au XVIII siècle en Savoie et Dauphiné," 126.
41. Peuckert, *Der vielförmige Hintzelmann.*
42. Weiser, "Germanische Hausgeister," 3.
43. Bringsværd, *Phantoms and Fairies from Norwegian Folklore,* 93.
44. Paulson, "Die Hausgeister," 144.
45. Ibid., 145.
46. Ertlé, *Sorciers, Magiciens et Enchanteurs,* 159.
47. Honko, *Geisterglaube,* 170.
48. Johansons, *Der Schirmherr,* 124.
49. Honko, *Geisterglaube,* 183.
50. Arnaudov, "Der Familienschutzgeist," 135.
51. Honko, *Geisterglaube,* 176ff.
52. Sylvie Mougin, "Neptune et satyre en gallo-romain," (forthcoming). I would like to thank the author for sending me the manuscript of her article.
53. Ronsard, *Œuvres complètes,* vol. VIII, verses 243–50. It is worth noting that the poet attributes these acts to "Larves, Lémures, Pénates et Succubes," thus to the dead and to demons.
54. Cf. Grimm, *Deutsche Mythologie,* vol. 1, 415, 424; vol. 3, 144.
55. Cf. Haavio, *Suomalaiset,* 400 ff; Sydow, "Övernaturliga väsen," 124.

56. Sand, *Légendes rustiques,* 198, 83ff.
57. Cf. Shakespeare, *King Lear,* Act II, 3: "Elf all my hair in knots!"
58. For Germany, see Linhart, *Hausgeister,* 164ff., 169. For France, see Sébillot, *Le Folklore de France,* vol. 3, 115ff.
59. William of Auvergne, *De universo* II, 3, 24 (p. 1066).
60. Honko, *Geisterglaube,* 241.
61. Eis, *Medizinische Fachprosa,* 241.
62. Cf. Vinogradova, "Les croyances slaves," 241. There is material for study on the interferences between the domestic spirit, the spirit lover, the nightmare, and the vampire, who are often commingled in folk traditions.
63. Kelch, *Liefländische historia,* 29.
64. Johansons, *Der Schirmherr,* 129.
65. Grimm, *Deutsche Mythologie,* nos. 87 and 97.
66. Johansons, *Der Schirmherr,* 120.
67. Honko, *Geisterglaube,* 180.
68. Dubois, *Les Contes du Petit Peuple,* 295. In the folklore of the Dauphine and Savoy regions, the household spirit (*matagot, follet, servan . . .*) also displays his discontent by tossing the cattle into the hayloft or onto the roof.
69. Dubois, *Les Contes du Petit Peuple,* 298ff. Other examples can be found in Bringsvaerd, *Phantoms,* 98ff, 1.
70. Johansons, *Der Schirmherr,* 129.
71. "Once she enters the house, the young bride is led through all the parts of the home—rooms, chambers, stables, gardens—and is obliged to toss there, even in the wells, ribbons or money if she has her heart set on prosperity and her husband's good fortune," Grimm, *Deutsche Mythologie,* vol. 3, no. 11.
72. *Domum puerum in ostio ovum sub scopa concluant,* Klapper, "Deutscher Volksglaube in Schleisen in ältester Zeit," *Mitteilungen der Schlesischen Gesellschaft für Volkskunde* 17 (1915), 31.
73. Conte, *L'Héritage païen,* 230.
74. Honko, *Geisterglaube,* 181.
75. Conte, *L'Héritage païen,* 225.
76. Grimm, *Deutsche Mythologie,* vol. 3, no. 69.
77. Cf. Abry and Joisten, "La Servante punie pour avoir touché à la part de l'esprit domestique," with many documents and local names for these kinds of spirits: *matagot, mandrigole,* familiar, devil, *servan,* will o' the wisp, sprite, *moune, foulletou . . .*
78. Paulson, "Die Hausgeister," 99.
79. Ibid., 97.

80. Conte, "La fourrure," 214ff.
81. Paulson, "Die Hausgeister," 100.
82. Cf. Déchelette, *Manuel d'archéologie,* 300ff.
83. Paulson, "Die Hausgeister," 126.
84. Ibid., 134.
85. Bächtold-Stäubli, *Handwörterbuch,* 6: 1188.
86. Johansons, *Der Schirmherr,* 147.
87. Ibid., 145.
88. Ibid., 145ff.
89. Rantasalo, *DerAckerbau,* 14.
90. Honko, *Geisterglaube,* 235 and especially 338ff., 377.
91. Lindig, *Hausgeister,* 85.
92. Paulson, "Die Hausgeister," 103ff.
93. Honko, *Geisterglaube,* 176.
94. Ibid.
95. Cf. Joisten, "Quelques attestations," 125.
96. Jacquinot, *Adresse chrestienne,* 189–93. I would like to thank Alice Joisten, who provided this text.

CHAPTER 8.
THE PURVEYOR SPIRITS

1. Cf. Auning, "Uber den lettischen Drachen-Mythus (Puhkis)," 1ff.
2. On this entire development, see Linhart, *Hausgeister,* 213–67; the entry for "Drache" in Bächtold-Stäubli, *Handwörterbuch,* 2: 391–404; 6: 1188; Johansons, *Der Schirmherr,* 120ff.
3. Grimm, *Deutsche Mythologie,* vol. 3, 833ff.
4. Johansons, *Der Schirmherr,* 121.
5. "The drac brought it to him," "It is the Alf that always brings him so much," "He has the drac"; cf. Linhart, *Hausgeister,* 265, which should be compared with pages 158 and 213.
6. Grimm, *Deutsche Mythologie,* vol. 3, no. 102; other beliefs, nos. 6; 253; 520; 858.
7. Cf. Bächtold-Stäubli, *Handwörterbuch,* 3: 625ff.
8. Cf. the entry "*Alraun*" in Bächtold-Stäubli, *Handwörterbuch,* 1: 312ff; 3: 613ff. (*Heckethaler*), and col. 625ff. (*Heckemännchen*).
9. Wossidlo, *Mecklenburgische Sagen,* no. 840; 847; 862. During the fifteenth century, the chronicler Froissart recounted the story of Orthon, the spirit-familiar of the lord of Coarasse.

10. Lasicius, *De diis Samagitarum libellus,* 47.
11. Tettau and Temme, *Die Volkssagen Ostpreussens, Lithauens und Westpreussens,* 258.
12. Johansons, *Der Schirmherr,* 121.
13. Cf. Dömötör, *Volksglaube und Aberglaube der Ungarn,* 93ff.
14. Greimas, *Of Gods and Men: Studies in Lithuanian Mythology,* 53–54. Author's italics for emphasis removed.
15. Johansons, *Der Schirmherr,* 120.
16. Honko, *Geisterglaube,* 171–79; Lindig, *Hausgeister,* 149–51.
17. Paulson, "Die Hausgeister," 151.
18. Honko, *Geisterglaube,* 229–38.
19. Johansons, *Der Schirmherr,* 126.
20. See the index entry for "Alp" in Rantasalo, *Der Ackerbau,* 238. In the Basque country, Inguma, who visits sleepers with evil intent, causes nightmares by smothering them. To counter her attacks, appeal is made to Gauargi, the household spirit. Inguma is another form of the *Chauchevieille* or *Caucavielha,* the *Pesadilla* of the Catalans, and the Occitan *Sarra-Mauca.*
21. Honko, *Geisterglaube,* 177.
22. Ibid., 202.
23. Rantasalo, *DerAckerbau,* 12; Grimm, *Deutsche Mythologie,* vol. 3, no. 367.
24. Honko, *Geisterglaube,* 265; Haavio, *Suomalaiset,* 388.
25. Sébillot, *Folklore de France,* vol. 3, 115.
26. Honko, *Geisterglaube,* 257–67.
27. Conte, *L'Héritage païen,* 148.
28. Wagner, *Le cheval dans les croyances germanistiques,* 73.
29. Rantasalo, *DerAckerbau,* 66–71.
30. Linhart, *Hausgeister,* 117 and 120.
31. Ibid., 135; on other animal shapes, 136ff.
32. Conte, *L'Héritage païen,* 225.

CHAPTER 9. HAUNTED HOUSES

1. Grossi, *La Vie de la Vénérable Mère Louise-Blanche Terese de Ballon,* 223–25. I would like to thank Alice Joisten for bringing this marvelous text to my attention.
2. Baethgen and Brun, *Chronica Iohanni Vitodurani,* 51.
3. Hinzelin, *Contes et Légendes populaires d'Alsace,* 293ff.

4. Sébillot, *Le Folklore de France,* vol. 4, 188ff.
5. Ibid., 189.
6. Ibid., 219.
7. Collin de Plancy, *Les Légendes des esprits et des démons qui circulent autour de nous,* 324–26.
8. Ertlé, *Sorciers, Magiciens et Enchanteurs,* 70–73.
9. This can also be seen in stories about vampires; cf. Lecouteux, *The Secret History of Vampires.*
10. This topic is fully developed in my book *The Secret History of Poltergeists and Haunted Houses.*

APPENDIX 1. SAYINGS AND BELIEFS

1 Schmidt, *Die gestriegelte Rockenphilosophie,* 2 vol.

APPENDIX 2. THE ALF

1. Pohl, *Die Volkssagen Ostpreussens,* 182ff.

APPENDIX 3. A BRIEF SUMMA

1. Gheradi, *Le Théâtre italien,* vol. 1, act I, scene 6, 395. Quoted in Martineau, *Les Nains dans la littérature,* 364.

Bibliography

Abraham, Maryvonne. "Les Pierres oubliés de la maison bretonne." *Bulletin de la Société de mythologie française* 159 (1990): 19–24.

Abry and Joisten, *Êtres fantastiques des Alpes*. Paris: Entente, 1995.

———. "La Servante punie pour avoir touché à la part de l'esprit domestique. Un récit-type pour un espace social." *Les Êtres imaginaires dans les récits des Alpes*. Aosta: 1996.

Amilien, Virginie. *Le Troll et autres creatures surnaturelles*. Paris: Berg, 1996.

Annuae litterae Societatis Jesu. Antwerp: Nutti, 1618.

Apuleius. *The Golden Ass*. Translated by P. G. Walsh. Oxford: Oxford University Press, 1994.

———. *Metamorphoses*. Paris: Les Belles Lettres, 2007.

Arnobius, *Adversus nationes*.

Arnaudov, Mikhail. "Der Familienschutzgeist im Volksglauben der Bulgaren." *Zeitschrift für Balkanologie* 3 (1967): 127–37.

Auning, Robert. "Über den lettischen Drachen-Mythus (Puhkis)." *Ein Beitrag zur lettischen Mythologie*. Mitau: Steffenhagen & Sohn, 1892.

Bächtold-Stäubli, Hans. *Handwörterbuch des deutschen Aberglaubens*. Berlin and Leipzig: De Gruyter, 1927–1942. 10 volumes.

Baethgen, Friedrich and Carl Brun, eds. *Chronica Iohanni Vitodurani*. In *Monumenta Germaniae Historica*. Scriptores, nova series 3. Berlin: Weidmann'sche Buchhandlung, 1924.

Barack, Karl August, ed. *Zimmersche Chronik*. Stutgart: Litterarischer Verein, 1869. 4 vols.

Bauer, Ingolf. "Zwei Stuben aus dem Tannheimer Tal (Tirol) im Bayerische Nationalmuseum." In Dieter Harmening and Erich Wimmer, eds., *Volkskultur–*

Geshichte–Region. Festschrift für Wolfgang Brückner. Würzburg: Königshausen und Neumann, 1990.

Beresnevičius, Gintaras. *Religijotyros įvadas*. Vilnius: Aidai, 1997.

Berge, Rikard. *Husgudar i Noreg*. Supplement to *Norsk Folkekultur* 7. Risør: Gunleikson, 1921.

Berger, W. *Bayrische Schlangentore. Der Zwiebelturn (14. Jht.)*. Regensburg: N. p. 1959.

Berlioz, J. "Pélerinages et Pélerins." *Le Pays cathare. Les religions médiévales et leurs expressions méridionales*. Fanjeaux: Le Grand livre du mois, 1998.

Bernstam, Tatiana A. "Le conte dans la vie et dans la culture de la paysannerie slave orientale." *Ethnologie française* 1996/4: 619–27.

Biezais, Haralds. *Die Hauptgöttinnen der alten Letten*. Uppsala: Almqvist, 1955.

Birkeli, Emil. *Huskult og hinsidighetstro*. Oslo: Norske Videnskaps-Akademi, 1944.

Boberg, Inger M. "Gardvordens seng i dansk tradition." *Maal og Minne* (1956): 109–20.

Bø, Olav, and Arne Berg. *Faksar og kyrkjerestar: serleg pa Rygnestad*. Oslo: Norsk folkemuseum, 1959.

Brelie, Hans J. von. *Haus und Hof in den französischen Zentralpyrenäen*. Hamburg: Evert, 1937.

Bremer, Ernst, ed. *Vocabularius optimus*. Tübingen: Niemeyer, 1990. 2 vols.

Briggs, Katherine M. *A Dictionary of British Folk-Tales in the English Language Incorporating the F. J. Norton Collection*. Part B: Folk Legends. London: Routledge, 1991.

Bringsværd, Tor Åge. *Phantoms and Fairies from Norwegian Folklore*. Oslo, Tanum: 1979.

Broendegaard, Vibeke Jansen. *Folk og fauna. Dansk husdyr etnologi*. Copenhagen: Rosenkilde Bagger, 1992.

Burchard of Worms. *Decretum*. Cologne, 1548. Facsimile edition. Aalen: Scientia Verlag, 1992.

Burenhult, Göran. *Arkeologi i Sverige* II. Stockholm: Verbum, 1983.

Camiglieri, Laurence. *Contes et Légendes du Lyonnais, de la Bresse et du Bugey*. Nancy: F. Nathan, 1975.

Cherepanova, Olga A. "La Profondeur de la mémoire. Etudes ethnolinguistiques." *Cahiers slaves* 2 (1999): 156–68.

Christiansen, Reidar T. "Gårdvette og markavette." *Maal og Minne* (1943): 137–60.

———. *Folktales of Norway*. Chicago: University of Chicago Press, 1964.

Cicéron. *Traite des lois*. Paris: Les Belles Lettres, 1959.

———. *La nature des dieux*. Paris: Les Belles Lettres, 2002.

Collin de Plancy, Jacques Auguste Simon. *Les Légendes des esprits et des démons qui circulent autour de nous.* Nîmes: Librairie Lacour, 1991.

Conte, Francis. *L'Héritage païen de la Russie. Le paysan et son univers symbolique.* Paris: Albin Michel, 1997.

———. "La Fourrure." *Cahiers slaves* 2 (1999): 203–18.

Coomaraswamy, Ananda K. *Traditional Art and Symbolism.* Edited by R. Lipsey. Princeton: Princeton University Press, 1977.

Cuisenier, Jean. *La Maison rustique. Logique sociale et composition architecturale.* Paris: P.U.F., 1991.

Cuvelier, André. *Contes et Légendes de Suisse.* Nancy: F. Nathan, 1955.

Dachler, Anton. *Das Bauernhaus in Niederösterreich und sein Ursprung.* Vienna: Seidel, 1897.

———. *Das Bauernhaus in Österreich-Ungarn und seinen Grenzgebieten.* Dresden: Österreichischer Ingenieur- und Architektenverein, 1906.

Déchelette, Joseph. *Manuel d'archéologie.* Paris: Picard and Sons, 1908.

Delavigne, Anne-Hélène. "Sur la piste des êtres de la basse mythologie. Présentation des travaux de Claude Lecouteux, professeur à l'université de Paris IV (Sorbonne)." *Antrœpotes* I (4): 31–40.

Delpech, François. "Légendes généalogiques et mythologie porcine." In Philippe Walter, ed. *Mythologies du porc.* Grenoble: Jerôme Millon, 1999.

Dictionnaire encyclopédique de la mythologie slave. Moscow: 1995.

Dieterich, Albrecht. *Mutter Erde.* Berlin: B. G. Teubner, 1905.

Dioscorides. *De materia medica.* Translated by Lily Y. Beck. Hildesheim: Olms, 2005.

Dömötör, Tekla. *Volksglaube und Aberglaube des Ungarn.* Budapest: Corvina, 1981.

Doulet, Jean-Michel. "Quand les démons enlevaient les enfants." *Les Changlelins: Etude d'une figure mythique.* Paris: P.U.P.S., 2002.

Downer, Ann. *The Book of the Keepers.* New York: Atheneum, 1993.

Dubois, Pierre. *Les Contes du Petit Peuple.* Paris: Hoëbeke, 1997.

Duvernoy, Jean. *Le Recueil d'inquisition de Jacques Fournier, évêque de Pamiers (1318–1325).* Toulouse: privately published, 1961. 3 vols.

Edvardsen, Erik Henning. *Gammelt nytt i våre tidligste ukeblader.* Oslo: Aschehoug, 1997.

Eis, Gerhard. *Medizinische Fachprosa des späten Mittelaters und der frühen Neuzeit.* Amsterdam: Rodopi, 1982.

Eliade, Mircea. *Cosmos and History: The Myth of the Eternal Return.* New York: Harper Torchbooks, 1959.

———. *Patterns in Comparative Culture.* New York: Meridian, 1965.

———. "Briser le toit de la maison: symbolisme architectonique et physiologie subtile." In *Studies in Mysticism and Religion Presented to Gershom G. Scholem.* Jerusalem: Magnes, 1967.

Ertlé, Jean Marie. *Sorciers, Magiciens et Enchanteurs de nos terroirs.* Paris: Jean de Bonnot, 1996.

Les Évangiles des Quenouilles. Edited by Madeleine Jeay. Montreal: Presses de l'Université de Montréal, 1985.

Feilberg, Henning Frederik *Nissens historie.* Copenhagen: Det Schønbergske Forlag, 1919.

———. "Der Kolbold in nordischer Überlieferung." *Zeitschrift des Vereins für Volkskunde* 8 (1898): 1–20; 130–46; 264–77.

Forêt, Phillipe. "Les Concepts géomantiques des trois capitals Qing." In Flora Blanchon et al., *Aménager l'espace. Asie* II, Paris: P.U.P.S, 1993.

Gennep, Arnold van. *The Rites of Passage.* London: Routledge & Kegan Paul, 1960.

Gervase of Tilbury. *Otia Imperialia: Recreation for an Emperor.* Edited and translated by S. E. Banks and J. W. Binns. Oxford: Oxford University Press, 2002.

Gieysztor, Aleksander. "Les Divinités lettones." In Pierre Grimal, ed. *Mythologie des peuples lointains ou barbare.* Paris: Larousse, 1963.

Giraldi Cambrensis (Gerald of Wales). *Giraldi Cambrensis Opera.* London: Longman, Green, Reader and Dyer, 1861.

———. *Itinerarium Cambriae* I. Edited by James F. Dimock. London: Longmans, Green, Reader and Dyer, 1868.

———. *The Journey through Wales and the Description of Wales.* Translated by Lewis Thorpe. Middlesex and New York: Penguin, 1984.

Grambo, Ronald. "The Lord of Forest and Mountain Game in the More Recent Folk Traditions of Norway." *Fabula* 7/1 (1964): 33–52.

———. *Svart katt over veien. Varsler, tegn og overtro.* Malmö: Cappelen Damm, 2012.

Greimas, Algirdas J. *Of Gods and Men: Studies in Lithuanian Mythology.* Translated by Milda Newman. Bloomington and Indiana: Indiana University Press, 1992.

Grimm, Jacob. *Deutsche Rechtsaltertümer,* 2 vols. Hildesheim and New York: Olms, 1992 [1899].

———. *Deutsche Mythologie,* 3 vols. Darmstadt: Wissenschaftliche Buchgesellschaft, 1965.

Grimm, Jacob, and Wilhelm Grimm. *Deutsche Sagen.* Edited by Heinz Rölleke. Frankfurt: Deutscher Klassiker Verlag, 1994.

Grossi, R. P. Jean. *La Vie de la Vénérable Mère Louise-Blanche Terese de Ballon.* Annecy: Humbert Fontaine, 1695.

Grubmüller, Klaus, and Bernhard Schnell et al., eds. *Vocabularius ex quo,* 5 vols. Tübingen: Niemeyer, 1988–1989.

Haavio, Martti. *Suomalaiset kodinhaltiat.* Helsinki: WSOY, 1942.

Haefele, Hans Frieder, ed. *Notkeri Balbuli Gesta Karoli Magni imperatoris.* In *Monumenta Germaniae Historica.* Scriptores rerum germanicarum, nova series 12. Berlin: Weidmann'sche Buchhandlung, 1962.

Hagen, Fredrich Heinrich von der, ed. *Minnesinger: Deutsche Liederdichter des zwölften, dreizehnten und vierzehnten Jahrhunderts,* 5 vols. Leipzig and Berlin: J. A. Stargardt, 1838–1861.

———. *Gesamtabenteuer.* Stuttgart and Tübingen: Litterarischer Verein, 1850.

Happ, Erich. *Kommentar zum zweiten Buch von Wolframs Willehalm.* Dissertation. Munich: 1966.

Haust, Jean. "Les Gnomes dans les parlers de la Wallonie." *Enquêtes du musée de la vie wallonne* 41–42 (1946): 141–46.

Herberstein, Sigismond de. *Moscovie du XVIe siècle vue par un ambassadeur occidental.* Edited by Robert Delort. Paris: Calmann-Lévy, 1965.

Higounet, Charles, ed. *Géographie historique du village et de la maison rurale.* Paris: Éditions du C.N.R.S., 1979.

Hildebrandt, Rainer, ed. *Summarium Heinrici,* 2 vols. Berlin and N.Y.: De Gruyter, 1974–1982.

Hinzelin, Émile. *Contes et Légendes populaires d'Alsace.* Paris: Club France-Loisirs, 1978.

Holzmann, Robert. *Die Chronik des Bischofs Thietmar von Merseburg und ihre Korveier Bearbeitung* in *Monumenta Germanias historica, Scriptores, Rerum Germanorum.* Berlin: Nova Scriestix, 1935.

Honko, Lauri. *Geisterglaube in Ingermanland.* Helsinki: Academia Scientiarum Fennica, 1962.

Hultkrantz, Åke. *The Supernatural Owners of Nature.* Stockholm: Alqmvist and Wiksell, 1961.

Jacquinot, Barthélemy S. J. *Adresse chrestienne pour vivre selon Dieu dans le monde, avec Méditations pour chaque jour du mois, divisée en quatre semaines.* Lyon: Reginauld Chaudière, 1621.

Jeanton, Gabriel, and Antonin Durafour. *L'Habitation paysanne en Bresse.* Tournus: Amis des Arts et des Sciences, 1935.

Johansons, Andrejs. *Der Schirmherr des Hofes im Volksglauben der Letten. Studien über Orst-Hof-und Hausgeiter.* Stockholm: Almqvist and Wiksell, 1964.

———. "Das Heimchen und der lettische Hausgeist." *Scando-Slavica* 7 (1961): 127–32.

Joisten, Alice. "Croyances au diable at à la sorcellerie dans la vallée du Freissinières."

Bulletin de la Société d'Etudes des Hautes-Alpes (1985–1986): 33–41.

Joisten, Charles. "Quelques attestations de récits légendaires antérieurs au XVIIIe siècle en Savoie et Dauphiné." *Le Monde alpin et rhodanien* 2 (1974): 119–30.

Jouet, Philippe. *Religion et Mythologie des Baltes. Une traditions indo-européenne.* Milan and Paris: Belles Lettres, 1989.

Jünger, Ernst. *Auf den Marmorklippen.* In *Sämtliche Werke,* vol. 15. Stuttgart: Klett-Cotta, 1978.

Kabakova, Galina I. "Adam et Eve dans la literature des Slaves de l'Est." *Cahiers slaves* 2, 1999: 219–33.

Karagiannis-Moser, Emmanuelle. *Le Bestiaire de la chanson populaire grecque moderne.* Paris: P.U.P.S., 1997.

Kelch, Christian. *Liefländische historia.* Revell: Johann Mehner, 1695.

Klapper, Joseph. "Deutscher Volksglaube in Schlesien in ältester Zeit." *Mitteilungen der Schlesischen Gesellschaft für Volkskunde* 17 (1915): 19–57.

Klintberg, Bengt af. *The Types of the Swedish Folk Legends.* Helsinki: Adademia Scientiarum Fennica, 2010.

Kottje, Raymund. *Die Bußbücher Halitgars von Cambrai und des Hrabanus Maurus. Ihre Überlieferung und ihre Quellen.* Berlin and New York: De Gruyter, 1980.

Kramer [Institoris], Heinrich, and Jacob Sprenger. *Malleus maleficarum.* Speyer: 1487.

Kristni saga, Þáttr Þorvalds ens viðförla, Þáttr Ísleifs biskups Gizurarsonar, Hungrvaka. Edited by Bernhard Kahle. Halle: Niemeyer, 1905.

Kulturhistoriskt lexikon för Nordisk medeltid från vikingatid till reformationstid 22 vols. Malmö: Allhems Förlag, 1982.

Labba, Andreas. *Anta: Mémoires d'un Lapon.* Paris: Plon, 1989.

Laisnel de la Salle, Germain. *Croyances et légendes du Centre de la France,* 2 vols. Paris: Maisonneuve, 1901.

———. "Myrdinn ou l'enchanteur Merlin." *Croyances et Légendes du Cœur de la France,* 2 vols. Paris: Jean de Bonnot, 1994.

Lasicius, Johannis. *Die diis Samagitarum libellus.* Vilnius: Vaga, 1969.

Le Braz, Anatole. *La Légende de la mort chez les Bretons armoricains.* Marseille: Lafitte, 1982.

Lecouteux, Claude. "Der Bilwiz: Überlegungen zur Entstehungs-und Entwicklungsgeschicte." *Euphorion* 82 (1988): 238–50.

———. *Mondes parallèles: l'univers des croyances du Moyen Age.* Paris: Honoré Champion, 1994.

———. *Au-délà du merveilleux: des croyances au Moyen Âge.* Paris: P.U.P.S., 1995.

———. *Démons et Génies du terroir.* Paris: Imago, 1995.

———. *L'Allemand du Moyen Age.* Turnhout: Brepols, 1996.

———. "Les bruits de l'au-delà." *Revue des Langues romanes* 101 (1997): 113–24.

———. *Les Nains et les Elfes au Moyen Age,* 2nd edition. Paris: Imago, 1997.

———. *Eine Welt im Abseits. Zur niederen Mythologie und Glaubenswelt des Mittelalters.* Dettelbach: J. H. Roll, 2000. (Quellen und Forschungen zur europäischen Ethnologie, XXII).

———. *Witches, Werewolves, and Fairies.* Rochester, Vt.: Inner Traditions, 2003.

———. *The Return of the Dead.* Rochester, Vt.: Inner Traditions, 2009.

———. *Nos bons voisins les lutins.* Paris: J. Corti, 2010.

———. *The Secret History of Vampires: Their Multiple Forms and Hidden Purposes.* Rochester, Vt.: Inner Traditions, 2010.

———. *The Secret History of Poltergeists and Haunted Houses.* Rochester, Vt.: Inner Traditions, 2012.

Lecouteux, Claude and Philippe Marcq. *Les Esprits et les Morts: croyances médiévales.* Paris: Honoré Champion, 1990.

Legros, Élisée. "A propos des lutins et des fées." *La Vie wallonne* XXIII (1949): 183–90.

Le Quellec, Jean-Loïc. *La Vendée mythologique et légendaire.* Mougon: Gestes Editions, 1996.

Leroy, Emmanuel. *Montaillou, village Occitan de 1294 à 1324.* Paris: Gallimard, 1975.

Lichtblau, Karin. "Kobold." In Ulrich Müller and Werner Wunderlich, eds., *Mittelalter Mythen 2: Dämonen, Monster, Fabelwesen.* Saint Gall: UVK, 1999.

Liebrecht, Felix. *Des Gervasius von Tilbury. Otia imperialia.* Hanover: Rümpler, 1856.

———. *Zur Volkskunde.* Heilbronn: Gebrüder Henninger, 1879.

Lindig, Erika. *Hausgeister. Die Vorstellung übernatürlicher Schützer und Helfer in der deutschen Sagenüberlieferung.* Frankfurt and Bern: Peter Lang, 1987.

Linhart, Dagmar. *Hausgeister in Franken. Zur Phänomenologie, Überlieferungsgeschichte und gelehrten Deutung bestimmter hilfreicher oder schädlicher Sagengestalten.* Dettelbach: J. H. Röll, 1995.

Loorits, Oskar. *Das mißhandelte und sich rächende Feuer.* Commentationes Archivi traditionum popularium Estoniae 1. Dorpat, Tartu: N.p., 1935.

Luther, Martin. *D. Martin Luthers Werke. Kritische Gesamtausgabe, Tischreden, Schriften,* 6 vols. Weimar: H. Bohlaus Nachfolger, 1912.

Magnus, Olaus. *Historia de gentibus septentrionalibus.* Rome: N.p., 1555.

Marie de France. *Die Fabeln.* Edited by Karl Warnke. Geneva: Slatkine, 1974.

Marliave, Olivier de. *Petit dictionnaire de mythologie basque et pyrénéenne.* Paris: Édition entente, 1903.

Martineau, Anne. *Les Nains dans la littérature arthurienne française du Moyen Âge*. Paris: P.U.P.S., 1998.

Martino, Ernesto de. *Italie de Sud et Magie*. Paris: Gallimard, 1963.

———. *Sud et Magia*. Third edition. Milano: Feltrinelli, 1978.

Mazalova, Natalia Evguéniévna. "La Médecine populaire dans les villages de la Russie du Nord." *Ethnologie française* 26:4 (1996): 666–76.

McIntosh, A., and M. Laing. "Middle English windown, 'window'—a World-geographical Note," *Neuphilologische Mitteilungen* 97:3 (1996): 295–300.

Mélétinski, Eléazar. "La Poétique historique du folklore narrative." *Ethnologie française* 26: 4 (1964): 611–18.

Merceron, Jacques. "Recherches sur le symbolisme cosmique de la toiture et métaphysique de la cheminée et de la toiture." *Bulletin de la Société de Mythologie française* 167 (1993): 2–9.

Mommsen, Thedor, and Paul Martin Meyer. *Theodosiani Libri XVI*. Berlin: Berolini, 1905.

Müllenhoff, Karl. *Sagen, Märchen und Lieder aus Schleswig-Holstein*. Schleswig: Julius Bergas Verlag, 1921.

Müller, Josef. *Sagen aus uri*, 3 vols. Basel: G. Krebs, 1929–1945.

Näsman, Ulf. "Hus, landsby, bebyggelse." In Johs Hertz, ed., *Danmarks længste udgravning: arkæologi på naturgassens vej 1979–86*. Copenhagen: Nationalmuseet, 1987, 69–86.

Ogle, M. B. "The House-door in Greek and Roman Religion and Folklore." *American Journal of Philology* 32:3 (1911): 251–71.

Olive, Jean-Louis. "La Salutation au soleil. Notes d'ethnographie héliotropique en Pyrénées catalanes." *Bulletin de la Société de Mythologie française* 183 (1996): 1–25.

Ovid, *Metamorphoses* VIII. Edited by R. Merckel. Leipzig: Teubner, 1875.

———. *Tristes*. Paris: Les Belles Lettres, 2008.

———. *Ovid's Fasti*. Cambridge: Harvard University Press, 1959.

Pape, John. "Studier om kyrkogrimen." *Folkkultur Meddelanden från Lunds Universitets folkminnesarkiv* 7 (1946): 11–240.

Patlagean, Évelyne. "L'Histoire de l'imaginaire." *La Nouvelle Histoire*. Edited by Jacques Le Goff, Roger Chartier, and Jacques Revel. Paris: Retz CEPL, 1978.

Paulson, Ivar. "Die Hausgeister und ihre idole in Norderasien." *Tribus* 12 (1963): 125–58. [Includes a bibliography of all earlier books focusing on the Scandinavian and Baltic countries.]

———. "Haus- und Hofgeister im Volksglauben der Esten." *Arv* 23 (1967): 95–113.

Petzoldt, Leander. *Kleines Lexikon der Dämonen und der Elementargeister*. Munich: C. H. Beck, 1990.

Peuckert, Will-Erich. *Sagen, Geburt und Antwort der mythischen Welt.* Berlin: Erich Schmidt Verlag, 1965.

Pohl, Erich. *Die Volkssagen Ostpreussens.* Hildesheim, New York: Olms, 1994.

Pitz, Louis. *Contes et Légendes de Lorraine.* Nancy: F. Nathan, 1966.

Plautus. *Aulularia.* (Plaute, *La Marmite*). Paris: Les Belles Lettres, 1932.

Pliny. *Natural History.* Edited by Ludovicus Janus. Leipzig: Teubner, 1864–1875.

Plutarch. *Quaestiones Romanae.* Edited by John Scheid. Darmstadt: Wissenschaftliche Buchgesellschaft, 2012.

Pourrat, Henri. *Contes et recits du Livradois.* Paris: Maisonneuve and Larose, 1995.

Prätorius, Johannes. *Anthropodermus Plutonicus. Das ist, eine Neue Welt-Beschreibung von allerley wunderbahrlichen Menschen.* Magdeburg: Lüderwald, 1666.

Quinel, Charles, and Adhémar de Montgon. *Contes et Légendes d'Ecosse.* Nancy: F. Nathan, 1962.

Rabuzzi, David Allen. "Some Notes on the Household Spirits in Norway." *Arv* 38 (1982), 87–101.

Rhamm, Karl. *Urzeitliche Bauernhöfe im germanisch-slawischem Waldgebiet.* Braunschweig: Vieweg und Sohn, 1908.

———. *Die altslawische Wohnung.* Braunschweig: Vieweg und Sohn, 1910.

Rank, Gustav. *Die heilige Hinterecke im Hauskult der Völker Nordosteuropas und Nordasiens.* Helsinki: Suomalainen Tiedeakatemia, 1949.

Ranke, Kurt, ed. *Enzyklopädie des Märchens.* Berlin: De Gruyter, 1977.

Rantasalo, Aukusti Vilho. *Der Ackerbau im Volksaberglauben der Finnen und Esten mit entsprechenden Gebräuchen der Germanen verglichen.* Helsinki: Academia Scientiarum Fennica, 1925.

Raudvere, Catharina. *Föreställningar om maran i nordisk folktro.* Lund: Lund Universitet, 1993.

Richard, Nicolas Louis Antoine. *Traditions populaires, Croyances superstitieuses, Usages et coutumes de l'ancienne Lorraine.* Remiremont: Mougin, 1848.

Robertson, Ronald MacDonald. *Selected Highland Folktales.* Nairn: House of Lochar, 1993.

Rolland, Eugène. *Faune populaire de la France,* vol. 4. Paris: Maisonneuve et Larose, 1967.

———. *Faune populaire de la France,* vol. 6. Paris: Maisonneuve et Larose, 1967.

Romanus-Büchlein. Translated by Claude Lecouteux in *Le livres des grimoires.* Paris: Imago, 2008.

Ronsard, Pierre de. *Songs and Sonnets of Pierre de Ronsard.* Translated by Curtis Page. Boston: Houghton Mifflin & Co., 1903.

———. "Les demons." In *Œuvres complètes,* vol. VIII, Hymnes. Edited by Paul Laumonier. Paris: Didier, 1963.

"Russie. Rossija. Paroles russes." *Ethnologie française* 26:4 (1996).

Rybakov, Boris. *Le Paganisme des anciens Slaves.* Paris: P.U.F., 1994.

Sand, George. *Légendes rustiques.* Paris: Calmann-Lévy, 1877.

Sartori, Paul. "Über das Bauopfer." *Zeitschrift für Ethnologie* 30 (1898): 1–54.

———. *Sitte und Brauch,* 3 vols. Leipzig: Wilhelm Heims, 1910–1914.

Schilling, Robert. "Les Lares grundules." In *Mélanges offerts à J. Heurgon,* 2 vols. Rome: École française de Rome, 1976.

Schmidt, Johann Georg. *Die Gestriegelte Rocken-philosophie oder aufrichtige Untersuchung derer von vielen super-klugen Weibern hochgehaltenen Aberglauben,* 2 vols. Leipzig: VCH Verlagsgesellschaft, 1988. [Originally published 1718–1722.]

Schmidt, Peter, ed. *Liber ordinis rerum,* 2 vols. Tübingen: Niemeyer, 1983.

Schmitz, Hermann Josef. *Die Bußbücher und die Bußdiziplin der Kirche.* Mainz: Kirchheim, 1883. Reprint edition, Graz: Akademische Druck-und Verlagsanstalt, 1958.

Schönwerth, Franz. *Aus der Oberpfalz. Sitten und Sagen,* 3 vols. Augsbourg: Olms, 1857–1859.

Schott, Arthur, and Albert Schott. *Rumänische Volkserzahlungen aus dem Banat. Neuausgabe besorgt von Rolf Wilh. Brednich und Ion Taloş.* Bucuresti: Kriterion Verlag, 1971.

Schramek, Josef. *Das Böhmerwaldbauernhaus.* Prague: J. G. Calve, 1908.

Schröder, Edward., ed. *Kleinere Dichtungen Konrads von Würzburg,* 3 vols. Berlin: Weidmann, 1959.

Schönwerth, Franz. *Aus der Oberpfalz. Sitten und Sagen,* 3 vols. Augsburg: Rieger, 1857–1859.

Schulz, Rose-Clarie. "'Il vaut mieux souffrir du froid maintenant. . . ,' le purgatoire dans les glaciers." In *Imaginaires de la haute montagne. Documents d'ethnologie régionale.* Grenoble: Jerôme Millon, 1987.

Schwerin, Claudius von. "Leges Saxonum und Lex Thuringorum." *Monumenta Germaniae historica, Fontes iuris,* vol. 4. Berlin: N.p., 1918.

Sébillot, Paul. *Les Travaux publics et les Mines dans les traditions et les superstitions de tous les pays.* Paris: J. Rothschild, 1894, 85–120.

———. *Le Folklore de France,* 4 vols. Paris: Imago, 1968.

Seignolle, Claude. *Les Évangiles du diable.* Paris: Belfond, 1978.

Servius. *Servianorumin Vergili Carmina Commentariorum.* Edited by George Thilo and Hermann Hagen. Leipzig: Editio Harvardiana, 1878–1902.

Sikes, Wirt. *British Goblins: Welsh Folklore, Fairy Mythology, Legends, and Traditions.* London: Sampson Low, Marston, Searle, and Rivington, 1880.

Silicus Italicus. *La guerre punique,* vol. 2. Paris: Les Belles Lettres, 1981.

Simon, Jean-François. *Tiez, Le Paysan Breton et sa maison: La Cornouaille.* Douarnenez: La Chasse-Marée de l'Estran, 1983.

Sjövall, Harald. *Om byggnadsoffer och besläktade bruk hos greker och romare.* Lund: N.p., 1915.

———. *Zeus im altgriechischen Hauskult.* Lund: Ohlsson 1931.

Stahl, Paul-Henri. "L'Organisation magique du territoire villageois roumain." *L'Homme* XIII/2 (1973): 150–62.

———. "L'habitation rurale traditionelle des Roumains." *Archéocivilisation* 7–8 (1969–1970): 47–56.

———. "L'Organisation magique du territoire villegeois roumain." *L'Homme* XIII/3 (1973): 150–62.

Steinmeyer, Elias von, and Eduard Sievers. *Die althochdeutschen Glossen.* Berlin: Weidmann Buchhandlung. 1879–1922, 5 vols.

Strange, Joseph, ed. *Caesarii Heisterbacensis Dialogus miraculorum.* Cologne, Bonn and Brussels: Lempertz, 1851.

Strömbäck, Dag. "Die Wahl des Kirchenbauplatzes in der Sage und im Volksglauben mit besonderer Rücksicht auf Schweden." In Wayland D. Hand and Gustav O. Arlt, eds., *Humaniora, Essays in Literature, Folklore, Biography Honoring Archer Taylor on His 70th Birthday.* Locust Valley, N.Y.: Augustin, 1960.

Sverdrup, Georg von. "Die Hausurnen und die Heiligkeit des Hauses." *Avhandliger utgitt av Det Norske Videnskaps-Akademi i Oslo II. Hist. Filos. Klasse,* no. 1, 10 (1939).

Sydow, Carl Wilhelm von. "Övernaturliga väsen." *Nordisk kultur* XIX, "Folktro" (1935): 95–159.

Taloş, Ion, *Meşterul Manole. Contributie la studiul unei teme de folclor European,* 2 vols. Bucharest: Minerva, 1973–1997.

———. *Petit dictionaire de mythologie populaire roumaine.* Paris: Ellug, 2002.

Temme, Jodocus Donatus Hubertus. *Die Volkssagen von Pommern und Rügen.* Berlin: Nicolaischen Buchhandlung, 1840.

Tettau, Wilhelm Albert Johann von, and Jodocus Donatus Hubertus Temme. *Die Volkssagen Ostpreussens, Lithauens und Westpreussens.* Hildesheim and New York: Olms, 1994.

Thiers, Jean-Baptiste. *Traité des superstitions. Croyances populaires et rationalité à l'Age classique.* Reprint edition, text established and annotated by J. M. Goulemot. Paris: Hachette, 1984.

———. *Traité des superstitions selon l'Écriture sainte, les décrets des conciles et les sentimens des saints Pères et des théologiens.* Paris: Chez Antoine Dezallier, 1679.

Thyraeus, Petrus. *Loca infesta, hoc est, de infestis, ob molestantes daemoniorum et defunctorum hominum spiritus.* Cologne: Goswin Cholinus, 1598.

Trimberg, Hugo von. *Der Renner.* Edited by Gustav Ehrismann. Tübingen: Literarischer Verein, 1908–1909. 2 vols.

Tubach, Frederic C. *Index Exemplorum: A Handbook of Medieval Tales.* Helsinki: Suomalainen Tiedeakatemia, 1969.

Der vielförmige Hintzelmann. Leipzig, 1704. Reprint edition, Göttingen: Otto Schwartz, 1965.

Vinogradova, Lioudmila Nicolaïevna. "Les croyances au démon dans la structure du calendrier populaire." *Ethnologie française* 26:4 (1996): 738–47.

Vintler, Hans. *Bluome der tugent.* Edited by M. Bartel and O. Ebermann: "Zur Aberglaubensliste in Vintlers Pluemen der tugent." *Zeitschrift des Vereins für Volkskunde* 23 (1913), p. 1–18, 113–136.

Vorreux, Damien. *Un symbole franciscain: le Tau. Histoire, théologie et iconographie.* Paris: Éditions franciscaines, 1977.

Wagner, Marc-André. *Le cheval dans les croyances germaniques. Paganisme, christianisme et traditions.* Paris: Champion, 2005 (Nouvelle Bibliothèque du Moyen Âge, 73).

Wall, Jan. *Tjuvmjölkande väsen.* Uppsala: Acta Universitatis Upsaliensis, 1977–1978.

Walter, Philippe. *Le Bel Inconnu de Renaut de Beaujeu. Rite, mythe et roman.* Paris: P.U.F., 1996.

Wasserschleben, F. W. H. *Die Bußordnungen der abendländischen Kirche.* Halle: Graeger, 1851. Reprint edition, Graz: Akademische Druck- und Verlagsanstalt, 1958.

Weinmann, Cornelia. *Der Hausbau in Skandinavien vom Neolithikum bis zum Mittelalter.* Berlin and New York: De Gruyter, 1994.

Weyer, Johann. *De praestigiis demonum. Von Teuffelsgespenst, Zauberen und Giffbereytern.* Frankfurt: N.p., 1586.

Weiser, Lily. "Germanische Hausgeister und Kobolde." *Niederdeutsche Zeitschrift für Volkskunde* 4 (1926): 1–23.

———. "Das Bauernhaus im Volksglauben." *Mitteilungen der anthropologischen Gesellschaft in Wien* 56 (1926): 6ff.

William, E. "The Protection of the House: Some Iconographic Evidence from Wales." *Folklore* 89:2 (1978): 148–53.

William of Auvergne. *De universo.* In *Opera Omnia,* 2 vols. Paris: Pralard, 1672.

Wirth, Alfred. "Von Bauernhaus und-hof in Anhalt." *Mitteldeutsche Blätter für Volkskunde* 1/8 (1926): 117–36; 1/9 (1926): 134ff.

Wolfram, Richard. *Die gekreuzten Pferdeköpf als Giebelzeichen.* Vienna: Verlag A. Schendl, 1968.

Wossidlo, Richard. *Mecklenburgische Sagen. Ein Volksbuch,* 2 vols. Rostock: Carl Hinstorff Verlag, 1939.

Wundt, Wilhelm. *Mythos und Religion.* Leipzig: Kroner, 1910–1914.

Wuttke, Adolf. *Der Aberglaube der Gegenwart.* 3rd edition. Berlin: Wiegandt and Grieben, 1900.

Zell, Franz. "Eine Renaissancestube vom Jahre 1588 im Kistlerhaus zu Grünwald." *Altbayerische Monatsschrift* I (1899): 22–29.

Ziegler, Konrat, and Walther Sontheimer, eds. *Der Kleine Pauly: Lexikon der Antike* 5 vols. Munich: Deutscher Taschenbuch Verlag, 1979.

Index

Page numbers in *italics* represent illustrations.

BOOKS OF RELATED INTEREST